JOEL & ETHAN COEN

The Contributors:

Brigitte Desalm is a film critic with the *Kölner Stadt Anzeiger* newspaper, and also writes for *Steadycam* and WDR radio in Germany. She has contributed to books on Kim Novak and Clint Eastwood.

Sabine Horst, born in 1960, is an arts editor with the *Journal Frankfurt* magazine and the *Frankfurter Rundschau* newspaper. She has contributed to books on Woody Allen and Johnny Weissmuller.

Peter Körte, born in 1958, is an arts editor and film critic with the *Frankfurter Rundschau*. He has written books on Humphrey Bogart and Quentin Tarantino.

Daniel Kothenschulte, born in 1967, writes for a variety of publications including *film-dienst, Frankfurter Allgemeine, Frankfurter Rundschau, Süddeutsche Zeitung* and *Steadycam*. He has contributed to books on Kim Novak and Ennio Morricone.

Ulrich Kriest, born in 1961, writes for *film-dienst, Spex* and *Weimarer Beiträge,* and has edited several books on film.

Stefan Reinecke, born in 1959, is an editor at the *tageszeitung* newspaper. He has written several books on film, including two on Hollywood's portrayal of the Vietnam war.

Georg Seesslen, born in 1948, writes for *Die Zeit, Frankfurter Rundschau* and *Der Tagesspiegel* and has published books on Clint Eastwood, Quentin Tarantino and pornographic films.

JOEL & ETHAN COEN

Edited by Peter Körte and Georg Seesslen

Translated by Rory Mulholland

TITAN BOOKS

JOEL & ETHAN COEN
ISBN 1 84023 097 5

Published by
Titan Books
42-44 Dolben Street
London SE1 0UP

First edition July 1999
10 9 8 7 6 5 4 3 2 1

Published by arrangement with Dieter Bertz Verlag.

Joel & Ethan Coen © 1998 by Dieter Bertz Verlag, Berlin.
English translation © Rory Mulholland 1999.

Front cover pictures:
Fargo © PolyGram/Pictorial Press
The Big Lebowski © PolyGram/Pictorial Press

Photo credits:
Filmbild Fundus Robert Fischer (FF)/Circle Films: 121, 248 below; FF/Concorde: 143, 160 above, 207 above;
FF/Twentieth Century Fox: 64, 65, 69, 75, 77, 79, 81, 89, 93 below, 102, 103, 206 (2 and 3 above); FF/Gramercy
Pictures: 12, 166 above, 180-182; FF/Manifesto Film Sales: 206 above; FF/Warner Bros: 150, 161; FF/Working
Title Films/PolyGram Filmed Entertainment: 15, 195, 197, 199, 200, 202, 204, 205, 207 below; FF: 19-21, 29, 37
below, 271 above; Foto- & Filmung-Sammlung Manfred Thurow (Thurow)/Circle Films: 9, 126, 127, 129 above,
130, 140, 221, 237 above; Thurow/Concorde: 216 below; Thurow/Twentieth Century Fox: 71, 85, 97, 99, 105, 106,
236 middle and below, 216 above, 233 above; Thurow/Gramercy Pictures: 166 below, 171, 186, 217 below;
Thurow/Metropol: 42, 43, 48, 49, 53, 59, 61, 242, 248 above; Thurow/Monopole Pathé: 116, 129 below, 266;
Thurow/Warner Bros: 11, 151, 217 above, 233 middle, 237 middle; Thurow: 45, 51, 236, 237; Yves Klein: 148
above; Zitty-Archiv (Zitty)/Concorde: 145, 153, 207 middle, 233 middle, 251; Zitty/Twentieth Century Fox: 93
above; Zitty/Metropol: 57, 206 above; Zitty/Prokino: 25; Zitty: 18, 37 above; Archiv des Verlages: 58, 81, 88, 142,
144, 145 below, 155 below, 158, 160 below, 163. Photo sequences: Dieter Bertz/original copyright holders.
Also: Columbia Pictures Corporation, Disney, Embassy Films, Palace Pictures, Paramount Pictures, Renaissance
Pictures, River Road, RKO Radio Pictures, Silver Pictures, Working Title Films.

Rory Mulholland would like to thank Wolfgang Mittelmaier for his lucid unravellings of knotty German
constructions, Karl Golden for his knowledge of pulp, Helen Bradley for her artistic input, Michael Kane and
Neil O'Brien for their editorial comments, David Barraclough, Gillian Christie, Simon Furman, Bob Kelly, Simon
Oliver and Katy Wild at Titan, Kim Newman for the videos and everyone else who put up with me during my
brief but intense visit to Coen County.

Thanks to Robert Fischer and Herbert Klemens at *Filmbild Fundus*, Hans-Joachim Neumann and Sabine
Rutkowski at *Zitty* and Manfred Thurow for supplying the pictures. Thanks also to Ines, Graf Haufen and Oliver
at *Videodrom*.

A CIP catalogue record for this title is available from the British Library.

Printed and bound in Great Britain by MPG Books Ltd, Victoria Square, Bodmin, Cornwall.

Contents

INTERVIEW

'We don't want everybody to love us'

Peter Körte

When I was preparing for this interview, I began to wonder how you feel when you look back over your work, over the seven films you have made so far. Are you proud, or maybe sad at the missed opportunities, or do you simply not recognise yourselves?

Ethan Coen: It's hard to say, because we don't really think about our films much once we've finished them. You spend so long on a film, worrying about all the details, you spend two years living with a film, and you're quite relieved when you don't have to think about it any more.

Joel Coen: I'm surprised that we've already made seven films. It depresses me a little to think about it because it makes me feel old. We try not to get too caught up in thinking about what we have done. Now and again, if we watch a bit of one of our films, then… We hardly ever look at a film once we've completed it. But if we do notice anything, it's usually something we might do differently today, usually something to do with the editing. But there's nothing in the films we've made so far that really bothers me.

EC: There's nothing I find particularly embarrassing when I watch them again.

The Big Lebowski *is a mixture of typical Coen motifs, but it reminded me most of* Raising Arizona.

JC: Yeah, that's true.

EC: That doesn't surprise me, but I don't know why it's so.

JC: Maybe it's the tone that's most like *Raising Arizona*. *The Big Lebowski* is also one hundred per cent comedy.

The narrator's parodic voiceover is another thing they have in common.

EC: Yeah. But we've used that several times.

JC: That's right. It reminds me of the scene in *Raising Arizona*, where Nic Cage is in the convenience store. Maybe it's also because of the contemporary ambience, after all the period pieces we've done.

In The Big Lebowski *was there some initial inspiration, a key scene, a specific image, such as Gabriel Byrne's hat in* Miller's Crossing *or the peeling wallpaper in* Barton Fink?

EC: Hmm, oh boy…

JC: I can't think of anything specific [mutters something unintelligible to Ethan, we just hear: 'What *was* it in *Raising Arizona*?']. It was when we were working on the characters of Dude (Jeff Bridges) and Walter (John Goodman) that the film really got rolling for us, that it got off the ground. But there was no specific image, no specific idea like in the other films.

EC: I recently came across the first or second draft of the screenplay for *The Big Lebowski* on my computer. The opening scene also had Dude in a convenience store.

I asked that because I'm interested in how you work

together. *Does one of you have an idea, which then sparks something off in the other, which in turn needs modifying, and so on until you arrive at an agreed solution? Can you describe the chemistry between you?*

John Turturro, Ethan and Joel Coen during the making of *Barton Fink*

JC: Generally speaking, a lot of things come into play. But in the case of *The Big Lebowski* it was different. Firstly, because the characters were very loosely based on people we both knew. Secondly, we wanted to make something that would generate a certain narrative feeling – like a modern Raymond Chandler story, and that's why the film had to be set in LA. We wanted to have a narrative flow, a story that moves, like in a Chandler book, through different parts of town and different social classes. That was the backdrop that interested us when we wrote the screenplay.

I immediately thought of Chandler's The High Window, *in which one detective spies on another. But, in fact, there are lots of little references to Chandler's novels.*

EC: Yeah, there was definitely more than one book that we had in the back of our minds.

JC: I think the story about the rich old guy in Pasadena, who sparks off the entire plot, is typical Chandler for me. In *The Big Sleep* it's the two daughters who set everything in motion, here it's the fake kidnapping.

Chandler, but also Hammett and pulp fiction generally, is obviously an inexhaustible source of inspiration for you. On the one hand it is a relatively closed genre, but on the other it provides a literary aspect that is well suited to your style of story-telling.

[both:] That's very true.

EC: It's funny, because people who write about our films always refer to other films whenever they want to make comparisons. It's often down to contemporary narrow-mindedness that these literary references are overlooked.

But it's almost impossible to miss the references in Miller's Crossing. Hammett's heirs could even have sued you for plagiarism.

[both laugh]

JC: Yeah, it does look like a wild mix of *The Glass Key* and *Red Harvest*.

And the title Blood Simple *could have been put in quotation marks, since it comes directly from Hammett.*

JC: Yeah, but the story is more James Cain.

I'm still wondering about how you work together. Maybe the key lies in your childhood. Did you read a lot – there is this penchant for language, for complicated narrative structures in your films – or did you watch TV all the time? You must have some sort of common ground, and the age difference between you is not that great.

EC: We did watch a lot of TV, a lot of films, and mostly we watched them together.

What about books? You come from an academic household, where presumably you were encouraged to read.

JC: That's right. Our father was an economics profes-

The Hudsucker Proxy: Joel Coen, cinematographer Roger Deakins, Joel Silver and Ethan Coen

sor and our mother taught art history. Sure, as academics they wanted to see their kids reading books, and they encouraged us to do so. You shouldn't make too much of this common background, but then again you can't pretend it's unimportant. Also, the three-year age difference [Joel was born in 1955, Ethan in 1958] is really important when you're a teenager, you have different friends etc. It wasn't until after college that we started spending a lot of time working together. Ours is simply a professional collaboration between adults, even if we do share a common history as well as countless cultural points of reference.

Your humour at least must have a common root. Do you think your Jewishness has anything to do with it? Were you brought up traditionally, or was religion not important in your household?

EC: We were brought up relatively traditionally. Our mother made sure of that, but it wasn't very important to our father. Moderately strict, I would say.

Fargo: the Coens with
Roger Deakins

Are you perhaps reminiscing when, in The Big Lebowski, *John Goodman so stubbornly refuses to work
on the Sabbath?*

JC: No. Only our grandmother on our mother's side
was as strict as that.

*But you did have to go to the rabbi, and he must have
taught you some Hasidic jokes, among other things?*

[both laugh]

*Still on the subject of Jewish humour, one could very
crudely say that there is more Billy Wilder than Woody
Allen in your films.*

Both: Yeah, that's probably right.

JC: But I'm not sure you could trace this back to Hasidic
jokes. Yeah, maybe, why not? I'm not even sure what is
so specific about them.

*Maybe it's the fact that there are certain rules your char-
acters must learn about life, even Dude Lebowski. Like
Barton Fink, they want things that are way beyond their
capabilities. And that's why they keep getting into trouble, particularly the men.*

EC: They're idiots, that's true.

JC: That's funny... [the rest of their answer is swamped by laughter]

You went your very different ways after high school. Joel went to film school, Ethan studied philosophy. It obviously wasn't pre-destined that you would hook up again after college. Or perhaps there is some secret connection between philosophical analyses and editing horror films?

EC: It's a fairly oblique connection.

JC: We had a common interest in watching and making films. And then it got to the point where we had to do something, where we had to produce something.

So your philosophy studies were not a significant influence?

JC: I really can't say [laughs].

EC: It's like our Jewish origin. It belongs in the background, you have the feeling that it's important but you can't say exactly why.

JC: It's like the fact that we're brothers. It would be absurd to deny any influence. We have far too many common reference points and interests, but it would be simplistic to make any direct connections.

Is this why you've never made a film about brothers? Would this be too Woody Allen for you?

JC: Probably. Woody Allen draws on his own life a lot, which you can't really say about the stories we write.

EC: As you said, we're more interested in playing with different genres in the style of Billy Wilder.

Your play with genre runs through your work like a leit-motif, particularly the references to film noir. And the visual side of your narratives is also very important to you. It's as though you were already tired of middle-of-the-road Hollywood realism before you even started making films.

EC: That's right. We were never really interested in realism or reportage or documentary-type work. *Fargo* might, at least partly, be an exception. It's a little more naturalistic than our other films, but it's still very stylised.

A lot of people complained about the humour in Fargo. Time *magazine, for example, said your attitude towards your characters was condescending. Do you find it hard to get your humour across, particularly in America?*

JC: It's very easy to offend people. There's always going to be someone who feels affronted, for regional, ethnic or whatever sort of reasons. In Minnesota the public was split in its reaction to the film. The locals who liked it saw in it something specific that could not have been made by someone who does not or has not lived there. But there were others who were deeply insulted. It's hard to make something without somebody misunderstanding it.

But you do choose your targets very carefully. I wonder, isn't it Cindy Sherman, among others, that you're sending up in The Big Lebowski *when you show Julianne Moore in her studio surrounded by display dummies?*

JC: No. Julianne's character is based more on a 1960s Fluxus artist. There was a painter who also worked, naked, from a swing or a rope construction, like Julianne in the film. We liked the retrospective element of this art form, the fact that it links into Dude's hippy mentality or Walter's Vietnam vet attitude. Curley Schneeman was the guy's name, that's right, I remember it now. But it's interesting that you thought of Cindy Sherman. You see how easy it is to offend people, even by accident. By the way, Yoko Ono was also a Fluxus artist...

This attack is fairly harmless compared with the scene where Walter decides old Lebowski is a malingerer, pulls him out of his wheelchair, stands him up and then lets him collapse onto the ground.

[both laugh incessantly]
JC: Of course people are going to get excited about it, but what can you do?

On the set of
The Big Lebowski

Does it sometimes bother you that your work, your humour, is appreciated more in Europe than in America?

JC: We're just glad that anyone likes our stuff… But we don't go and make films with huge expectations about their commercial potential. It doesn't upset us, we don't want everybody to love us. Of course we want more people to go and see our movies, who wouldn't. But on the other hand…
EC: If you make a film like *Fargo* there's no point in trying to convince yourself that you're going to have a *Titanic* audience.
JC: We were really surprised at how many people went to see *Fargo*, honestly.

Has there ever been a point in your careers where a producer has tried to talk you into doing bigger, more conventional projects? Maybe along the lines of: you're talented, now how about something more mainstream?

JC: Sure, when we were starting off we had a few offers. But with time, people understood what interested us and what didn't.

So you're going to carry on using just your own stories, your own material?

JC: Exactly.

What your films have added to the cinematic landscape might best be described as Coen County. Your movies are all radically different, but they also have many things in common. Were you perhaps surprised to discover just how closely linked they are?

EC: It is pretty surprising when you look back on it. Particularly when it's pointed out to us that we have a lot of raging tycoons and fat men that scream at each other. *Is it a sort of hallmark, a forgery-proof trademark?*

JC: Yeah, you just can't escape it, for good or for bad. And there's nothing you can do to change it. How can we help it if we feel the need to put dream sequences into our films?

This interview took place in New York on 12 December 1997. Many thanks to Albert Wiederspiel and the Polygram team for arranging it. ■

JOEL & ETHAN COEN – THE FILMS

Crimewave (dir. Sam Raimi)

t is night in Detroit. A goddamn windy, rainy, blue, film noir, comic strip, studio night. A night torn by flashes of lightning. An early 1950s-style car roars past. Brakes screeching, it tears around the corner of the deserted street. Cut. Close-up of the car. In it sit more nuns — frightened, wildly determined nuns — than have ever been seen in one car at once. The beat-up car radio, meanwhile, tells us how the whole story began:

Victor Ajax (ah, those names!) is about to be executed. It is twelve minutes to midnight, and at midnight the electric chair will launch him into eternity. Yet he doesn't look much like a mass murderer, and won't stop protesting his innocence. Victor (Reed Birney) was a repair man for the security systems that were meant to protect the townsfolk from a rising crime rate and which enabled his bosses, Trend (Edward R.

The murderous pest controllers: Coddish (Brion James) with Nancy (Sheree J. Wilson); Crush (Paul Smith)

Pressman) and Odegard (Hamid Dana), to amass a small fortune. Now he is accused of killing half a dozen of these same townsfolk. How did such a nice young man end up facing a mass murder rap? There is only one person in the world who can prove his innocence, and that is his sweetheart Nancy (Sheree J. Wilson). But she has been missing since the night the terrible events took place, finding refuge in a convent and believing Vic to be dead. Now she is rushing, along with a group of her fellow sisters, to save the condemned man.

Cut to the prison, which happens to be called the Hudsucker State Penitentiary (this Hudsucker was clearly a versatile chap). Everything in the jail is as we expect it to be. No, it is more than that. The harsh circles of light that the naked bulbs cast onto the floor, the

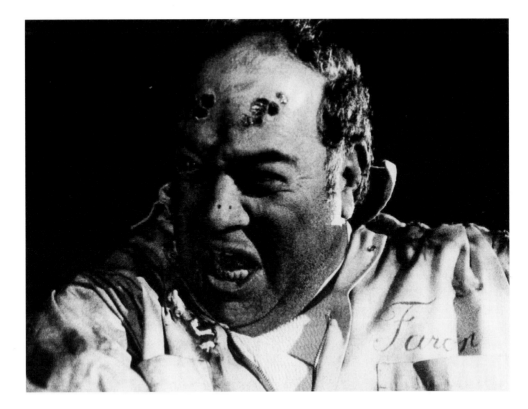

menacing pattern of the bars, the screaming of the men on death row — we have seen all this before, but never quite so distinctly. The black convict with the melancholy expression on his face, tells our hero in his bass voice (as though he were about to start singing the deepest blues): 'Don't give 'em the satisfaction.' Victor, desperate, ignores his advice and, on the way to the chair, tells the guards the story of what really happened. They are as unmoved as they always are in prison movies by Victor's sorry tale. Cut to flashback:

He has just installed another security system for Trend and Odegard when the lovely but distressed Nancy rushes into his arms, having nearly been run over by a truck driven by the mad and unscrupulous pest controllers Crush (Paul Smith) and Coddish (Brion James), the Center City Exterminators. The exterm-

How to Talk to Girls: Vic (Reed Birney) tries to hit it off with Nancy

inators tear through town in a van with a giant stuffed rat on top and the slogan 'We Kill All Sizes' painted on it. Gratifyingly, they both look like rats, and they are as unpleasant to each other as they are to everyone else (there is a running gag where one tries to pinch a Kool cigarette from the other and invariably gets his hand crushed). The exterminators have invented a highly effective method of electrically executing their favourite animals, and they occasionally try their equipment out on humans, with deadly results. (Their death machine has three levels: one for rats, one for people and a third for heroes.) Vic is, of course, still unaware that Bob Odegard and the heel Renaldo (Bruce Campbell) are plotting against Odegard's business partner Trend. It doesn't take Trend long to find out about it, however, and he promptly hires Crush and Coddish to murder

his associate, which they proceed to do.

Trend's wife (Louise Lasser) looks across at her husband's shop through a pair of binoculars. Something is going on there... After some time, Trend also gets up and inspects the scene of the crime, apparently in all innocence, playing the part of a film noir killer who thinks he has carried out the perfect murder.

Vic, meanwhile, is in the Rialto café, making vain attempts to get a little closer to the lovely Nancy, but he is no match for Renaldo, whose favourite pick-up line is: 'Why don't you come up for a scotch and sofa.' Renaldo has to laugh himself when he says it, and he usually gets a clip round the ear for his efforts, but it doesn't seem to bother him. Renaldo makes the indecent advances toward Nancy, but it is the hapless Vic who manages to get both soaked and thumped. Vic thinks he might be

A happy ending?

getting somewhere with her, but, even as he tries out lines from his book *How to Talk to Girls*, Nancy's eyes are wandering once again to her playboy seducer, who is already chatting up somebody else at the bar.

Crush and Coddish decide they might as well kill Trend too. They do so, and then go for his wife, who fights off Crush with the help of a fork. Coddish, meanwhile, is threatening Nancy, and Vic has just left her apartment. Mrs Trend, Nancy and Vic then flee the killers. The rest of the plot is taken up by their escape, which is punctuated by a series of bizarre coincidences. Vic, as usual, has no idea what's going on.

A long car chase and a perilous struggle on the truck leaves the pursuers out of action, the highway littered with car wrecks and a couple of people quite literally flattened. Victor hangs helplessly from a bridge over a river. Above him, a stolen car, with Nancy inside, threatens to topple over. Vic is miraculously saved, but just as he is asking who the people chasing them actually were and what they wanted, he falls into the river, together with the parapet he has been clinging to.

That is Victor's story, at least as far as he can figure it out, but nobody is interested. Tell it to Saint Peter, says a rather fiendish prison guard, who looks as if he thoroughly enjoys executions. Another equally pleasant guard puts the clock, which marches inexorably towards electrocution time, forward by a few minutes.

The governor (Wiley Harker) appears at the last moment. Vic is saved! Alas, no! The politician is only there for the entertainment. The nightmare seems to have no end, but luckily the nuns are still racing through the city, to the chords of 'Hallelujah'. They reach the prison seconds before the execution is scheduled to take place — Nancy protests his innocence, and the sisters can verify her claim, but no, they can't! They have, after all, taken a vow of eternal silence. 'HERO EXECUTED,' announce the headlines the next morning, '…ALMOST!!'. And then we see Vic and Nancy's wedding photo, with Vic grinning and

Nancy gritting her teeth, and suspect that he is already getting on her nerves. ◆

Life cartoonery in the film noir

The Coens wrote the *Crimewave* screenplay with director Sam Raimi, who achieved minor cult status with his *Evil Dead* movies, and who doesn't really go in for story-telling in his films. He weaves situations together, situations that appear both abstract and somehow typical for the genre. European critics don't seem to mind the fact that his cinematic aesthetic, which is simultaneously trashy and arty, is significantly removed from the American mainstream. They have, however, complained that his films 'go nowhere'. But where should a film 'go'? Towards the development and resolution of a theme, naturally, towards an end that suggests a truth has been revealed to us, or at least that we have been entertained. A film should perhaps have the rigour of the three-act drama of discord, sacrifice and redemption, or maybe the familiar sequence of exposition/intensification/climax/retardation/resolution, but there is little of this in Sam Raimi's work. His films are submerged in an underworld, a world of symbols where they bloodily bang their heads and refuse to find their way out. They quickly ditch dramatic convention and begin to play feverishly with the building blocks they have generated like a thing possessed. Towers are erected only to immediately collapse again, and the blocks often comically refuse to fit together at all. Raimi must have been dozing over a comic book the day the film professor, to inevitable but sympathetic laughter, told his students that a good film has a beginning, a middle and an end. Raimi is said to have a collection of 25,000 comics, including a few real rarities, and have you ever tried discussing Sergei Eisenstein's ideas on montage with someone who owns 25,000 comics? You should try it some time. You'll be surprised.

It's far easier to talk about attitude than about plot when dealing with Raimi's films. His work is much more reminiscent of that European master of fantastic anti-dramaturgy, Georges Franju, than it is of the great era of Hollywood genre films. Raimi's *Darkman* (1989), which comes closest to having a traditional storyline, is like a mixture of *Judex* (1963) and *Les yeux sans visage* (*Eyes Without a Face/The Horror Chamber of Doctor Faustus* [1959]), and his Western *The Quick and the Dead* (1995) is, in its consistent rejection of any real dramaturgy, comparable only to *L'Homme sans visage* (*Shadowman* [1973]).

The Raimi and Coen universes may well have developed in radically different ways, but it does seem logical that the director of *The Evil Dead* (1983) and the Coen brothers should have come together at least once (they did in fact collaborate occasionally afterwards, though, and their bond is not merely a professional one). Their meeting of minds produced one of the strangest films in the history of B-movies, and *Crimewave* is so weird that not only did it leave Raimi fans nonplussed, but Coen fans would later refuse to acknowledge it. The film breaks down the usual relationship between cause and effect, becoming a sort of cinematic cartoon nonsense which, unlike the later Coen films, does not lead one deeper into ever more riddles and connections but instead remains resolutely focused on the surface (which is by no means meant as a criticism). It is a film with not so much a theme as a formal task: to use the means of modern cinema to establish a link between the aesthetics of the comic strip and the aesthetics of film noir. To carry out such a task, one naturally needs 'material', material which will, at the very least, provide an internal justification for the formal event. It is here above all that the Coens' contribution to the film lies.

Inside jokes and a fascination for the superficial: Bruce Campbell in *The Evil Dead*

The whole thing is, of course, a parody — fooling around. A particular way of playing with autobiographical, mythical and aesthetic material, with the

result that one can never quite tell what is a gag, a little private joke or an allusion to films made by their friends, or to comics, advertisements, television programmes, classic films etc. Raimi had already cultivated this link between inside jokes and his fascination for the superficial in *The Evil Dead*, and he could, of course, count on his loyal and knowledgeable fans, who not only understood every allusion and gag but could also instantly recognise when the director was going beyond the aesthetics of his predecessors.

There is no such following for either the crime thriller or the comedy. The cinemagoer is left alone and unprepared to tackle a hotchpotch of brilliant individual scenes, internal and external references, aesthetic experiments and parodic *élan*. Unlike the film spoofs of Mel Brooks, Zucker and Abrahams or John Landis, *Crimewave*'s genre parody functions through the satirical subversion of visual codes rather than the exaggeration or contravention of clichés. This type of cinematic humour undoubtedly demands more from the viewer than frequent cinema attendance. To appreciate the lunatic camera movements, it is necessary to have thought at some time about how and why a movie camera moves at all. In short, *Crimewave* had to remain an inside joke, a curious hybrid of commercial product and film student project, as often found in the early works of the first generation of film school directors in the USA. It is a film forged from enthusiasm, a film in which little thought was given to who would be able to read the messages it contained.

The film is set in Detroit, where Sam Raimi, Robert Tapert (the producer) and Bruce Campbell (the co-producer and actor) went to school, and it was chosen as a backdrop mainly because it is the town that most resembles the cities seen in the films of the 1940s. It is darker and older than other American cities, or so says Sam Raimi, but it has nothing that amounts to either a proper centre or a monument (no Empire State Building, for instance). The story takes place today, but it is

Detroit in *Crimewave*

shot in the style of movies from the 1930s and 1940s, and features props from the 1950s, and what it sets in motion is just as dubious as what it aims to achieve. *Crimewave* reveals itself as inhabiting a system in which there is neither a reliable linear time scale nor a reliable link between the portrayal and the portrayed, or between code and experience — the code itself becomes the theme. What, for Raimi, was above all a formal challenge, later became, for the Coens, a theme: a narrative that generates itself and at the same time explodes its own narrative time.

The sharp blue and white at the start of the film evokes many things — gangster films of the 1930s and 1940s; silent expressionist films; daily crime strips in the papers, Dick Tracy or Secret Agent Corrigan; wanted posters and vaudeville shows. The vile and lecherous Renaldo exhales his cigarette smoke and it forms a naked woman, just like in the old Tex Avery cartoons. Raimi even eschews the classic use of fade-out in his flashbacks and opts instead for the kind of obvious distortions used in the old serials (when it was also important not to give the characters too much depth).

Examining the film's narrative structure won't get us far, but it is worth investigating how Raimi handles visual codes. Everything is blue and white, dark blue and light blue, as Victor is being dragged to the electric chair, and there is only a single red line above the characters in the walkway. It's difficult to describe the effect it has, although there is something funny about it, just as there is in certain works of art whose point lies not in the contradictoriness of their literary and visual codes, as with the Surrealists, but in the visual code itself, as in the work of Paul Klee, for example. And something similar happens with the background sound too. Trend taps his cigarette on his matchbox, producing a jarringly loud noise as muffled thumps reverberate through the room. The sound is amplified and seems to go on and on until it is interrupted by the

Lecherous: Bruce Campbell as Renaldo

sound of a telephone ringing quite normally, making another significant acoustic point. Finally, there is also the dramaturgy of colour, which reminds us of comic strips in the Sunday supplements of American news-papers, and the distinction between 'coloured' and 'in colour'. The colours want to tell their own story, which often means that, for comic authors and artists, the colourist is the least popular figure, after the publisher. Raimi uses this aesthetic not only to mock classic colour symbols (such as red/blue for the interior/exterior, day/night, sex/hate, hot/cold dichotomies), but also to see just how lime green and royal blue go together when there is enough black in the picture. In doing so, he is being just as merciless towards the form as the Sunday funnies colourist.

The film is also riddled with 'mistakes'. Why doesn't Trend's shadow move when he makes the lampshade swing? The frames should blend into each other logically and harmoniously, but instead they stand side by side throughout, like the panels of a comic. Worst is the constant violation of filmic grammar. The camera is either somewhere where it has no business to be, using a viewpoint which may amaze or baffle, but doesn't draw us into the action, or else utilising such a classic, Renaissance perspective that even the most turbulent scenery is endowed with the static appearance of a painting. Internal and external movement are not synchronous; Raimi tends to employ 'difficult' devices whenever nothing of importance is happening. And there is, of course, the montage, which very definitely brings us back to Eisenstein. The montage refuses to allow an unambiguous cinematic space by creating unreal distances between the objects in that space, setting the protagonists' line of sight against the direction of the frames, among other things. Instead of a sequence of objective and subjective experience (I see the room where the protagonists are interacting / cut / I see the protagonists reacting to each other in this room / cut / I see the others through

We Kill All Sizes: the exterminators and their tools

the eyes of one of the protagonists) comes a barrage of actions which apparently stand alone. In the scene where Crush attacks Trend's wife Helene, for example, their eyes never meet, as though we are turning an imaginary page between the two takes.

This deconstruction goes far beyond merely quoting from the comic book aesthetic. It also concerns the stylistic device at the heart of *Crimewave,* namely a particular type of 'life cartoonery' — the technique of having real actors behave as though they were cartoon characters. They have no psychological depth, nor are they entirely bound by the laws of nature, and, because they are drawings, they can be killed off and brought back to life at will. Life cartoonery, as developed by the likes of Frank Tashlin and Jerry Lewis, also means that objects are given their own independent existence and are basically equal to the 'human' actors. The acting style is also thoroughly object-bound. Bruce Campbell has been particularly successful in using gesture and facial expression to create what might be described as a machine of rudimentary feelings, whose repertoire is as limited as it is expressive. Above all, he can dispense with emotional transitions, being instantly aggressive, fearful, happy or hurt. And what he is, is, like Popeye, all that he is.

Naturally, this becomes a little tiring after a while, since life cartoonery quickly suppresses any signs of a symbiotic relationship, of growth or development. The viewer is never so well served as in, let us say, a *Naked Gun* film, where he might be allowed to like the idiot the plot revolves around. *Crimewave* is so radical in laying bare its devices that it is uninhabitable. The principle of life cartoonery functions in mainstream comedy largely because the most well-known protag-onists (such as Inspector Clouseau in the *Pink Panther* films) behave in the manner of a cartoon character, while those around them are clearly inhabitants of the normal world where the laws of nature apply.

Crimewave, on the other hand, is played out in a

world where objects and symbols rule, a little like Wonderland without Alice. Or, to put it the other way around, it is a world full of Alices. Somebody falls a couple of storeys onto the street, lies there, looks up and realises that he is still alive and, what is more, he hasn't a scratch on him. As he gets up, he is run over by a car and literally sticks to its windscreen. The man has not lost his 'I've survived!' grin as his murderer, none other than Coddish, tries desperately to dispose of the corpse, bundling him into a lift which signals that it is going up but counts the storeys down to the ground floor (where two policemen have appeared, wearing sun glasses and filmed from below in the style of movie cops). Coddish, who is trying to get rid of the dead man, Crush, carrying the bound and gagged Helene on his back and Vic, who is taking the uncon-scious Nancy to her flat, finally bump into each other on one floor of the apartment block. Doors open, doors close, and they all startle each other, without really knowing why. A small boy finds the body and schleps it along with him, as small boys do when they find things, until he runs into the police officers, who realise straight away that the dead man can only be the victim of a paranoid schizophrenic. 'My Dad!' cries the boy, and when the father looks out of the door he is immediately arrested. The structure of this gag is so abstract that it is able to dispense with psychological timing. The gags simply cannot be reduced to their mechanics — the lovingly costumed father and son, who wear almost exactly the same checked tank tops and bow ties, for example — yet another point that works exclusively on the level of the code and not of the coded (as long as we aren't tempted to venture too analytically into the Coen family history).

Life cartoonery corresponds to a form of human behaviour that is instinctual and perceptual on a pure-ly mechanical level. Vic leaves Nancy's flat to fetch some washing powder (an action which itself is anoth-er joke). She hears a noise and assumes he has not yet

Life cartoonery: objects rule

gone, so she tries to tell him, in a careful and very flattering way, that he's a really nice guy, but... The killer, Coddish, imitating Vic's voice so as not be discovered, is so moved by her words he completely forgets she is not addressing him. When he reveals himself to her in the bathroom, his voice naturally changes, but it goes far beyond the typical reversed voice change from something like *The Nutty Professor* when the hero is torn from his Buddy Love existence. The *Crimewave* villains have grating cartoon voices consisting of little more than childish, primitive sounds and high-pitched whining or sardonic-sadistic bass laughter.

This slapstick cartoonery becomes pure poetry in one of the film's best chase scenes. Helene Trend flees Crush through a series of doors that have been lined up one behind the other in order to demonstrate a security system. She opens each door and then closes it again behind her in a sort of panic-stricken ballet, dancing with the doors while the camera follows her in a tracking movement interrupted only by an end shot and an overhead shot, both distorting proportions and perspective to an Alice in Wonderland extent. Crush smashes through each door with his head as he chases her. She reaches the end and thinks that all is now lost, but this door is clearly more solid than the others. It withstands her pursuer's headbutts, and then begins to sway backwards and forwards until the individual doors fall down like a row of dominoes right on top of the pursuer-turned-pursued, squashing him.

The villain's behaviour in this scene can only be 'understood' if one remembers that he is an animated character. In the cartoon world, a danger exists only if it is recognised as such. The last door is actually made of the same material as the dummy doors, and Helene has no difficulty in making it tip over, but Crush acknowledges it purely as a symbol, and as such it becomes a heavy iron door that is capable of flattening even someone like him. As Helene congratulates herself on her triumph ('I got you!'), she tumbles into an enormous box and is sent as air freight to Uruguay, disappearing from the film once her story is of no more interest to us. Only after the final credits have rolled are we reminded of her fate.

This sequence reveals how the film as a whole functions, with the protagonists subjected to an endless chain of absurd but mechanically linked catastrophes. These events move in the same direction as the domino game with the doors — Nancy, Vic (albeit unknowingly), Helene and the others are at first on the run from the two killers, and their movement is from right to left. Later, when circumstances radically change, although they are still in danger of being murdered by the malefactors, the movement is reversed to match the direction from which the violence now emanates. Everything suddenly starts moving from left to right, and it is Crush and Coddish who are copping it. A similar principle is at work in *The Hudsucker Proxy*, where the silver balls of the Newton's cradle on Paul Newman's desk crash into each other as they swing to and fro. This mechanical, predictable chain of cause and effect produces an almost abstract rhythm, as time in both films shows itself to be an abstruse and arbitrary force.

Coencidences

The techniques of deconstructive life cartoonery and montage used in *Crimewave* are to be found, in a less excessive and more subtle form, in all the later Coen films, liberating the codes from the constraints of representation and tradition. Such stylised techniques are a protest against film that is habitable in time or space, but in the later films there is at least some degree of self-reflection (and the codes themselves work towards rebirth and consciousness). Barton Fink, for example, ends up in a world where the catastrophes pile up, arriving one after another, where the codes used are

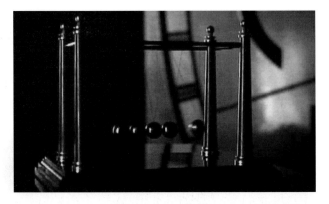

The Hudsucker Proxy

similarly on display (instead of being neutralised by everyday life). We suspect, however, that this happens not because he is a human cartoon figure, but because it's also exactly what is happening inside him. Alice, in comparison, doesn't know if her Wonderland is an external or an internal world either. She just knows that it exists, because she has been excluded from another environment — the good, respectable world of the grown-ups.

There are many other elements in *Crimewave* that lead directly, and literally, to later Coen films. From something as trivial as the names, such as Hudsucker or Odegard (which anticipates *Fargo*'s Lundegaard, another cheated and cheating businessman) to the portrayals of the naïve hero and the two killers — the scene featuring the two mean Laurel and Hardy types screaming wildly will be repeated in *Raising Arizona*, for instance. Even the family and marital relationships seen in *Crimewave* overlap with those depicted in other Coen films. Furthermore, there is, as in *The Hudsucker Proxy* (also a Sam Raimi collaboration), the long fall from a window, the old-fashioned facades of the industrial buildings and the 'miracle' that takes place at a point which is as pivotal as it is unexpected. (Here it is the rebirth of the kind-hearted black man, who has had to do so much as both a living being and as a corpse, suddenly reappearing as a taxi driver,

A change of direction: Vic strikes back

Cheated cheaters: Odegard (Hamid Dana);
Lundegaard (William H. Macy)

causing Vic to slowly raise his eyes towards the heavens in gratitude at the very moment that a comet is drifting past, and then to grab a baseball bat before setting off to save his beloved.) It's sometimes hard to resist the temptation to see *The Hudsucker Proxy* as a remake of *Crimewave*, but there are plenty of tracks in *Crimewave* that lead to other Coen films.

It is as though the Coens rather hurriedly and enthusiastically dipped into their collective reserve of ideas — the results are seen here in a very raw state that shows few signs of the sophistication with which it will later be put to work. To understand the later films it is clearly not necessary to know that the symbols have been used before and are being reproduced in a new form, but they can, on a certain level (on one of many levels), be 'read' in this way, as a Rosebud-type game with signs from a cinematic childhood that is referred to again and again within a system of self-quotation and self-parody. Or, to put it another way, the Coens can allow themselves to use certain codes in a very familiar way for their own personal reasons. These codes may well appear out of place within a particular narrative, but the ease with which the Coens employ them is always somehow transmitted to the viewer.

They also like to use techniques such as the sub- and supercoding of symbols through ingenious camera movements, which move fluidly between distant and distancing overhead shots and close-ups from the side or from below. These ideas are, of course, introduced at the screenplay stage, and the narrative construction simply wouldn't work without them. The *Variety* critic was absolutely right when he pragmatically remarked in his review of *Crimewave* that it was 'more storyboarded than directed' . The relationship between the actual story and the storyboard is turned on its head, though, and 'plot' is at best a pretext for the picture. *Crimewave* achieves far more than just this — it arrives at a new structure, a new narrative with a grammar that could only be possible in the cinema.

Despite frequent collaboration, Sam Raimi and the Coens have developed in entirely different directions. While Raimi continues to work on a 'skeletonisation' and an abstraction of material drawn from popular mythology, the Coens have fleshed out their visual style with ever more narrative, structural and cultural detail. Raimi has stuck to cartoonery, while the Coens have turned more towards life.

Crimewave

Any discussion of the directors' careers or the development of their methods must not, however, lose sight of the fact that *Crimewave* is a genre parody (in which the necessary Hitchcockian suspense-resolutions are driven to a formal, superficial excess). It is a genre parody that suffers not so much from its limited budget as from the pleasure its creators take in experimentation, an experimentation that leaves behind it quite a few structural and narrative loose ends, and we might occasionally feel we are watching the silliest film in the history of cinema. There is also another important point to be made — the contradiction that exists between an autonomous work of art and a product of popular culture, a contradiction the Coens deal with so masterfully in their later films (not least because they turn it into a major theme), has not really been addressed here. The kids have lost themselves in their game, and the game has begun to play back. Again and again we are delighted by some detail, only to lose interest in it immediately because there is no heart (a heart which will, however, emerge in later Coen films) to bestow any significance on the codes and enable them to retain their aesthetic value. Only in *Raising Arizona* do the Coens once again project their grotesque material in a similarly two-dimensional, linear fashion. After that, they move on. ■

The Hudsucker Proxy

Blood Simple

Blood Simple makes an impact straight away. As in a film noir, we are quickly drawn into a specific ambience and are supplied with false information, even a false perspective. A worm's-eye view of a country road shows us the remains of a burst tyre in the foreground.

Texas. A broad sky frames the rumbling derricks. A gigantic advertising hoarding stands in the middle of the prairie. In the lethargic, spiteful singsong of the Texan drawl, a male voiceover draws up the moral co-ordinates of this universe: 'The world is full of complainers. The fact is, nothing comes with a guarantee.' And Texas isn't Russia, where everyone pulls for everyone else. Here you pull for nobody but yourself, and even that is too much. As the picture darkens from cut to cut and night takes hold of the road, we know that we need not bother with any false hopes. In Texas you have to

The heart of the intrigue:
M. Emmet Walsh as the detective

look after yourself, and you can't even count on nature. Heavy rain sets in as the opening credits roll. A man and a woman in a car drive through the stormy night.

The couple are Abby (Frances McDormand), the young wife of the wealthy but unattractive bar owner Julian Marty (Dan Hedaya), and strong, silent bartender Ray (John Getz), who works for Marty. It is more of an escape than a conspiracy. Ray tells his companion that he has liked her for a long time, and Abby looks as she will look throughout the film — disturbed and determined to survive. The trip, briefly interrupted by a mysterious Volkswagen Beetle, ends in a motel bed. Ray is woken by a phone call... 'Had a good time?' asks a voice. 'Who was it?' asks Abby. 'Your husband.' But it was, of course, the detective (M. Emmet Walsh). And it was the detective who spoke the film's first words to us, who has

trailed the couple in his Beetle, who may even have set the whole thing up to gain some advantage. We are none the wiser after the conversation between Marty and Ray, when Marty sneers at the idea that Abby has come back on account of the other man.

Julian Marty (Dan Hedaya) with the incriminating photographs

The shabby, bloated detective, who specialises in divorce cases, is then introduced, having slowly become a menacing presence in the film. We now see him in the flesh as he sits with his feet on the table and an immense Stetson on his head, as country and western music plays in the background. He hands over to Marty an envelope containing photographs which confirm Abby's adultery with Ray. The cowboy detective, who is never named, is rebuffed at first, but he knows he will get the job. Marty, the entrepeneur, surprises his wife with her lover, with whom she is now living. (Already, relation-

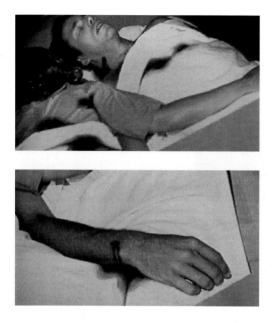

See what you want to see: the
manipulated photos

Abby (Frances McDormand)

ships seem to have been strangely invert-
ed — is Ray behaving like a jealous husband?) Marty drags her out of the house
to try to force her to come back to him —
she tries reaching for her gun but he prevents her, and she eventually manages to
break free, after biting his finger and
kicking him in the groin. Marty throws
up violently before beating a retreat
along with his German shepherd dog
(from whose point of view we followed
the action for a few moments).

Marty meets the detective in a lover's
lane high above the town. He wants to
have his wife and her swain killed, but
the detective has other plans. He doctors
photographs he has taken of the pair in
bed to make it look as though he has shot
them dead. This is easy, as we know, and not only from
Coen films, since people see what they want to see. He
meets Marty in the back office of the bar, presents him
with the 'proof', and collects his remuneration. Marty
feels ill at the sight of the pictures and has to retreat to
the toilet. When he returns, the detective shoots him,
using Abby's pistol to do the deed. Throughout the
scene the ceiling fan spins, cutting noisily through the
air.

Ray calls in at the bar and sees what has happened.
The gun goes off when he knocks it with his foot, and he
fishes it out from under a cupboard. Because he thinks
Abby is the killer, he tries to erase all traces of the crime,
removing his boss's body along with his lover's weapon.
He cleans up the room while his colleague Meurice
(Samm-Art Williams) amuses himself in the bar proper
with a woman, and decides to bury the body. Ray drives
into the desert, to the sounds of a soul song that grows
ever louder. On the way, he discovers that Marty is still
alive (barely), and is horrified to find him missing when
he returns to the car after a reconnaissance trip. But

Marty has not gone far. The car's headlights pick him out as he crawls along the road, Latin American music blaring out from the radio (or from somewhere). The expression on Ray's face as he looks at Marty drives away any sympathy we may still have for him. He feels obliged to end the matter himself, and considers running over his boss with the car, but he can't bring himself to do it. So he takes a shovel from the boot and prepares to beat him to death, but again he hesitates. Headlights grow larger in the distance, and Marty grabs hold of Ray's trouser leg for a brief moment. A truck is approaching fast. Ray drags Marty back to the car, and in doing so gets blood all over him. He finally digs a grave in a field with giant furrows and starts to bury Marty, still alive and still twitching. From the grave, half-covered in earth, Marty raises his pistol and tries to shoot Ray. He pulls the trigger twice, but the chamber is empty. Ray starts shovelling again while Marty covers his face with his hands and screams. When Ray has buried him, he bashes down the mound with the shovel. Not since Wolfgang Kieling's death in the gas oven in Hitchcock's *Torn Curtain* (1966) has anyone taken so long to die on screen.

Suddenly it's morning, and it looks like a pretty cold one. The furrows in the field stretch off into infinity. Ray smokes a cigarette and looks like a man who no longer wants to be an advertisement for jeans. The images that follow are both sad and beautiful: the tracks of the car across the field; the mist around the farmhouse in the background; Ray, as he drives along the highway; a flock of crows that casts an unexpected shadow on the road. A very simple piano motif is heard; simple, but with an unexpected and unsentimental resolution. At the end of the road a light comes towards him — a car drives by with an old hillbilly at the wheel, who grins and gives the Texan greeting (shooting him with an imaginary pistol). He stops at a garage so emblematic of his angst and desolation that it might have been put there especially, and phones Abby to tell her that she doesn't have to worry any more, that he has taken care of everything. Unfortunately, she has no idea what he is talking about, and so begins the mistrust that will lead to more deaths.

The detective burns the photos of Abby and Ray, but taking them out of the envelope he finds a notice saying: 'All Employees Must Wash Hands Before Resuming Work'. Shit! He realises he has left his lighter behind, the one with the lasso initials on it. He will have to return to the scene of the crime.

Cut to Ray and Abby. The telephone interrupts the moment of the incipient schism between them. There is no voice at the other end of the line. Abby can only speculate: 'It's him!' — 'Who?' — 'Marty!' Ray knows it must be someone else. He moves to leave the room, through dusty beams of early morning sun, like in a little cathedral. A Mexican song can be heard in the distance again. 'You left your gun behind,' he says, and lays the pistol down before he shuts the door behind him.

Meurice finds a strange message on his answering machine. It's from Marty, saying that money is missing from the till. Meurice goes to Ray's place, accuses him of theft and tells him to put the money back, overlooking the bloodstains in Ray's car in his excitement. Now it's Ray's turn to be clueless about what is going on around him. We now suspect there is something dubious about his past, just as there seems to be about Abby's.

Abby, meanwhile, has gone to the bar to try to find out what has happened, but the detective got there first, and is now hiding, watching her. She looks around, seeing scattered papers, the hammer the detective used to try and open the safe, and some fish.

Back home, she sinks exhausted onto the bed, but then she hears something. 'Ray!' she calls. She goes into the living room and finds Marty sitting there. 'I love you. That's a stupid thing to say, right?' he says. 'I love you too,' she whispers, and he replies, 'No, you're just saying that 'cause you're scared'. He throws the gun to her, spewing torrents of thick, black blood onto the floor. Then Abby wakes up.

'I'm not afraid of you, Marty': Abby nails down the detective's hand

Ray, who has packed his things, will not tell her what really happened, but she figures out that Marty was still alive when he buried him, and she goes to Meurice, who has a dreadful hangover following the loss of his job — perhaps his headache makes the thudding of a pneumatic hammer in the background seem so loud. Meurice tells her that Ray took Marty's money, but Abby is certain that Marty is dead. The net begins to close in. Meurice doesn't believe Marty is dead, and goes out to look for him — in the meantime, he advises Abby, she should keep away from Ray. Ray is busy searching through Marty's office, where he finds the photos that show he and Abby 'dead'.

Ray is waiting for Abby when she gets home, urging her to turn off the light. She is afraid of him and turns it back on again, then the bullet hits him and the telescopic

sight is directed towards her. At the last moment she jumps to the side, and manages to knock out the light bulb with her shoe. Moonlight glitters on the broken glass; a sad Mexican song plays, as though death were a temptation from the other side of the border; steps are heard; the ventilator fan rotates. The detective searches Ray's corpse, and starts looking for Abby. In the bathroom he sees that she has escaped through the window. He puts his ear to the wall, reaches outside and opens the next window along, but she jams his arm and stabs a knife right through his hand and into the wooden window frame (just like Mrs Trend and Crush in *Crimewave*). Here, the pain caused by each act of violence, which is also psycho-sexual in its nature, goes much deeper, and the cowboy detective digs more maliciously into America's poetic mythos than dim-witted, thuggish bad guy Crush. He shoots blindly through the wall, causing ever more holes to appear, and rays of light burst through them, forming strange and beautiful patterns in the dark room. When his gun runs out of bullets he begins to scream in desperation, pounding the thin wooden wall until he eventually punches a hole through it and can pull the knife out of his hand. Abby, meanwhile, has grabbed her pistol and is cowering in a corner in the next room.

Before the detective goes to find her, he must of course put his hat back on. He is about to walk into the room when Abby shoots. We hear him scream, and another beam of light appears. 'I'm not afraid of you, Marty,' she says. The detective lies there as if dead, but lets out a last spine-chilling laugh as the blood pours from his stomach. This is the last deception of the film — the detective does not believe in his own death. He is lying on his back under a washbasin, and a drop of water frees itself from the pipes and falls slowly down onto him. 'You're sweet...' goes The Four Tops hit 'Same Old Song' as the closing credits roll: directed by Joel Coen / produced by Ethan Coen / written by Joel Coen and Ethan Coen.   ◆

Simply bloody

Blood Simple is almost shockingly simple in its structure, much simpler at least than its supposed literary and cinematic models, the hard-boiled novel and the film noir. Love betrayed, murder and intrigue, double-crossing and resolution. The dramatic structure that was abandoned with such relish in *Crimewave* appears to be at least approximately respected here. The exposition presents us with the estranged husband and wife, the lover and the tempter in the form of the cowboy detective who pushes the intrigue to its deadly conclusion. After Marty's comparatively unbloody attempt to abduct his wife comes the plot which eventually leads to the first crisis, Marty's excruciating murder. The retardation leads us through the misunder-

standing between the two lovers and Abby's search for the truth, to the second and final crisis, which brings about the only possible resolution — the duel between Abby and the murderer. Using the right actors and pacing, it would be entirely possible to use these elements to produce a very effective, if conventional, genre piece. This option is, however, ruled out by several opposing factors:

Love without passion: Abby with Ray (John Getz)

1. The construction of the drama is both diachronically and synchronically open. It begins not with the adultery that establishes the tragic triangle, but with the return of the wife. Where has she been? Has she attempted to escape, or was her absence due to something as brutally trivial as an abortion? Marty sneers at Ray for thinking she has come back for him. And when Ray and Abby are together, there are so many little things that suggest they are at the end rather than the

beginning of their love affair. The characters don't 'explain' themselves as the heroes in *The Postman Always Rings Twice* and its various film versions do, for instance, through their obsessive passions. Minor characters and subplots carry the seeds of their own stories in themselves, which may or may not have some connection to the main plot.

2. Neither the emotional nor the intellectual structure keeps pace with the dramatic action. Instead of working to resolve their situation, the characters appear to fall apart emotionally. Instead of finding out more about themselves, about the other characters and about their relationships with each new step, the protagonists actually know less about what is really going on with every turn of the plot, enabling the final conflict to coincide with a process of painful recognition. In the Hitchcockian scheme of things there are, however, two missing elements in the way the suspense is constructed in *Blood Simple*: firstly, the viewer's sympathy or, failing that, pity for at least one of the characters; and secondly, the viewer's assurance that he or she knows more than the protagonist.

3. The composition of images and the presentation of objects does not match their function in the plot. There are always the red herrings that pepper Hitchcock films, and the sort of false shock or suspense devices which we are used to finding in thrillers and horror films, when every second or third 'real' threat turns out to be a harmless misunderstanding — in this case it is the practical legibility of the world that is blurred. It is no coincidence that in this film each character can see every other character as a murderer while the real murders are carried out in ignorance of the victim/killer relationship. The most terrible aspect of the final duel is that Abby does not know the identity of the person who is trying to kill her, and whom she ends up killing.

4. There is an autonomy in the film's stylisation, whereby the story both tells itself and 'reflects' upon itself, and thus on the narrative form of the film noir.

This is done by means of exaggeration and caricature — one can clearly see *Blood Simple* as a parody — and multiple levels of coding. Sometimes the film almost seems to come to a halt in order to admire its own aesthetic potential. When it has got moving again, we then notice that a change of tempo also conceals things that are important for the development of the plot, or for comprehension of it. And if we don't wish to regard the protagonists' motive as pure, mechanical desire for gratification (as in *Crimewave*), then we have to try to understand them through recurring images such as the highway, the field, or the window pane.

5. Each individual player in the game — the young, frustrated wife, the hot-blooded lover, the vengeful husband and the shabby private detective — is deconstructed, and none more so than the figure of the Westerner/detective. As soon as their inner, iconographic affinity is brought to the surface, the lonely

cowboy and the shabby private eye both turn out to be semiotic deceptions.

6. Finally, this is not a story of morality or redemption. It seems clear right from the start that there is no hope. None of the characters can absolve themselves, and even the female sacrifice is not really accepted. The myth is not broken on the back of 'reality', as in the modernistic, late phases of the genre, but undermines itself instead .

The storyboard again

L ike *Crimewave*, *Blood Simple* relies heavily on an incredibly detailed storyboard (although the charge that it is 'more storyboarded than directed' can certainly not be made here). Working so closely from the storyboard not only enables speedy work once on the set (which is particularly important when the budget is limited), but is also in keeping with the Coens' distinctive style of visual composition.

The recurring elements used here are not so spectacular in themselves but achieve some very particular effects in their dramatic repetition. Take, for example, the view over the prairie from the arched windows of Ray and Abby's living room. The colour and the mood of the landscape, of the outside, is different each and every time it is seen. The ventilator fan, with its penetrating noise, is repeatedly used as a harbinger of death. The sound of gunfire is heard several times throughout the film, but it generally turns out to be harmless, and became a threat only because the viewer's overwrought perception made it one (it also happens when a newspaper is blown against the window pane). And, finally, there is the acoustic flash forward, a device that will be stylistically polished in later Coen films, largely through their use of music.

Overlapping sound effects, match cuts and a camera that never stops moving but manages to avoid seeming too hectic (a 'Texan' camera, if you like), give the film a dynamic which is generally absent from productions in this price range. Classic techniques for leading the viewer astray and for creating suspense are routinely employed. There is no dialogue in the twenty minute long sequence when Ray kills Marty, but unlike in *Du rififi chez les hommes* (*Rififi* [1956], dir. Jules Dassin), the impression created is not one of obsessive concentration but rather the feeling of time stretching mercilessly out — as though we are to understand that the awfulness of the act is surpassed only by the awfulness of the non-act (bearing in mind that Ethan Coen was once a philosophy student). The constantly moving camera means that the viewer never gets his bearings. Despite repeated takes of

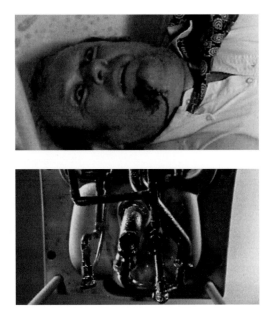

the same objects from the same angle, the plot has no fixed point and the movement no fixed direction. The camera moves, and what is in front of it also moves. Movement along a line in one direction is followed by movement the opposite way, and progress along a vertical line comes after progress along a horizontal one, until it resembles nothing more than the spinning of an ever tighter web. At the end of the film, the inevitable trajectory of the falling drop of water both complements and contradicts the horizontal vector of the blind journey through the rain at the beginning, and water, the symbol, has increased in intensity from a general condition to a single point.

Such visual compositions can only be achieved by deliberate planning and forethought, not by 'thinking with the camera' or by handing responsibility over to a set or costume designer — even if the Coens are able to call on Jane Musky, a production designer whose fine work deserves tribute in itself. In the room which forms the centre of Ray and Abby's relationship with each other and the outside world (a space which is all too

open, yet feels like a fortress), we are repeatedly presented with a 'naked' interior wall, a brick wall one would normally expect to see on the outside of a building, and we can only read this as a sign that leads off in all sorts of directions. We might read the house as a head whose inside has been revealed, just as the inner skin of Barton Fink's room will also be exposed; an interior design trend of the post-Reagan era of the American aesthetic, a style that is simultaneously derelict and ostentatious; the dwelling place of people who have turned the outside in; a construct which, like the film itself, does not need to conceal its inner structure — or perhaps this space, which determines the relationship between Ray and Abby, is simply not complete.

It is at the same time an 'abstract game', which, through its rhythm, takes the form of a dialogue between the point and the line (as Sergei Eisenstein would have said); or the angular against the round, the artificial against the organic (as seen even more explicitly in the shots of the land art in the furrowed field after Marty's murder).

The land itself plays a leading role, the prairie that lies far away from the world where the 'biiiiig buildings' are, the buildings Meurice, the barman, described as though he were telling some visiting hillbilly a fantastic fairytale. The border between the wilderness and the garden has again become fluid. It is either shimmeringly hot or wet or pitch black, or all these things at once. This affects perception of where boundaries really lie, and also has consequences for relations between the various characters. Everything is pretty sweaty and dirty, which is why it seems so difficult to get a hold on any particular person or thing.

The dissolution of form is both the driving force and

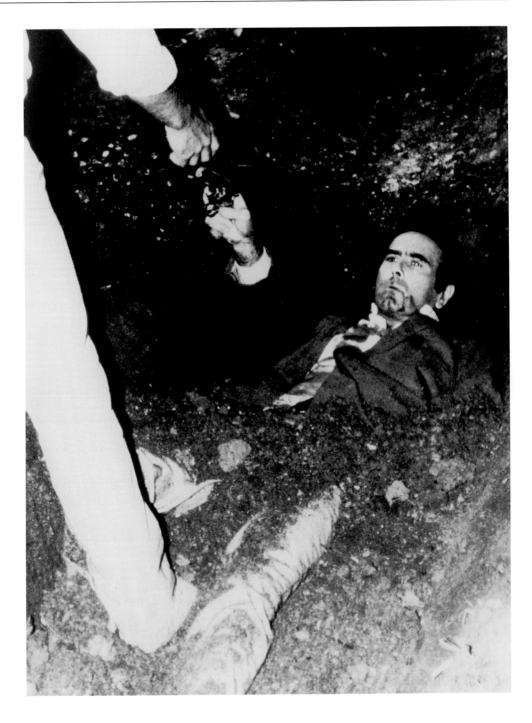

John Garfield and Lana Turner, and Jack Nicholson and Jessica Lange in different versions of the James M. Cain novel *The Postman Always Rings Twice* (1946 and 1980); Juan De Landa, Massimo Girotti and Clara Calamai in *Ossessione* (1942, dir. Luchino Visconti)

the aim of the film, but it is also something which is present as a direct sensory experience. In *Crimewave* it's the creators' sadistic play instinct alone which deconstructs a genre, but here the disruption, the destruction, stems directly from the characters themselves, from the very aura of the place. *Blood Simple* completes a 360 degree turn to arrive at a new form of realism. It's possible that there is a mythical place called 'Texas' which engenders anti-logical and anti-melodramatic fantasies, but it's equally possible that the *real* Texas can only be described by constructing such anti-logical and anti-melodramatic fantasies. Which brings us once again to that author who is much alluded to in *Blood Simple*: Edgar Allan Poe.

A fake film noir

The common ground between *Blood Simple* and James M. Cain's novel *The Postman Always Rings Twice*, and its film versions on both sides of the Atlantic, is considerable. The plot kicks off in an apparently straightforward fashion with the mechanical inversion of the exposition — it is not the lovers who try to get the husband out of the way (the obsessive reacting to the normal), but the husband who seeks the death of the adulterers (the normal defending itself brutally against the aberration). Homage to Hitchcock is, however, never far away, and the film bids again and again to construct negation. The reversal leads to a series of at least partly unforeseeable effects which appear to be out of everyone's control (including the director, the genre's conventions, even our own rationalisation). Within a three-dimensional aesthetic-moral model, the inversion of a premise leads not only to a negative reflection of the model itself but also to a chaotisation of the entire system. What occurs in *Crimewave* through its series of collapsing doors leads, when is transferred to a three-dimensional world, to the fracture and the eclipsing of the intensifying, breaking (crime) waves.

Blood Simple is a film noir without an emergency exit.

The mechanical inversion of the exposition does not in the end lead to a revolt against the mythos, and the Oedipal drama is reinstated. The 'son', who steals the woman/child from the powerful father, is pursued by his terrible double and reduced to a state of 'speechlessness' that will eventually kill him. This violation of the family saga, the theme of so many films noir, is different in *Blood Simple* in so far as it does not present itself as a linear drama (which can be resolved through guilt, sacrifice and atonement), but as normality, as part of the system itself. And the 'dark fairytale' is shattered, because the erotic and the material crime itself falls apart, among other things.

The classic voiceover or flashback in the film noir usually harks back to some guilt-laden past, to some

Inversion of the exposition: Marty hires a contract killer

crime that can only be judged in the present established at the end of the sequence. But in *Blood Simple* the voiceover leads into the space where the action is yet to take place, representing not a false testimony but a false institution. The film is 'told' by the murderer and it ends with his death. We are familiar with the absurd construction in Billy Wilder's *Sunset Boulevard* (1950) of a narrator who turns out to be lying dead in a swimming pool, but it is even more absurd to have a dead man begin the tale with some general philosophical statements, laying down some rules. He has either contradicted himself by his own death or else he has, with his very last words, delivered his death sentence.

Voiceovers or flashbacks lead to structural clarity at best, not to analytical explanations. Instead of being a confession, in this instance the construction becomes a confirmation of moral equanimity, a laconicism of complete failure. 'Texas', the heart of the United States of America, thus behaves just like the main character in the film — if 'Texas' really is Texas, then it isn't worth saving.

The joke is that this film noir finds itself existing in a Western environment, in a world where modernisation hasn't taken hold (modernisation as an attempt to imitate *Dallas*, that is). The second joke is that the characters don't behave like the overwrought, melancholy heroes of the film noir, with their deadly obsessions, nor like the archetypal men and women who inhabit the Western, but like wicked, unsympathetic, very ordinary people. At one point, Abby says that her psychiatrist told her she was as normal as anyone can be. This is not only quite true but also totally absurd. How can you have a normality that you don't believe in yourself, and which you regard as the most peculiar thing?

Blood Simple is a film full of fear rather than violence. The characters are beside themselves because ultimately they are as hollow as the architecture of their world. The careful, expressive arrangement of isolated images, in which neon signs look like works of art; shattered glass like a puzzle; the ventilator fan on the ceiling

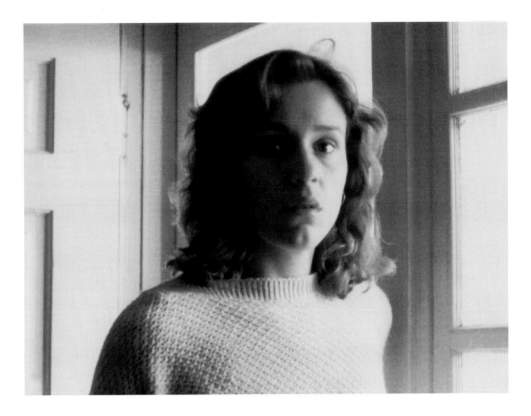

A film full of fear: Frances McDormand

like a metronome for the bloody ballet, hints at the continuation of the identity of the characters inside their masks. It is Frances McDormand's expression, along with the misdeeds of the fat cowboy detective, that lays bare the heart of *Blood Simple*. It is a childlike, covetous, want-to-be-happy look that combines a terrible fear of anything that moves with a sadistic curiosity, neutralising the conflicting impulses of flight and resistance.

Blood Simple really is a nasty film. The Coens don't appear to have the slightest consideration for any of their characters, and are quite happy to take them apart, mercilessly, both physically and morally. It as though the love triangle story serves only to display the characters' most unattractive traits. This also goes for the setting, Texas, which at first seems to be no more than a pile of clichés, a place, as Joel Coen puts it, 'where you wear a gun and shoot anyone who looks at you funny'. But what emerges is not the reality *behind* the cliché, but rather the reality *within* it.

Freedom's just another word

The opening voiceover presents us with an unappealing definition of what freedom means in the state of Texas, and the rest of the film can be seen as an exploration of this definition. Each of the characters is, in his or her rather painful way, free to make their own moral and material decisions. It is not the case, either in *Blood Simple* or the other Coen films, that a character can be aware of the sinfulness of his action but unable to stop himself carrying it out. It is precisely because the characters are able to make free decisions that this structure of inexorable evil emerges.

This obscene idea of freedom, alongside the swipe at Russia, is a résumé of the Reaganism of the time. The fact that it is formulated by the most immoral and unappetising figure in the film gives the movie a thoroughly political accent. It shows what is behind this façade of freedom, and not only in Texas, a barbarism that does not even understand its own nature. *Blood Simple* is, among other things, a radically anti-American film. ∎

Raising Arizona

Prison officer Edwina 'Ed' (Holly Hunter) and inept petty crook and natural born loser H.I. 'Hi' McDunnough (Nicolas Cage) meet and fall in love in the county lock-up in Tempe, Arizona. They get married and settle down in a trailer on the edge of town, and all they need to complete their happiness is a baby, but to their great distress it turns out that Ed is barren. When the pair hear that the wife of wealthy furniture dealer Nathan Arizona (Trey Wilson) has just been blessed with quintuplets, they see the solution to their problem. They manage, not without difficulty, to abduct Nathan Jr, and suddenly become a 'proper' family. Hi doesn't appear to be entirely comfortable with the lower middle-class family idyll, though, even saying at one point that he comes from a long line of frontiersmen and needs freedom just as other people need their daily bread. His recent past, in the form of

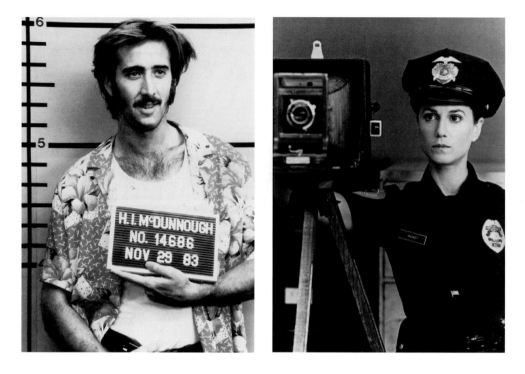

Professional encounters: Hi (Nicolas Cage) and Ed (Holly Hunter)

two infantile former cellmates, Gale (John Goodman) and Evelle (William Forsythe), the unusual sexual preferences of young parents Glen (Sam McMurray) and Dot (Frances McDormand) and Hi's subconscious in the shape of terrifying, bounty-hunting biker Leonard Smalls (Randall 'Tex' Cobb) all combine to provide new obstacles and a series of bewildering plot twists. Hi has decided to fall back into the familiar arms of lawlessness when Gale and Evelle steal the child in order to claim the reward its father has offered. A wild hunt for baby Nathan ensues, at the end of which Hi and Ed, exhausted and disillusioned, decide to return the infant to its lawful parents and then split up. Nathan Sr catches them as they try to bring back his baby, but, instead of calling the police, he takes pity on them and advises them to think again before they separate. The film ends on a conciliatory note with Hi's dream. It is a simple dream that shows a happy family celebrating

Thanksgiving, but we have seen from the Lone Biker of the Apocalypse the power Hi's dreams can have.　◆

Domestic bliss: a longing for conformity

Children, dogs, hand grenades

When asked what the vital ingredients of *Raising Arizona* were, Joel Coen said it contained all the essential elements of popular cinema: 'Babies, Harleys, and explosives.' He could also have mentioned dogs, car chases and Laurel and Hardy (as W.C. Fields said, anyone who hates children and dogs can't be all bad). *Raising Arizona* is a turbulent, high-speed cartoon, laced with surreal effects, which quotes liberally from all sorts of popular genres, mixes them together and stands back in amazement to observe the result. But the film also examines the longing for conformity that is expressed through the desire to have children, and with the contradictions that emerge on

In the footsteps of W.C. Fields: children...

...and dogs

the way to the fulfilment of this desire. This longing is condemned at the same time, and the fundamental mythical institution of the American Dream, the 'holy family', is subjected to a satirical endurance test which makes it appear to be what Alexander Kluge and Oskar Negt called a 'terror relationship' in more ways than one.

'More than we can handle,' jokes Nathan Arizona for the benefit of the press when he is interviewed about the Arizona quints. Nathan Sr, the wily, self-made businessman ('My motto is do it my way or watch your butt!') thinks it highly amusing that there might be a situation that he is unable to handle. It is his off-the-cuff remark that leads Hi and Ed to address the obvious imbalance in God's world. Abducting the baby will enable the unfruitful to multiply, to found their own 'state' (*Raising Arizona* would have made a great title for a 'how we snatched the forty-third state from the Mexicans' frontier myth), to become a 'proper' family. Where did they get their ideas from? It is the prison psychologist Doctor Schwartz who tells Hi that there is an alternative to prison life in a therapy session at the start of the film: 'Most men your age, Hi, are getting married and raising up a family. They wouldn't accept prison as a substitute.' Hi does not know how to respond to this, and his fellow prisoners Gale and Evelle jump in. There are situations, they say, in which your job has to come first. And with this we have an important theme of the prosperous 1980s and its yuppie ideology: career or kids? Hollywood reacted around the middle of that decade with a string of movies mawkishly exploring the longing for a family and the promise of happiness through reproduction. And they examined the dilemma so simply stated by Ed: 'We got a child now, everything's changed!'

The theme was omnipresent. There was the stressed career woman, who through sudden yearning or simply by coincidence unexpectedly discovers the joys of motherhood, through adoption, if neces-

sary (*Baby Boom* [1986, dir. Charles Shyer]); the three men who have to deal with a foundling (*Three Men and a Baby* [1987, dir. Leonard Nimoy]); the young couple who are forced to face up to their responsibilities by an unwanted pregnancy (*For Keeps* [1987, dir. John G. Avildsen]); and the 'interior monologue' of a talking embryo (*Look Who's Talking* [1989, dir. Amy Heckerling]). But *Raising Arizona* stands out like an alien body in the midst of this trend because the child-wish appears as a clear sign of a heteronomous conscious-ness and because babies are treated as a consumer product that is in very short supply. Here, the issue is not that major moral problem of the 1980s, the choice between career and kids, but rather the telling fact that Nathan Arizona, the already highly successful busi-nessman, is further validated through his fertility, which can be seen as a natural legitimisation of radical Reaganomics. When Hi and Ed rebel against what

Serial production: baby boom in the Arizona household

they see as the unfair distribution of goods, they are also rebelling against nature, which is in bed with power. In the films that deal affirmatively with the theme, economic or emancipatory rationality is counteracted by a discourse made in the name of nature, but Hi and Ed's childlessness appears to be a direct biological and sociological result of their underdog status.

More than he can handle. An insert provides the viewer with more precise information. The scene: the Arizona household. Date: 17 September 1985. Time: 8.45pm. Characters: Hi and babies Harry, Barry, Larry, Garry and Nathan Jr. The choice in the children's bedroom is wide, but we have seen from his convenience store-robbing days that Hi is notoriously undiscriminating. He is only supposed to take one, but it proves harder than expected because he has to pacify the entire brood, and the room is soon swarming with liberated babies. A nightmare! The hopeless battle against the five infants is captured by a series of point of view shots taken from a baby's perspective, more than a little reminiscent of Larry Cohen's cult baby-horror film, *It's Alive* (1973).

More than they could handle. Hi and Ed, defeated, bring the stolen child back at the end. Ed's elemental wish ('I just wanted to be a mama') triggered a long chain of violence and action because the couple did not have enough time or resources to establish a watertight image of normality. Her improvised family is shattered, and all that remains is Hi's conciliatory final dream — and the status quo.

White House, white trash

It's quite possible to trace a political theme through *Raising Arizona,* but it is at the same time difficult to try to define the 'political' jokes. The question that lies at the centre of the Coen enigma is this — do their films have a heart? Cinematographer Barry Sonnenfeld, whose contribution to *Raising Arizona* should not be underestimated, has said the Coens could deliver an excellent screenplay on any given theme because themes are 'incredibly unimportant' to them, and they are more, though not exclusively, concerned with 'structure and style and words'. It is reported elsewhere that the Coens' infamous press conferences, with their perplexing allusions and unintelligible murmuring, are not merely a pose, and that they really 'don't believe in much of anything'.

One populist theory in *Raising Arizona* (which Woody Allen warned us about in *Annie Hall* [1977, dir. Woody Allen]: 'You know the ethics those guys [politicians] have. It's like a notch underneath child molester') says that politicians in Washington are all crooks with whom even professional criminals will not associate. There is no room in the world of outlaws for state gangsters. Hi legitimises his astonishing recidivism by referring to that 'son'bitch' Ronald Reagan in the White House. Pictures of Barry Goldwater and JFK can be seen in the background in the opening sequence (incidentally, these never change, even though quite some time passes between Hi's various stints in jail). Later, Gale and Evelle draw Hi into their plan to rob the 'Farmers and Mechanics Bank of La Grange'. They explain that they got a tip that the place was worth robbing from 'Lawrence Spivey, one of Dick Nixon's under-secretaries of agriculture'. After the heist, when the Snopes brothers notice that they have 'forgotten' Nathan Jr and left him sitting in the road, they rush screaming back to the scene and stop their car just inches from the child. On the left side of the frame, under the car's bumper, is an election sticker for Walter Mondale.

Nathan Arizona (Trey Wilson): self-made businessman or East Coast mobster?

The furniture dealer Nathan Arizona is the only representative of the Establishment who appears in the film. He distinguishes himself through sharp business practices, vulgar language and a thorough lack of respect in his dealings with the authorities. His hack-

The kidnap attempt: baby-horror

'Very structured': fingerprinting, the Mopping Convict, the therapy session, the parole board

neyed advertising slogan, 'And if you can find lower prices anywhere my name ain't Nathan Arizona', is somewhat undermined by the fact that his real name is Nathan Huffhines. When Nathan Jr is abducted, he doesn't forget to plug his business while talking to the press, but such pragmatism can only be dreamed of by the other characters in the film, who resort to hysterical screaming when faced with complex situations. The movie merely hints, however, at one particular aspect of Nathan Sr — FBI agents arrive after the kidnapping and want to take his fingerprints in order to be able to distinguish them from those of the kidnapper, but he is conspicuously resistant to the procedure, which leads us to wonder whether there was more behind his name change than simply optimising his sales strategy ('Would you buy furniture at a store called Unpainted Huffhines?'). Has an East Coast mobster found himself a new identity in the furniture trade?

When we hear the narrator's voice for the first time — 'Call me Hi' — he is being photographed and fingerprinted. Hi may be a notoriously unsuccessful petty criminal, but he likes to talk big. He appreciates the camaraderie and the *esprit de corps* he finds in prison, but we see none of this in the film. What we do see is an unappetising mix of routine and ritual which parallels Hi's life in so far as it is 'very structured'. The impressive opening minutes of *Raising Arizona* make this clear, because within a very short time we are presented with three

cycles of the photographing and fingerprinting process, accompanied by Hi's commentary which draws us into 'his' world. The sessions with Doc Schwartz do, however, have an effect on Hi. One arrest later he is ready to fall in love with the woman he sees the most frequently, whereupon jail loses its homeliness. 'The joint is a lonely place after lock-up and lights out when the last of the cons has been swept away by the sandman.'

The repeat offender's life turns in a circle, a fact which again becomes clear when Hi, at last a free man, asks Ed to marry him. As he does so, he also greets Curt, who is being photographed before being sent back into the can. There is no great difference between Hi and Ed's social status. Their first (and last) home is mobile, and they are white trash who live out on the edge of town, where the desert begins. Hi's new life — he gets a mindless job in the steel processing industry — may well be little different to the one he knew in jail,

White trash on the edge of town: 'That was beautiful!'

75

but the couple do manage to have their 'salad days'. In one picturesque scene they lie on folding beds and watch the sun go down. When it has finally disappeared, we hear Ed's voice in the darkness: 'That was beautiful.' It is Ed who decides that their happiness is big enough for three: 'There was too much love and beauty for just the two of us.' The outlaw Hi reacts to these words with apparent indifference, but he knows they are about to change his life: 'My lawless years were behind me; our child rearin' years lay ahead.'

In the first photo they take of their new family unit, after they've kidnapped Nathan Jr, Hi looks like he very definitely wants to be somewhere else. And when he takes his 'son' on a tour of the trailer, his words are like an estate agent's sales patter: 'Lookahere, young sportsman. That there's the kitchen area where Ma and Pa chow down. Over there's the TV, two hours a day maximum, either educational or football so's you don't ruin your appreciation of the finer things. This here's the divan, for socialisin' and relaxin' with the family unit. Yessir, many's the day we sat there and said wouldn't it be nice to have a youngster here to share our thoughts and feelin's.'

It is not Doc Schwartz who is the inspiration for this little lecture, but, we assume, *Dr Spock's Baby and Child Care* manual. The rest comes from the Beach Boys. Convincing it is not, and we can only agree with Gale and Evelle that Hi is not being 'true to his own nature'. On the other hand, a baby offers the possibility of making a copy of oneself, an idea with which Hi and Evelle seem to concur when they call Nathan Jr a 'little outlaw'. This is an appalling prospect for Ed, who, as one critic has pointed out, can already see Nathan Jr's future sitting in her living room in the form of Gale and Evelle; two big babies who feed on crisps and beer.

Circle jerks

In *Raising Arizona*, as in all slapstick comedies, the cyclical structure is a vital characteristic. We enc-ounter it in both the major and minor elements of the film (as we do later, in *The Hudsucker Proxy*). The life of an unsuccessful petty criminal appears to follow an almost natural cycle — Hi repeatedly meets the bald-headed Mopping Convict in exactly the same spot in the cell block as the man goes about his 'natur-al' activity of mopping. The convicts meet one another on the fixed day of their sessions with the prison psy-chologist, who very successfully provides them with the terms they need to be able to describe their own existence. Despite the breakneck speed of some of the film's individual episodes, neither the plot nor the characters ever get anywhere. In one of *Raising Arizona*'s most appealing scenes, Gale and Evelle, who have by now abducted baby Nathan for themselves, hold up a store. They are looking for nappies and bal-loons that blow up into funny shapes, and the nice old man working in the shop says his balloons are only funny if you think round is funny. He finds himself looking down the barrel of a gun, is told to lie on the floor, count up to 825 and then back down to zero, and is warned that the gangsters will be keeping an eye on him in order to promptly punish any violations: 'I'll be back to check — see y'ain't cheatin'.'

Kidnapped and almost forgotten: Nathan Jr (T.J. Kuhn)

We recognise the threat from countless cinematic hold-ups, and experience tells us that the gangsters never actually come back. But Gale and Evelle leave Nathan Jr in the middle of the road and, as soon as they realise what they've done, return to the scene of the crime at top speed, where the old man ('Sevenhun-dredninetyone Mississippi') has just decided to stop counting. As he is getting up he sees Gale and Evelle.

We hear him start counting again as he moves out of the frame. Gale, sitting in the car and looking at the balloons, asks Evelle if they can be blown up into funny shapes, and Evelle replies that they only come in round. The circles are completed — the depressed Snopes brothers return on their own initiative to the familiar world of prison, and Hi and Ed are once again childless.

Cyclical structures are also evident in individual episodes. For example, after a breath-taking chase through the front gardens, back yards, living rooms and hallways of suburban normality, Hi arrives right back at the packet of nappies he left lying on the street just a few minutes previously. *Raising Arizona* has a plot that is continually turning in circles, concealed by the speed of the action (and by a constantly moving camera). This is perhaps why a comment made by a *Sight & Sound* critic with reference to the Coen films in general — that they are like a 'sphinx without a riddle' — is particularly relevant to *Raising Arizona*.

The doll inside the doll

Wanting to have a family makes you tired. We are repeatedly shown Hi and Ed sleeping, completely exhausted. Hi is a dreamer — even when he's in prison he likes to do his thinking in bed. Hi dreams dreams, but he doesn't decide where they begin or end. Nor does the film itself mark the transition from the dream world to the real world — there are no wobbly fades or slow zooms onto faces. When Gale and Evelle are holed up in his trailer, Hi dreams of a terrifying creature, the Lone Biker of the Apocalypse, who drives through the world on a Harley. This Leonard Smalls appears to ride from Hi's dark side directly into the film. Hi himself says that although he doesn't know whether Smalls is a dream or a vision, he thinks he has unleashed him.

Gale and Evelle's bizarre 'birth scene' is also cine-

The Wild One: Lenny Smalls,
Hi's untamed side

matically ambivalent. The two rockabilly compadres
crawl out of the primeval slime, uttering infernal cries,
into the film and into Hi's private life. But where have
they come from? Prison? Or from one of Hi's instinctively anti-family fantasies? The potency of Hi's dreams
stems from another very important fact — he is also the
narrator of the film. If Smalls looks as though he has
just stepped out of a *Mad Max* movie, and if the long,
light-coloured dustcoats that Gale and Evelle wear
when they hold up the bank call to mind certain
spaghetti Westerns, then this may well be because they
are products of Hi's imagination. It is worth considering that the entire film could be a dream Hi has in his
prison cell, which he uses to 'work through' his family-
versus-outlawry dilemma. And there is, of course, Hi's

A strange 'birth': Gale (John Goodman) breaks out of jail

question in the middle of the family apotheosis: 'This whole dream, was it wishful thinking? Was I just fleein' reality, like I know I'm liable to do?'

Viewed from this angle, there are a whole series of signs in *Raising Arizona* that can be traced directly back to Hi's subconscious. Let us suppose that during his many prison sojourns he spent a lot of time in front of the television, and in so doing underwent a thorough programming in Americana. We might then see the references to cowboy and action movies as products of Hi's subconscious, a subconscious which has absorbed the codes of film history.

If we add to that the parallelism of prison and industrial routine, we might arrive at a sort of all-embracing self-delusion, within which even the scenes which try to transcend it are themselves a rip-off of conventional Hollywood models. It would then be interesting to note that 'the system' is represented here by a president, Ronald Reagan, who is said to have been unable to distinguish between celluloid and reality.

In prison, floors are scrubbed and conversations psychologically guided. The prisoners are taught everything they need to know for life on the outside. Many of these 'insights' come in the form of maxims delivered by Doc Schwartz, whose counselling sessions clearly have a big impact on the delinquents. We know that Lenny Smalls' mother didn't love him, because it says so on his tattoo, which is a sort of bodily

The bank job: Gale and Evelle (William Forsythe) in Western outfits

Pale Rider (1985, dir. Clint Eastwood)

explanation for his behaviour. But Lenny is the product of Hi's imagination, and Hi in turn is a victim of Doc Schwartz's therapy sessions. It is quite useful to suppose that Doc Schwartz is behind every situation analysed by the characters in *Raising Arizona*, as is evident from their choice of language. Take, for example, the following dialogue between Ed, Gale and Evelle — Ed: 'You mean you busted out of jail?' Gale: 'Waaaal...' Evelle: 'We released ourselves on our own recognisance...' Gale: 'What Evelle means to say is, we felt the institution no longer had anything to offer.'

Hi's domestic happiness is threatened not only by his jailbird friends and by Lenny, but also by the sexual revolution in the guise of the apparently respectable foreman Glen and his wife Dot. 'Decent' is the word Ed uses to describe the couple to Gale and Evelle, and 'decent' is, according to the promise she wrung out of Hi when they took their first family photo, how their

Sexual revolution in the heartland: Glen (Sam McMurray) and Dot (Frances McDormand)

future together will be. But, recounts Hi at the beginning of the film, people say that son'bitch Reagan is 'decent', and behind Dot and Glen's respectable façade lies the abyss of swingerdom. Glen's family descends like a plague upon Ed and Hi's trailer. Glen tells dim-witted Polack jokes, and manages to screw up the jaded punchlines, while his kids rampage through the place. When Glen suggests swapping partners, Hi reacts instinctively by breaking his nose. Of course, he loses his job because of it, but, for the first time in a long while, feels like a man again. To affirm his masculinity even more, he goes out and holds up the nearest convenience store.

Post-modern and so on

There's a great big mystery / And it's surely worryin' me / Yes, Diddy Wah Diddy, Mr Diddy Wah Diddy / I wish somebody would tell me / What Diddy Wah Diddy means.
(Arthur Blake/Ry Cooder [1974])

Whenever post-modern films are discussed there is a good chance that the Coen brothers will be mentioned. Some critics say that they take on popular genres (the film noir, the Mafia film, the 1940s-style comedy) in order to remove them from circulation once and for all. Taking a successful film or genre and transforming it into a parody, perhaps throwing in the odd excursion into film history, and thereby producing something which is so ambivalent that it can be seen as both a homage and a settling of scores, is the speciality of the Zucker/Abrahams/Zucker team (*Airplane!* [1980]). The competent viewer is expected to appreciate the speed of the narrative and the piling up of gags, and to be able to fill in any gaps with his or her knowledge of the genre. *Raising Arizona* is, however, probably closer in its narrative stance to *Top Secret!* (1984) than *Airplane!*, as the later

Zucker/Abrahams movie is a hotch-potch of elements from spy, war and romantic films and musicals. *Raising Arizona* for its part has easily identifiable ingredients taken from prison and gangster films, domestic and screwball comedies and apocalypse movies.

It is also a melodrama, with thriller elements and touches of social satire, in a cartoon-like format. The crude *mélange* works because the film makes no effort to conceal its component parts, nor does it ever try to marshal them into any sort of hierarchy. This allows the Coens to spin out their comic ideas as they choose. An example of their digressive narrative technique is the wild chase that ensues after Hi holds up a convenience store when he needs nappies. The sequence ends with an argument between Ed and Hi. Ed declares that this style of shopping for nappies has nothing to do with 'family life'. Whereupon Hi, in a rare lucid moment, replies that no, this is certainly not family life as seen on television.

Leonard Smalls is first seen riding along a lonely highway, trailing death and destruction. Rabbits and lizards are among his victims because he is 'especially hard on the little things'. His Harley leaves behind it a line of fire that burns up the only flower growing at the side of the road, and other shots highlight disturbing details about the mysterious biker. We see, for example, a pair of baby shoes hanging from his belt and wonder whether they are a memento or a trophy. Lenny is a cartoon figure, born

The Lone Biker of the Apocalypse: 'Hard on little things'

Raising Arizona, Mad Max

in the mind of another character who could himself be from a cartoon. The showdown at the end of *Raising Arizona* thus logically pits creator against creature, whose kinship is symbolised by the Woody Woodpecker tattoo they both bear. The brutality of their encounter segues seamlessly into the slapstick aspect of the film.

The movie uses elements of the spaghetti Western aesthetic, but retains the essential nature of a cartoon. When Hi is pulled away by Lenny, for example, he digs his nails into the dirt and leaves furrows behind him. And the showdown, even in its colour scheme, is teeming with references to *Mad Max*, which features one shoe lying in the street to indicate to Max that his wife is dead, and an explosion that kills off the surviving bad guy.

Although *Raising Arizona* never pretends to be anything other than a film of the 1980s, its images frequently appear to be from the 1970s. When Hi is not sporting a garish Hawaiian shirt, he wears a brown-green acrylic polo neck. *Raising Arizona* is also about the moral sea-change of the 1960s finally arriving in the heartland, which Hollywood likes to see as a haven of Ur-American values. By 1970 many films had begun to question this belief in the purity of Middle America. Movies like *Easy Rider* (1969, dir. Dennis Hopper), *Deliverance* (1972, dir. John Boorman) or *Southern Comfort* (1981, dir. Walter Hill) showed the murderous potential of hillbillies and rednecks, and the myth of the family was destroyed by *The Texas Chainsaw Massacre* (1974, dir. Tobe Hooper) and *The Hills Have Eyes* (1977, dir. Wes Craven). By the 1980s the American heartland had moved so far out of sight that film-makers began to make ethnographic excursions back into it. There they found strange customs

(*Witness* [1985, dir. Peter Weir]), ruthless, small-time
gangsters (*Something Wild* [1986, dir. Jonathan Demme])
and even a bizarre new cosmos (*True Stories* [1987, dir.
David Byrne]). *Raising Arizona*, because it doesn't
shield us with a visitor to the scene to act as our media-
tor, allows us to see the heartland from within. If the
1970s raised awareness of such concepts as 'revolt' or
'social change', then *Raising Arizona* shows how these
ideas have arrived in Tempe, Arizona. Progress here is
represented by the 'sexual revolution', personified by
'swinging' couples, and the psychologisation of daily
life in the form of Doc Schwartz's analyses.

At the end of the film the characters are — in classic
tradition — gradually disassembled. Lenny Smalls is
blown to pieces, Nathan Jr is sent back to his family,
Gale and Evelle return to jail and Hi dreams the film to
an end. The soundtrack takes a turn for the sentimental because Hi is now only concerned by his future

Creator battles creature

with Ed. The tear-jerking pathos of Nathan Arizona's final words is matched by the schmaltz of the final scene — a family gathering, bathed in golden light, in Ed and Hi's trailer. Hi narrates the dream: 'And it seemed real. It seemed like us. And it seemed... like... well... our home... If not Arizona, then a land, not too far away, where all parents are strong and wise and capable, and all children are happy and beloved... I dunno, maybe it was Utah.'

Utah, the neighbouring Mormon state, instead of Oz. Hi's is a mid-range utopia, but the pathos of the final scene is also an ironic representation of the romantic Hollywood melodrama. Even the last gasp of this self-destructive review of the mechanisms of film comedy is itself a cinematic allusion. It's entirely possible to place *Raising Arizona* in a similar category to *Crimewave* — cinemagoers in the 1980s had to learn that their viewing contract could be continually renewed through the duration of the film they were watching. *Top Secret!, Something Wild* and *Wild At Heart* (1990, dir. David Lynch), and even *Raising Arizona* not only played with genre expectations, but also switched between those genres whenever it suited them. ∎

Miller's Crossing

Liam 'Leo' O'Bannion (Albert Finney), Irish gangland boss, club owner and uncrowned ruler of a
city 'on the East Coast of the United States, at the
end of the 1920s,' has a problem. Rival mobster Johnny
Caspar (Jon Polito) wants the head of Bernie Bernbaum
(John Turturro), a bookie whom Caspar suspects of fid-
dling the odds on boxing matches. But Bernie, like everyone else, pays protection money to Leo. Despite the
objections of his friend, advisor and protégé, the notoriously debt-ridden gambler Tom Reagan (Gabriel Byrne),
Leo insists on covering for Bernie, because Bernie is the
brother of the woman he loves. Although Leo loves
Verna Bernbaum (Marcia Gay Harden), he is still suspi-
cious enough to put a tail on her. When the man he
assigns to the job is murdered, Leo blames the hit on
Caspar, and that triggers a series of attacks which Leo
himself barely manages to survive. Tom does his best to

Return of the mob: Robert De Niro in *The Untouchables*, Ray Liotta in *GoodFellas*, Andy Garcia and Al Pacino in *The Godfather Part III*, and Warren Beatty in *Bugsy*

vilify Verna, even telling Leo that he is having an affair with her, but fails to persuade his boss to change his stance over Bernie. The pair fall out, and Tom offers his services to Caspar, who has both the police and the politicians in his pocket by now. Mistrusted by both his former and his current bosses, with his own bookie putting the screws on him, Tom is forced to prove his loyalty to Caspar by killing Bernie. He fakes the murder, however, and, to his good fortune, when Caspar's right-hand man, the killer Dane (J.E. Freeman), gives orders for the body to be brought back, his men find a corpse in the woods which they assume is Bernie. But then Bernie himself reappears and tries to blackmail Tom. After Tom has persuaded Caspar to eliminate Dane, he arranges a meeting between Caspar and Bernie which will culminate in Caspar's death. Then he murders Bernie himself and makes it look like the two of them killed each other in a shoot-out. After Bernie's funeral, Leo, who has the city back under his control and plans to marry Verna, asks Tom to work for him again. Tom manages to convince him that he has been working for his side all along, but nevertheless turns down the offer.   ◆

Gangster renaissance

1990 was a good year for the mob, in the cinema at least, where it was once again fashionable to wear a fedora and sport a Thompson sub-machine gun, to hang out in small restaurants with checked table-cloths and to run an alcohol or drug empire from the nearest public telephone. Martin Scorsese transformed the confessions of *Wiseguy* author Nicholas Pileggi into *GoodFellas*, and Francis Ford Coppola made *The Godfather Part III*. These movies, together with *Miller's Crossing*, formed the core of a Mafia wave that began in 1987 with the success of Brian De Palma's *The Untouchables*, branched off in various directions — comedies, modern gangster

A plush office: Tom Reagan (Gabriel Byrne) and his boss Leo O'Bannion (Albert Finney)

movies, nostalgic epics — and came to a worthy close with Barry Levinson's *Bugsy* (1991). These productions may have adapted the themes and iconography of the classic gangster film in radically different ways, but they do appear to have an underlying affinity. If experience shows that real Mafiosi always emerge in large numbers when the business practices of civil society and its governments come to resemble those of the underworld — as during the Depression or in the early 1970s, for example, when the United States was going through one of the most violent periods in its history — then we might also argue that the conservative revolution of the Reagan and Bush regimes, the Iran-Contra affair and a general 'political crisis' prepared the ground for the cinematic comeback of organised crime. 'Bull permeates everything' was the era's motto.

Gangster etiquette: Tom gets walloped by Leo, but hangs on to his hat

No other film in the 1990 crimewave looks quite so seriously at the idea of gangsterism as a model for the decline in political morality as *Miller's Crossing,* which is particularly ironic, since many critics took exception to the movie's polished surface. It was the Coen's most expensive film to date and definitely the first to bid for a place on the A-list. Roger Ebert's review in the *Chicago Sun-Times* led the chorus of those who wanted to see it as no more than self-referential narcissism. The plush office, where the opening shots contextualise gangster boss Leo, are for Ebert the key to a film which 'is continually looking over its shoulder instead of getting to the point... I don't think that Leo would have had such an office. I think this is the type of office that a good interior designer with contacts in England would design for a rich lawyer.' Ebert is right to describe the office as stylish, but its splendour is lugubrious, even a little military. And, because the Coens develop the scene as a pointed, if elegantly directed, allusion to the momentous opening of Coppola's *The Godfather* (1972), we can see it as an expression of two contradictory things: a fascination for the genre, which has always dealt with the glamour of living dangerously, and a modern disillusionment with it. The Coens said in an interview with *Tip* that of all the gangster films on offer at the time, theirs was the most 'mythical'. This is true only in so far as *Miller's Crossing* places such great emphasis on detail, from its reconstruction of contemporary argot, which even the American public could apparently not understand, to the finer points of the décor. Even the film's central motif points to the problem that a 'mythical' gangster movie has to confront today. The hat, which Tom Reagan constantly threatens to lose, represents a semiotic system that is itself disappearing. By the end, Reagan has managed to hang on to his hat, but has lost just about everything else — and thus the film marks, in its melancholy way, the demise of the old gangster etiquette, of the genre in its classic form. What distinguishes *Miller's Crossing* from Scorsese's contemporary *GoodFellas* is not its mythical but rather its almost philological perspective. While Scorsese moves the genre on by examining the modern Mafioso in terms of his life as an employee in a large organisation, the Coens develop their narrative by explicitly reflecting upon and criticising historic material.

The latitude and longitude of gangsterism

The very existence of the criminal, who does not feel obliged to honour any contracts and who has no respect for property, strikes at the foundation of society, challenges it, makes it recognisable by the very act of disregarding it. At the beginning of the 1930s, when the Mafia began making its fortune and classic gangster films started to emerge, Howard Hawks' landmark *Scarface* (1932) laid down the two poles between which the image of the gangster in popular culture was to move in the following decades. As a big-city reflection of the figure of the adven-

turer, as someone who lives on a knife edge and takes risks which the civilised world no longer knows, the gangster has certain heroic characteristics, and provides a foil to the societal norm as expressed through the law. There is often an underlying anti-bourgeois sentiment to the depiction of mobsters, but conversely, *Scarface* Tony Camonte's motto clearly suggests that the organised criminal, the mobster, is very definitely a part of the society that despises him. 'Do it first, do it yourself, and keep doing it!' — the election slogan identifies the racketeer as a social climber, a self-made man and entrepreneur, who is doing nothing more than taking the law of the market to its logical, ruthless extreme. As the law-gangsterism opposition began to recede in popular culture, criminality came to be presented as a mirror image of bourgeois-capitalist society. 'I was living in even greater circles of gangsterdom than I had dreamed, latitudes and longitudes of gangsterism,' says the narrator in E.L. Doctorow's mid-1980s Mafia novel *Billy Bathgate*.

The autocratic, violent, carnal Leo in *Miller's Crossing* brings to mind the heroic image of the gangster of the old school. The film reserves its most spectacular scene for the 'old man', who is 'still an artist with the Thompson'. When Caspar's hitmen burst in on him while he is in bed, the Irish boss shows, in a rare outbreak of 'action', that he is still a street fighter, despite the silk dressing gown and pyjamas. If such isolated scenes come across as comic strip flash panels in an otherwise very theatrical, dialogue-based film, then this is because *Miller's Crossing* is less interested in law-breaking as transgression than in the ubiquity of crime — the politician has become the public enemy and is now running the show.

The Coens found an early model for this viewpoint in the novels of Dashiell Hammett. In the classic gangster films there were still judges who battled with the public enemies, and bourgeois society still existed, if only to act as a foil for the hoods, but the crime stories

An autocratic gangster of the old school: Leo gets a visit from Caspar's killers

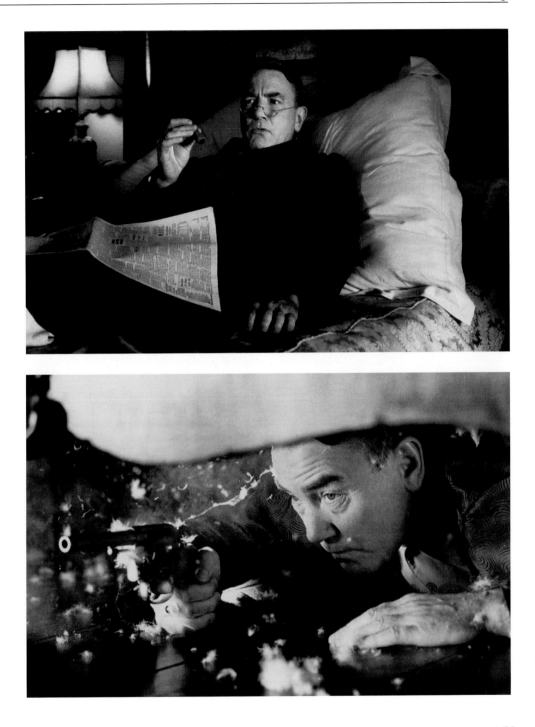

A rare outbreak of action: Leo, an artist with the Thompson

Hammett wrote around this time tended to exclude the external world. His 1929 novel *Red Harvest* — from which the Coens borrowed the title for *Blood Simple*, and which also inspired several scenes in *Miller's Crossing*, in particular the battle between the police and Leo's men in front of the Sons of Erin club — portrays a Prohibition-era, fictional American city ruled by terror. The political establishment, the police and the bootleggers have divided up the territory between them, and even Hammett's hero, the Continental Op, is no longer likely to help old ladies across the street. The novel that does most to hermetically seal the genre is Hammett's *The Glass Key* (1931), and strictly speaking the Coens should have applied for permission to make use of this work too — 'it's a wonder the Hammett estate didn't sue for plagiarism', remarked John Harkness in *Sight & Sound*. The novel distinguishes itself by being almost perfectly self-contained. The detective is reincarnated in the form of Ned Beaumont (the model for Tom Reagan), the mobster and the politician have become one, and there seems to be no other world outside of gangland. It is this distillation, this reduction of the world to a metaphorical, stylised criminal milieu which enabled the novel to serve as the model for a film that would be made some sixty years later. Not that Hammett's book was sitting around waiting to be turned into a film. There were already two adaptations — a 1935 version by Frank Tuttle, starring George Raft, and a 1942 version by Stuart Heisler, starring Alan Ladd — both of which perfectly captured the tone and the atmosphere of the original work.

The Coens, however, not only thematically enriched the original but also reinterpreted it. The basic elements of the plot, many of the characters, the jargon and some of the settings were retained, and it isn't necessary to name *The Glass Key* or even the author himself to identify Hammett as the source. When Tom Reagan says ''lo, Shad' into the phone, any ambiguity is

A *Red Harvest* scene: the siege of the Sons of Erin club

dispelled, because ''lo' is one of Ned Beaumont's mannerisms, and Shad is the name of his antagonist. We could dismiss such references as a sign of the complicity of the informed viewer, and some critics have dubbed them 'post-modern' and refused to see any originality in the film — Josef Schnelle, for example, wrote in *film-dienst* that it was a case of a 'copy of the copy of the copy'. But unlike mid-1980s genre pastiches such as Lawrence Kasdan's *Silverado* (1985) or De Palma's *The Untouchables*, *Miller's Crossing* is economic and in no way arbitrary in its use of allusion and quotation. It uses them both to advance the plot and to establish a certain distance from the original model, as well as to mark any deviations from this model. Thus the casually mentioned name, Shad, points to what has become of the figure in the hands of the Coens — Hammett's Irish gangster has been transformed into the Italian Johnny Caspar, or Giovanni Casparo. And there we have an example of one of the biggest shifts that takes place between the original work and this film adaptation — the movie transplants what was a purely Anglo-Saxon affair into an ethnically mixed and heterogeneous society.

Watch the hero thinking

There is one man at the heart of *Miller's Crossing*, but we are never sure if he has one himself. Tom Reagan's essential ambiguity can be understood only if we bear in mind his literary model. 'Friendship, character, ethics,' was still binding for Ned Beaumont — but, repeated ad nauseam in *Miller's Crossing*, it is used to support nothing more than the right to a calculable relationship between investment and profit. A notorious gambler who doesn't hesitate to take what is his due, and sometimes more, Hammett's hero makes his way independent and untouched through a corrupt world. Behind the tough guy façade there is a kind nature, however, which repeatedly gets him into

An ethnically mixed society: Irishman Tom and Italian Johnny Caspar (Jon Polito)

Tom's first appearance: the camera has to work out its position

trouble, and by the end his gentle persistence has won him the woman his friend and boss believe is meant for him. Tom Reagan seems, on first sight, to imitate his predecessor, but it soon becomes clear that the Coens went to some trouble to make his motives murkier. The viewer is, to a large extent, encouraged to identify with Tom, and is narratively tied to his perspective — whatever we learn about the intrigue, we learn at the same time as he does. We also suspect that we know less than he does, though, and we never find out much about him personally. The film restrainedly but significantly breaks with the conventions that establish a hero and psychologically underpin his actions.

Reagan is introduced indirectly by way of one of the props that almost seem to take on a life of their own in *Miller's Crossing*. First we see the glass, the ice cube, the drink that Tom is mixing. While Caspar and Leo continue their debate, he remains silent in the disturbingly blurred background. The first shot to show him alone is immediately replaced by a parallel shot of Caspar's henchman Dane, as the film arranges its dramatis personae and its criminal hierarchy — 'a man who walks behind a man, whispers in his ear', as Caspar later describes Tom. And when Tom finally does have something to say, while Leo awaits his comments and the viewer awaits a close-up, what we are shown is a lot of empty space between the camera and the sofa where Reagan is sitting, almost as if the camera operator has missed the crucial moment.

The camera is not allowed to be an inconspicuous companion or accessory to the hero, but must work for its position in relation to the protagonists, as will be seen again later. After Tom's tiff with Verna in the powder room of Leo's club, the camera pulls back quickly alongside the woman as she moves to the door. In the next shot, in Tom's flat, it has to bridge this distance again. In such moments the Coens stress the

A double betrayal: Tom with Leo…

external perspective on the action — the camera and the viewer know just as little as the characters about what will happen next. They have their own conjecturing to do, even when contemplating the hero himself. And Gabriel Byrne's highly controlled acting, his vague facial expressions and his physical passivity make it almost impossible to figure Reagan out. The most obvious signal that he sends out is the way he moves his eyes when registering some new piece of information, and because we never catch him doing anything where he might let his guard down — his 'passions', for gambling and for Verna, are pursued off camera — there is little we can do but watch him thinking.

What he is thinking can only be reconstructed, at best. The film maliciously takes at its word the old cliché that the American hero can be recognised by his actions. As advisor, as *consigliere* to the man in charge, Reagan sustains the illusion that he is above

...and with Verna (Marcia Gay Harden)

the business that is going on around him, or at least that he is able to control his own affairs (turning down Leo's offer to pay off his gambling debts, for example). He begins his career in *Miller's Crossing* by calling for somebody's death. Why? For the greater good? To keep the peace? To safeguard business? To split Leo and Verna up? Whatever the reason, he advises Leo to hand over the bookie Bernie Bernbaum to the opposition, and within a very short time Tom has gone on to betray those closest to him. He is disloyal to Leo by carrying on his affair with Verna, and he double-crosses Verna by telling Leo she is a tramp. Tom's intrigue turns out to be no more than an attempt to keep pace with events he has been unable to foresee, and which force him, the thinker, the only one who doesn't stop and furrow his brow when he has a problem to consider, into action, into getting his hands dirty. The Coens thereby destroy what we might call the leitmotif of the genre, the codified affirmation that

Repetitions: Tom and Bernie (John Turturro) at their first and second meetings; and in the forest near Miller's Crossing

beneath the hard exterior lies a soft centre. Reagan's model, Ned Beaumont, might well walk away untouched from some bloody episode — he has no murders on his conscience, and even manages to clear one up — but Reagan himself finally kills the man he began by proposing as a sacrifice, the man who begged him for mercy.

A stranger in his own land

Laurence Giavarini wrote in *Cahiers du Cinéma* that repetitions are a central structural characteristic of the film — they are 'more than obvious, they exhibit themselves, they make a system' — and noted that they lend the film an ambiguous character. That defining principle of the classic American gangster story, the double-cross, the betrayal already discernible in the title of the film, plays itself out not only on the level of dialogue and plot, but also visually. Each important motif is turned on its head at least once; confrontations between the characters are repeated in almost mirror image form — Tom and Bernie change places for their second conversation in Tom's apartment, and catchphrases and central concepts such as Tom's 'nobody knows anybody, not that well', or the 'et'ics' that Caspar says distinguish us from animals, take on a new meaning when repeated in new contexts. The subtle shifts in the semantics of the different parts, the strange changes in meaning, are matched by the 'invisible' editing. The montage connects rather than con-

trasts, and the transition from scene to scene is often made through the dissolve-like construction of inter-communicating images. This procedural variation culminates in a series of corresponding, yet differently coded, key scenes: Bernie's postponed death, the death that Tom narrowly avoids, and, finally, Bernie's murder in Reagan's apartment block.

In the forest near Miller's Crossing, the place where Reagan undergoes two existential tests, even the rules of the genre no longer seem to apply. The gangsters in their city clothes are completely out of place, as though they have walked into the wrong film. This departure from the characteristic iconography of the crime story brings a previously hidden narrative level to the surface. Reagan is supposed to murder Bernie Bernbaum, and it is a murder so anticipated by the viewer that in the end it seems as if it really was carried out in this place, but it isn't like a typical gangster flick murder. It is more like the execution of a man who, in Verna's words, is different, who is marked out as not the same as other people. The black car on the forest track, the men in the long coats, the screaming victim, the shot that Reagan fires at the fleeing Bernie — the whole scenario stirs up memories of fascist crimes, of Gestapo methods. These connotations were particularly strong for the critic Brigitte Desalm, who wrote in *Steadycam* that Bernie looked like 'one of those unfortunates in Poland or Russia who were brought to be executed at the edge of the lime pit'. And it is no coincidence that the film emphasises the fact that Bernie is both Jewish and homosexual.

His sister Verna is, of course, also Jewish, and Dane, who competes with Bernie for Mink (Steve Buscemi), is also homosexual. But such 'deviant' characteristics only become important in Bernie's case because his out of control gambling scams threaten the precarious balance of money and influence. Caspar's insistent denunciation of the bookmaker —

Jewish/homosexual: Verna, Dane
and Bernie

he calls him a *schmatte*, the Yiddish word for junk or cheap goods — shows that he regards him as an object that can be bought and sold, but it also reveals the barriers imposed by race and class. Bernie is quite clearly a small-time gangster, and belongs to the criminal underclass. The question as to whether or not Bernie is still under Leo's protection is shown to be merely a pretext. The bookie is just the excuse for a conflict which will decide whether the parvenu Caspar is in a position to compete with Leo's organisation, whether Giovanni Casparo is anything more than a 'guinea fresh off the boat'.

The multiculturalism of the city is an important theme in *Miller's Crossing*, even if it is only developed in passing. Various dialects (hardly anyone here speaks pure American) characterise a film that wants to be heard as well as seen. Reagan might act like a man of the world, but he still has not lost his guttural Irish accent, and the cultural spheres of the antagonists Caspar and Leo are conspicuously delimited. The former lives with his wife and relatives, who apparently only speak Italian, while the latter allows himself to be moved by a particularly kitsch rendering of 'Danny Boy', which Hollywood likes to suppose will evoke the roots of America's Irish community.

The multiplicity of voices is further enriched by what happens off camera — in one scene, where Tom is reading the morning paper in a café, we hear a couple having an argument in some soft European language. The families, the friendships and the interest groups show little evidence of assimilation, and the 'standard' white American does not appear to exist at all. What is 'standard' is the fact that whoever has power will exclude all others, and the others are, according to whoever is currently dominant, the 'guineas', the 'Micks' or the 'Hebrews'.

Bernie's central position in the plot can only be understood when seen against this background. He is labelled a weak link in the racial chain — his problem is that he has no membership card for the Sons of Erin nor for any other club. As John Turturro remarked about his role in an interview with *Film Comment*, 'He's a guy who's trying to be a survivor. He's constantly on the move. Which is kind of Jewish history'. Anti-Semitism, as a historical model for the suppression of anything different, gives *Miller's Crossing*'s multicultural commentary an edge that goes beyond the genre's usual parameters. The battle between Irish and Italian crime organisations, between groups that arrived in the first and in the second wave of immigration, began with Prohibition, and we might regard it as the Ur-conflict of the American gangster movie. It appears here as part of a more general situation, which must be assigned ethnic attributes because an economic and political battle is pitting all the players against each other. Following the template of a uniquely American genre, the Coens present a picture of a land of immigrants who have remained foreign to each other, even right up to the 1990s. So foreign, in fact, that in the struggle for dominance even the pogrom cannot be excluded — a gloomy prognosis, but one which was lent some credibility two years after the film was released by the race riots and deaths in South Central LA sparked by the Rodney King case.

A brilliant game

If the scene in which Caspar's men send Tom and Bernie into the woods emphasises difference or disparity, then the portrayal of his actual death is very definitely back within the rules of the genre. The bookie's pleading — 'Look in your heart!' — immediately calls to mind the earlier scene in the forest. The final act is, of course, carried out in the midst of 'civilisation', in one of those dark stairwells where the men in the long coats and hats feel so at home, and it is a calculated, cold-blooded murder. It is no longer Caspar's hitmen who push the gun into Tom's hand,

and Caspar himself, the only person who could still pose a serious threat, lies dead at his feet. If Reagan ever had a heart, then he loses it here. If his earlier decision not to kill Bernie was a moral one, then he has clearly revised it. The fact that he profits from the double murder, stealing Caspar's money to pay off his gambling debts, makes him doubly dubious and places him within a system where there are no longer any borders between economic and private life, between business and friendship. It is impossible to say whether Tom acts out of loyalty to Leo or not. In any case, what Leo admiringly calls a 'brilliant game' has now come to an end, with a shabby gangland killing, a murder heralded in the film's opening scene, and the gangster flick's bitter irony is complete. The killing might be described as an execution — if the Coens had not taken it one step further and involved the viewer.

Bernie, the petty criminal who becomes significant only because he has strayed across the front lines of a larger war, is negatively portrayed. Several elements encourage us to see his death as just reward for his own risky manoeuvrings — his switch from whining, pathetic victim to arrogant blackmailer, so brilliantly interpreted by John Turturro, and the symmetry between his own situation and the situation he lands Tom in. The film doesn't present Bernie as an innocent victim, and it doesn't allow the viewer to empathise with him, but rather demands that the victim be seen as someone who is only marginally more sympathetic and less corrupt than the men who are calling the shots. That Bernie Bernbaum has the right to beg for his life, that his refusal to go into 'exile' is legitimate, given that crime bosses have always bullied people like him, are facts that push against the traditional heroic constructions of the genre as much as they do against the politically correct view that the underdog should appear as a good person. Tom Reagan and Bernie Bernbaum are almost interchangeable under the trees at Miller's

Crossing, because the viewer himself must work out 'who is a friend and who is an enemy'. This, perhaps the most disturbing of the film's characteristics, shifts the focus away from the questioning of an individual's morality to the questioning of the morality of the situation as a whole. The Coens craftily destroy the assumption that, in a society controlled by ruthless interest groups, there can be any rules that do more than serve the interests of these groups.

Seen from this perspective, *Miller's Crossing* is superior to works such as De Palma's similarly stylised *The Untouchables*, which draws inspiration from many of the same models as the Coen film, or the melodramatic *The Godfather Part III*, in which an innocent is sacrificed in the final scene. There are no untouchables in the Coen movie, and, because everyone is 'touchable', no-one can be tragic. Thus the rise-and-fall-of-the-empire model, which the Mafia film felt obliged to adopt right up to the *Godfather* trilogy, has been superseded in *Miller's Crossing*. The Coens do allude to the infamous O'Bannion-Capone vendetta in Chicago, which marked the replacement of the Irish mob with its Italian counterpart, and which provided the genre with its most popular material, but their treatment of it deviates considerably from both the historical reality and previous representations on the big screen. In their film, nothing changes. The murders, the violence and the high-stake intrigues don't even result in a change of government in this emblematic city state. The business ethics of the 1980s, that gold-digging decade in which greed was positively encouraged, and which a stock market crash brought to an end three years too early, find a peculiar echo in Johnny Caspar's tirades — 'now, if you can't trust a fix, what can you trust?'. 'The party is over' was how car stickers greeted the end of Reaganism after the 1988 election, but the Republicans stayed in power, and, under George Bush, who rode roughshod over the Constitution during the Gulf

'Trying to be a survivor': someone like Bernie has
the right to beg for his life

War, the impression grew that American politics had become both inscrutable and secretive. The cool, self-controlled intimacy of *Miller's Crossing*, a rather atypical Coen production, and its recourse to an apparently outmoded milieu, are both entirely appropriate as they are used to portray a society that is at a standstill, a society that has failed to change, inasmuch as it is still run by racketeers.

Some critics did not allow themselves to be misled by the film's luxurious surface, by the period furniture in Leo's office, and instead recognised restraint, a sort of noble neo-classicism, as the basic stylistic principle at work. 'Miller's Crossing strives for a precision in its linking of form and content that is all too seldom found in contemporary cinema, and its obliteration of any sign of authorship makes the film all the more surely a product of a (two-headed) *auteur,'* wrote Tim Pulleine in *Sight & Sound.* The movie is breath-taking and bold not in its invention but in the meticulousness with which it displays its material, analyses, develops and ultimately transforms it. It does not persuade, it argues. And, through the fact that it assumes intelligence on the part of its audience, it gains a lustre that no production designer or special effects artist could ever give it. And the Coens succeed in doing what was described as true 'political alchemy' by a character in a Lizzie Borden film — 'turning shit into gold'. ■

Barton Fink

laywright Barton Fink (John Turturro) has made a big splash. He has sold Broadway a new subject — the common man, social romance, the poetry of the street. The year is 1941 (admittedly, the fiction lags somewhat behind literary history), and the public and critical applause for his play has barely died down when his agent shunts him off to Capitol Pictures in Hollywood.

Barton, however, fears that the well-paid work in California, which is supposed to finance his art, might actually distract him from his literary destiny. He worries that in Los Angeles he will be cut off from 'the well-spring of [his] success, from the common man'. But the viewer knows better. The cut from a bar counter in New York to the entrance hall of the Earle Hotel in Los Angeles shows that Barton has indeed arrived at his destination.

Barton Fink arrives: the Earle Hotel has
been waiting for him

He stands, a forlorn figure, in the unreal light of the
run-down, pompous lobby. The scene is shot from a
distance, which has the effect of suggesting that the
man has reached exactly the place where he belongs.
Barton Fink walks through the deserted space to the
reception, rings the bell, and the ringing doesn't stop

until a hatch in the floor opens (leading to the under-world, perhaps) and the bellboy (Steve Buscemi) appears, white as a ghost. A board bearing keys and messages suggests that although the hotel might not be operating at capacity, there is some business being done, but it soon becomes clear that the whole build-ing is really only there for Barton Fink. The Earle Hotel has been awaiting his arrival just as eagerly as the Overlook Hotel awaited Jack Torrance in *The Shining* (1980, dir. Stanley Kubrick).

Our writer, who could not have guessed what wis-dom he had expressed in his Broadway hit — 'Daylight is a dream if you live with your eyes closed' — will here find out about more than just the common man. He will be visited by the demon of reality, the demon who lives in the next room, in the form of voluminous sales-man Charlie Meadows (a terrifyingly good John Goodman), who turns out to be the mass murderer Karl Mundt (German and Jewish jokes feature promi-nently in this film). Trying to write here is futile. Barton's screenplay for a wrestling movie, which his boss at Capitol Pictures has ordered, doesn't get any further than the first few lines before he is engulfed by loneliness and despair. Madness and violence break out around him — Barton Fink has ended up in a nightmare from which he cannot escape. ◆

A Day or a lifetime — the Earle Hotel

If we take away the people and emphasise the emptiness, then the set piece of the shabby hotel lobby, immortalised in Raymond Chandler's 'Nevada Gas', is highly suggestive. Few films can be successfully transformed into literature, but *Barton Fink* actively invites the viewer to do so. It reveals a second layer of prefabricated imagination which has a more literary than a cinematic origin, and whose ele-ments are put through a process which attempts to make them unrecognisable as it distills them.

Slack-jawed and watery-eyed lift operator
Pete (Harry Bugin) with Barton Fink

> *There were two open-grille elevators but only one seemed to be running and that not busy. An old man sat inside it slack-jawed and watery-eyed on a piece of folded burlap on top of a wooden stool. He looked as if he had been sitting there since the Civil War and had come out of that badly.*
>
> *I got in with him and said 'eight', and he wrestled the doors shut and cranked his buggy and we dragged upwards lurching. The old man breathed hard, as if he were carrying the elevator on his back.*
>
> *The old man didn't look at me. His face was as empty as my brain.*
>
> (*The High Window*, Raymond Chandler)

The description in *The High Window* extract reads like a blueprint for the scene in the Coen movie. Bellboy Chet hands Barton his key, and Barton stumbles into the antiquated lift with his two cases. Pete (Harry Bugin), the hangdog lift operator who looks like he really has been there since the Civil War, reacts only when Barton says 'six, please', then hauls the sliding door shut and gets the lift cage moving. A trick on the soundtrack adds to the sense of alienation — the old man's heavy breathing becomes an inhuman, rattling groan, although his face remains stony and immobile.

Reality is nearly always at its most beautiful when perceived as an artefact, a self-contained object whose outlines we think we already know. Like the idea of a shabby hotel lobby, for example, whose best days are long gone, which automatically evokes words like for-lornness and sadness. Cinema can thus produce impressions by continually reconstructing these out-lines under new conditions. Joel and Ethan Coen are experts in manipulating appearance, at assessing its taste, its temperature and its associations. Marcia Gay Harden, the leading actress in *Miller's Crossing*, said she was amazed that the directors told her nothing about how to play the role she was given. They merely presented her with adjectives such as ambiguous, smoky and secretive.

The Coen brothers' films, which have been criti-cised for being both artificial and sterile, function enthusiastically and brilliantly on the level of extreme stylisation, at least for the first few movies, right up to *Fargo*, and they also emphasise the self-sufficient artistic space. They use stereotypes (eg the eccentric writer who is blind to reality) and plots that are not particularly subtle — with the exception of the Hammett-inspired *Miller's Crossing* and *The Hudsucker Proxy* (a remake of tried and tested Hollywood material, co-scripted by Sam Raimi). This isn't really important, though, because the *mise en scène* is the focal point of their work. And their originality lies in their ability to rigorously, inventively and indissolubly mix effect and material to arrive at a new formula.

Barton Fink is an excursion into literature and imagination which raises its literary, epistemological and biographical material to a genuinely cinematic level, and does so without submerging its sources. It is the story of a writer's block, a story that was born as a sort of therapy for the writer's block the Coens suffered during the making of *Miller's Crossing*, a film which itself is the most closely derived from literature (Dashiell Hammett's novels *The Glass Key* and *Red Harvest*) of all their work.

Richard T. Jameson, writing in *Film Comment*, saw the novelist Nathanael West as the model for Barton Fink, but the film, set in the mythical Chandler territory of Hollywood and downtown LA during the legendary early 1940s, also reveals just how far the Coens were influenced by Raymond Chandler's pithy sarcasm, how they adapt his technique of stressing details in order to mine their metaphorical resonance and how they have internalised his trademark mix of vitriol and poetry.

It is appropriate that, since the film was premiered at Cannes in 1991 (where a jury chaired by Roman Polanski awarded it the Palme d'Or), it has been compared with various works of literature — with books by Kafka, by James M. Cain or even by John Fante, the predecessor and 'godfather' of Charles Bukowski. Joel and Ethan Coen, however, deny any literary influences at all. They admit that Kubrick was a cinematic model, but play dumb and claim they know little of the novels variously cited as their inspiration.

We can't really buy this, though, since first-hand knowledge of a book is no longer a necessity in an age when even those who aren't well read know exactly what is meant by the term 'Kafkaesque', and are familiar with the characteristics of the 'hard-boiled' genre, without ever having read its authors, because they

Creator and medium of the illusion: John Turturro as Barton Fink

have been displayed in countless popular cinematic rehashings. Literature has, to an extent, lost some of its identity by becoming fodder for mainstream cinema, but cinema has also moved away from the unshakeable self-assurance of its physical existence, the belief that it is there to provide a landscape for impressions, a place for contemplation, a home for psychological drama. The new cinema wants to get away from this formula, and is prepared to make its escape a violent one if necessary. The unexploited space that offers itself up for exploration is the ethereal space of the memory; the infinite storage ability and the communicative levels of the human intellect.

Gilles Deleuze coined the term 'cerebral cinema' to describe modern classics such as those directed by Stanley Kubrick (*Cinema 2. L'image-temps*), and the

Coen brothers' films are a youthful, less earnest variation of this. They represent a multi-layered, but also lightweight, cinema of cerebral attractions, manufactured by jugglers and connoisseurs of a universe of references to which the media network is constantly adding. The fleeting essence is what interests this new cinema, the perfume of the masters that lingers in the air, the establishment of atmosphere — all this is more important than structure or background.

The Coens are the merciless puppet masters of this new cinema. The viewer cannot have a passionately serious relationship with any of the subject matter in their films, whether it be violence, or American literary history, or the familiar, sentimental figure of the lonely writer battling with the intricacies of language.

From the very first to the very last scene, everything in *Barton Fink* revolves around the fabrication of illusion, and the Coens' stroke of genius was to make the creator and the medium of the illusion come together in the figure of the main character. In the opening scene the camera descends from the flies of a New York theatre, that highly symbolic place where illusion is manufactured, then swings after a stagehand through the wings and catches Barton Fink as he stands engrossed in the experience of his own text. Turturro mouths the words of the actor who is on stage but off screen. We see only Turturro's enraptured face, almost hearing his inner voice. Hyperreality is established. From that point on the film sees with the eyes of its main character, and foists this viewpoint on the viewer so adroitly that he or she hardly even notices. But there is a price to be paid. Any occasion on which the film drops this perspective and moves towards a more standard viewpoint immediately stands out as a serious artistic error — the dance hall scene where Turturro flips out, for example.

Barton with his Underwood: Writer's block

So, to the author — the author alone with his typewriter and the blank, white sheets of paper that are meant to become a screenplay. The words 'Fade in' are

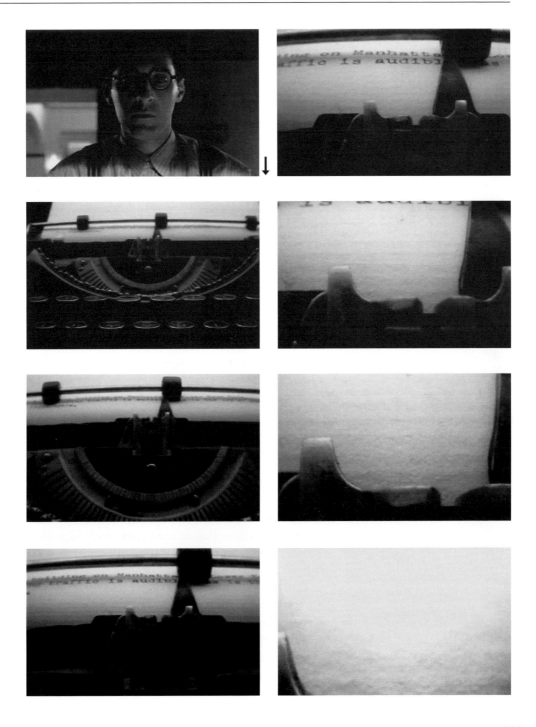

typed there, but not much else. Giant letters spring up before the camera, and the senses of sight and hearing are sharpened to the point of madness. The extreme passivity of the narrative situation — a hotel room, a man brooding over a typewriter — is balanced by the maximum of cinematic finesse. 'How do you bring movement into a static situation, how can you build drama and emotion to draw in the viewer?' was the problem that had to be solved in *Barton Fink*, declared the Coens in an interview with French magazine *Cahiers du Cinéma*.

The solution, as in most of their films, is to intensify the situation until it becomes a paradox. The barriers between the inner and outer world are permeable in *Barton Fink*. Just as the isolated, blocked writer's perceptions become monstrous, so the inside turns outward. The visual framework of the film is founded on long, steady takes, slow camera movements and magnified details, and the frequent point-of-view shots that work towards an identification of perspective with the protagonist. Barton's alienated stare is mirrored by static shots of almost empty spaces, which are interrupted by snatches of dialogue, as in the scene in Lipnick's office.

The special effects in *Barton Fink* are as simple as they are effective because they are rooted within the situation. With almost imperceptible tracking shots, sometimes combined with zooms, the camera shortens the distance from the objects it portrays and mediates our view, as we are sucked in towards the objects. There are a few virtuoso flourishes, though, such as the trip down the bathroom drainpipe; the significance of a mosquito in the room swells out of all proportion until it becomes a personal enemy; the walls have ears and they sweat so much that the paste runs down them and the corners of the wallpaper peel smoothly away.

The Shining

A feeling for the humorous, and a good sense of comic timing, are what distinguish *Barton Fink* from *The Shining*, Kubrick's take on a monstrous writer's block and a film from which the Coens drew some inspiration. Illusion and reality are just as hard for Barton to distinguish as they are for Jack Torrance (Jack Nicholson). The hotel corridor, that omnipresent feature of *The Shining*, is always filmed through a slow forward or backward movement of the camera in *Barton Fink*, as though it is creeping along the passage. The Earle Hotel, just like the Overlook before it, appears to have a life of its own. It perspires, gives off an unnatural heat and appears to have its guests — and judging by all the shoes outside the bedroom doors, it has many guests — under lock and key. The camera circles overhead as John Turturro lies pinned like a helpless insect on his bed, reinforcing the impression that he is being controlled by some greater force. In Stephen King's novel *The Shining*, and in Kubrick's adaptation, Jack Torrance, the writer who goes off the rails, turns into a maniac and becomes a serious threat to his environment. Perhaps more accurate is the figure of the autistic caveman that author Barton Fink regresses into.

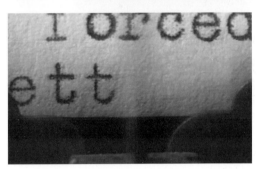

John Turturro, who is never better than when he's acting in Coen films, fuses with the character almost to the point of self-sacrifice. He avoids any hint of cliché in his portrayal of the author as an egocentric horror, alternating between self-pity and self-conceit, and complete ignorance of what is going on around him. The common man, imposingly embodied by the man in the next room, Charlie Meadows, turns up at his door and offers to tell him stories about the life of other common men, but Barton merely smiles graciously and turns back to his typewriter.

The common man, imposingly embodied
by Charlie Meadows (John Goodman)

Turturro's miserable caricature figure nevertheless appeals to our sympathy. We would like to think that he, too, is a victim, perhaps of some intrigue, or of his own feverish imagination. Even when he wakes up beside the murdered woman, the muse who had kissed him the night before, we still don't write him off. He swats the mosquito that is feasting on her flesh, and blood streams from the woman's lifeless, mutilated body. Barton is appalled, and the viewer is too (unless some unsporting critic has already given the game away). The discovery of Judy Davis dead is a typically brilliant Coen joke — both extremely heartless, because it disposes of this wonderful actress so quickly, and perfectly calculated. It also shows us what great use even a tiny mosquito can be put to if its final, deadly appearance is fittingly prepared. We admire this

perverse pirouette, and in doing so realise that in this film the viewer is getting none of the usual suspense-realisation-resolution business. Because the viewer is Barton Fink.

Slave Ship Hollywood

We could, and, out of respect for the Coens, should suppose that it is for dramatic purposes that the fictional aspect of the characters of Barton and Mayhew are emphasised — such allegorical exaggerations flourish best when their roots are unclear. Let there be no absolute resemblance to living or dead persons, then, although the parallels are considerable. Perhaps the fact that these are so actively played down is itself a diplomatic, evasive manoeuvre.

Battery hens: the Writers' Building

Capitol Pictures: Barton Fink and Lou Breeze (Jon Polito); Jack Lipnick (Michael Lerner)

The models, namely William Faulkner and Clifford Odets, are, after all, disembowelled in the film. What the Coens do with W.P. Mayhew (John Mahoney), for example, who wears a white suit of the kind favoured in the southern States, and is quite a convincing Faulkner figure, is not a demythologisation, though. It is simply tasteless. He vomits copiously in the men's toilet only to emerge the perfect gentleman and blithely begin making conversation with Barton before hurrying off to an urgent appointment with his hip flask. ('Anything that gets a laugh is good' is a key part of the Coen credo.)

'When he can't write, he drinks', says Audrey (Judy Davis), Mayhew's secretary and mistress. But he hasn't written anything in a long time — Audrey later confesses to Barton that she is the author of his latest screenplays and novels, and Mayhew himself is a burnt-out wreck. If he isn't drinking, he's bullying Audrey, Barton notes with outrage the first time he sees the couple together.

The Writers' Building is, in its battery hen architecture, a fairly accurate model of the infamously Spartan writers' residence in the Warner Brothers' studio in Burbank. The words 'Slave Ship' are written on Mayhew's door, a fitting metaphor and one that is rooted in reality. *Slave Ship*, a 1937 curiosity by Tay Garnett starring Wallace Beery as an underhand sailor, was scripted by Sam Hellman, Lamar Trotti and Gladys Lehman. The credits also state that the story is by a certain William Faulkner, but Faulkner has insisted he was involved merely as a 'script doctor'. His claim is characteristic of his assessment of the work he did in Hollywood, and of his pragmatic approach to his role: 'I'm a motion picture doctor. When they run into a section they don't like, I rework it and continue to rework it until they do like it. In

The Faulkner model: W.P. Mayhew (John Mahoney) with Audrey (Judy Davis)

Slave Ship I reworked sections. I don't write scripts. I don't know enough about it.' (*Some Time in the Sun*).

The Coens drew deeply from the rich well of historical Hollywood for *Barton Fink*, but this is not immediately obvious because they have so skilfully defamiliarised the borrowed elements and dovetailed them seamlessly into their own requirements. They exact their revenge on the industry for its contempt for and exploitation of its productive talent, its authors, with caustic satire. Their representatives of Hollywood power are exaggerated in the extreme, and are dazzlingly depicted by the actors. There is the ranting Capitol Pictures studio boss Jack Lipnick (Michael Lerner), his factotum Lou Breeze (Jon Polito), once a major shareholder and now Lipnick's chief bootlicker, and producer Ben Geisler (Tony Shalhoub), a man who is at once dynamic and neurotic, an allusion perhaps to a more contemporary stereotype.

The boss, the producer, the bootlicker:
Michael Lerner, Tony Shalhoub, Jon Polito

Lipnick is invested with the vulgarity of Columbia's Harry Cohn and the girth of MGM boss Louis B. Mayer, but the feature that characterises him most is the brusque directness he inherits from Jack Warner. Warner gained some notoriety after the Japanese entered the war by strutting about in an army uniform (which he borrowed from his costume department), and it was Warner who described script-writers as 'schmucks with Underwoods'. It is, of course, the classic Underwood typewriter Barton struggles with to produce a script for the wrestling film.

Barton's real-life model, Clifford Odets, was better able to adapt to his new circumstances, and found success immediately after his arrival in California with *The General Died At Dawn* (1936, dir. Lewis Milestone). His later attack on Hollywood, *The Big Knife*, earned him the industry's hatred. This 1947 Broadway hit was filmed eight years later by another Hollywood renegade, Robert Aldrich. In *Barton Fink*, the Coens parody the pathos of Odets' schmaltzy, social revolution play *Awake and Sing*, which gave him his Broadway breakthrough in 1935.

The Coens' depiction of Hollywood screenwriters as driven fools who are out of touch with reality rather than martyrs for their art makes even more of an impact in the case of Faulkner because his time in Hollywood was one of progressive humiliation. He worked for Warner for a weekly pay cheque of three hundred dollars, no more than the lowliest scribe there earned, and sank ever deeper into alcoholism.

By 1941, the year in which *Barton Fink* is set, both F. Scott Fitzgerald and Nathanael West had left the stage — they died within twenty-four hours of each other at the end of 1940. Faulkner was now back home in Jefferson, Mississippi, after working for both MGM and Fox, and, as the breadwinner for an extended family, was again unable to pay the bills. 'I will take anything above $100,' he said in a telegram to his agent. In 1942 he signed a strait-jacket contract with Warner.

There are also conspicuous echoes of Faulkner's life in the figure of Barton Fink himself, as well as Mayhew. Faulkner, like Barton, preferred a hotel to the Writers' Building, and he also showed little interest in the cinema, claiming that he only watched Disney films and news-reels. The first project Faulkner worked on in Hollywood was the Wallace Beery vehicle *Flesh* (1932, dir. John Ford), which was also a wrestling film. When the end product was being screened, he is said to have left the

Grave desecration: Mayhew's first appearance

Fairground attraction: *Devil on the Canvas*

projection room after five minutes — he knew how it would end, he said — and disappeared for a week's soul-searching in Death Valley. In the Coen film, Barton is shown a wrestling film to get him in the mood. The film is being shot for Capitol Films by 'Victor Soderberg', he is told, and it contains scenes of such absurdity that even the most idiotic fairground attraction couldn't compete with it.

The specialists of the spoken and written word,

whose help the film industry required after the arrival of sound films in 1929, numbered several hundred in the treadmill that was Hollywood in the 1930s. Once there, they disappeared from view 'like travellers on a moon rocket. Many of them joined Hollywood's proletariat', (*Literary History of the United States*).

If we pursue the narrative logic of Barton's tale, we can see that a similar miserable fate was probably reserved for him too. Lipnick refuses to sack him, contemptuously sneering that he won't do him the favour: 'You're under contract and you're going to stay that way. Anything you write is going to be the property of Capitol Pictures, and Capitol Pictures is not going to produce anything from you... You're not a writer, Fink, you're a goddamn write-off.'

The horror! The horror!

On the bed, which was down, a girl was lying, clothed in a pair of tan silk stockings... Above and inside her left breast there was a scorched place the size of a man's hand, and in the middle of that there was a thimbleful of blazed blood. Blood had run down her side but it had dried now.
(Raymond Chandler, 'Bay City Blues')

To wake up next to a beautiful, murdered woman is a perfectly perverse idea. There are definitely taboos for Joel and Ethan Coen — they avoid sex and sexuality like the devil avoids holy water, and will never crack a decent dirty joke. There has probably never been a more chaste love scene (though admittedly it's seen from the ironic perspective of the inhibited Fink) than their portrayal of Audrey's motherly seduction of him. Happily shocked, Barton eases himself back on to the bed. The camera wanders discreetly downwards to show shoes being slipped off, before tiptoeing into the bathroom, down the drain and through an endless shaft that leads to a wailing underworld.

Magic object: the framed photo

What happens to Barton and Audrey can only be seen as a punishment fantasy within the context of the puritanical Coen film universe. A vague psycho-analytic subtext runs through this tale of a writer whose loss of reality is portrayed as a sort of *déformation professionelle*. Their 'punishment' also has undeniably mythic undercurrents. For critic Klaus Theweleit it was quite clearly a case of the woman being sacrificed for the sake of art. Barton's block disappears the very moment he puts the sinister package, the legacy of neighbour Meadows-Mundt, which we may assume contains Audrey's head, on his desk. He places it beneath another magical object — the framed picture of the bathing beauty who sits on the beach and stares out at the Pacific. The camera has settled on this photograph several times since Barton arrived in the room, as though it were a window opening out from the cursed hotel on to his dreams.

A significant combination — an abstract picture of feminine beauty and a symbol of the feminine psyche which has been detached from the body and is thus deprived of its power. This is, of course, another version of the 'head in the box' joke, a gag that David Fincher and his script-writer Andrew Kevin Walker utilised again in *Seven* (1995).

At this point the film could easily disappear down its

The avenger: Karl Mundt rescues Barton

own hypertextual meanderings, but it doesn't, because John Goodman doesn't let it. *Barton Fink,* like every other Coen film, is a highly calculated construction where little is left to chance. Goodman, as Meadows-Mundt, ever the good friend, and dangerously honest, enables Barton to rise up to meet the challenges of the finale. He has become a serial killer in the role of a Wild West avenger who saves his struggling buddy, just like in a cop film. The whole thing is a Byzantine accumulation of genre allusions and wild excess. The scene's tight execution is an admirable feat given that we see it

through Barton's decelerated perception.

The real dream couple of this film is, of course, John Turturro and John Goodman, as they sit next to each other on the bed and exchange their mixed up shoes. They embody the alchemy of the non-relationship in this nightmare of isolation. The nightmare, however, ends in admirably paradoxical fashion at the edge of the blue expanse of ocean — Barton, the package and the bathing beauty, together in one of the most beautiful closing scenes of the 1990s. Orpheus united with Eurydice, who turns to face him. An inexplicable, and therefore perfect, enigma. It might be argued that the whole film was made simply as a means to end up with this image, to arrive at this place. But that might be too literary. ∎

The Hudsucker Proxy

New York, New Year's Eve 1958/59. The voice of Moses (Bill Cobbs), the keeper of the clock that tops the Hudsucker skyscraper, describes the rise and fall of Norville Barnes (Tim Robbins), who is about to fling himself from the forty-fourth floor. Just a month earlier he left his home in Muncie, Indiana to look for a job in New York. As he walked into the building to start work, the man who founded the company, Mr Hudsucker (Charles Durning), threw himself to his death. His right-hand man, Sidney Mussburger (Paul Newman), decided to put a pawn in the chairman's seat so stocks would plummet and he could buy them back more cheaply later and take control of the company. Norville Barnes displayed his aptitude for the job when he was despatched to deliver the last letter Mr Hudsucker sent Mussburger before he died, but managed to set Mussburger's office alight instead.

Hard-bitten hack Amy Archer (Jennifer Jason Leigh), undercover as Barnes' secretary to gather material for a scoop that would expose him as an incompetent, watched as Barnes found a totally unexpected success with a seemingly pointless toy. The hula hoop became a national craze, Hudsucker shares rocketed, and Mussburger made a final bid to get rid of the upstart Barnes — depressed after falling in love with his secretary and then discovering the truth about her — by declaring him insane.

We come in as Barnes leaps from the window ledge, but the clock-keeper brings him to a halt in mid-air by stopping time with a judiciously placed broom handle. While Barnes hovers helplessly in the air, the deceased Mr Hudsucker appears to him as an angel to remind him of his last, undelivered letter, which states that his share of the company is to be left to his successor. Moses has to fight off the devilish Aloysius (Harry Bugin), but his timely intervention nevertheless allows Barnes to reach the ground safely. It's Mussburger who ends up in an asylum, and Barnes who leads his company forward to new heights with the invention of the Frisbee.

The fall of Icarus

Stormy heights and snow-laden skyscrapers. The gleaming art deco conference table is the runway for the big jump straight through the window and into the abyss. Wide-angle lenses await their victim, one above and one below, and a third camera follows him straight down. The mechanics of dying has always interested the Coen brothers — in *Miller's Crossing* they aestheticised the highly ritualised gangster execution, and in *The Hudsucker Proxy* they opt for the traditional Wall Street suicide method. The film both starts and ends with a fall from the executive floor of a skyscraper, and if the viewer were to remember one particular image from the film, it would probably

Suicide risk: Gary Cooper (with Barbara Stanwyck) in *Meet John Doe*

Life cartoonery: the Hudsucker board's
second suicide candidate sticks to the
reinforced glass

be one of these leaps. The movie's German distributors
even chose to call the film *Hudsucker — Der grosse
Sprung* (The Big Jump).

The death leap has undergone something of a
demythologisation since Gary Cooper contemplated
suicide on top of a skyscraper in Frank Capra's *Meet
John Doe* (1941). The fashionably extreme sport of
bungee jumping must look like sheer mockery to the
despairing John Does of this world. The separation of
the fall from the necessity of impact is a typical invention of post-modernism, which likes nothing better

Harold Lloyd in *Safety Last*

Pinocchio

The urban canyon in *The Hudsucker Proxy* and its inspiration in *Clock Cleaners*

than to find the potential for fun in an activity that has not traditionally been regarded as especially entertaining. It is hardly surprising that the film's Swiss distributors organised a public bungee jumping session to mark the Zurich premiere. It is also worth noting that in 1958, the year in which the film is set, the Warner Brothers cartoon star Wile E. Coyote had a popular routine in which he fell into canyons only to quickly re-emerge from the coyote-shaped crater made by his impact.

The tidy hole Mr Hudsucker leaves in the window pane, a testament to his bodily proportions, is just one of several cartoon-like elements in *The Hudsucker Proxy*. The view into the exaggerated urban ravine is very similar to a background painting in Walt Disney's Mickey Mouse cartoon *Clock Cleaners* (1937). Disney animators liked to show off the advantages they had over the people who made 'real-life' films, and a false perspective in a cartoon could easily outdo the vertigo induced by, say, Harold Lloyd, who shunned the use of camera tricks in films like *Safety Last* (1923). Today it is the digital post-production and computer animation experts who are charged with overcoming the limitations of classic camera perspectives, and in *The Hudsucker Proxy* it's not only the lunatic nose-dive that comes from Britain's Computer Film Company. The seemingly endless offices, the reflective surface of the conference table and, of course, the damaged window pane are all digitally generated. The Coens are notorious for making meticulous preparations before shooting their films, and one of the means they use is a very detailed storyboard, a technique pioneered by Disney studios. 'Joel and Ethan Coen draw up a storyboard for everything,' cinematographer Roger Deakins told Brooke Comer. 'They start with rough sketches and end up going through absolutely every scene and angle. Before we shoot we spend months preparing, working out details with the designer and with everyone else involved.'

Waring Hudsucker (Charles Durning) on the way down

'Leap into the Void' (1960)

A preliminary study: the fall from the
window in *Crimewave*

The opening scene of *The Hudsucker Proxy* fits into a long series of iconographic cinematic falls from windows. The powerful and deadly allure of the abyss was used to great effect by Powell and Pressburger in the final scene of *Black Narcissus* (1946) and, of course, in the Hitchcock thriller *Vertigo* (1958). Joel and Ethan Coen use it to lead into their comedy — after all, Lewis Carroll's Alice found her way into Wonderland through her fall down the rabbit hole, and in Disney's *Pinocchio* (1940), the wooden doll ties a stone to his foot to stop him rising up to the surface when he dives into the sea to look for the whale.

The critic Josef Schnelle saw this 'leap into the void' (the title of his review of *The Hudsucker Proxy* in the *Frankfurter Rundschau* newspaper) as a metaphor for the essential emptiness of which the film has often been accused: 'Without "love, pain and all that bloody stuff" the cinema is grey and empty.'

Yves Klein, the French artist of the *nouveau réalisme* tradition, created a work called 'Leap into the Void', a manipulated photograph produced for a daily newspaper that was published specifically for this purpose. Klein had a different view of the void — *le vide* for him was a spiritual space. Perhaps we can understand the Coen films a little better if we try not to look negatively at their interpretation of the void.

In many of their films there are signs that don't seem to be ruled by any sort of code, signs that appear empty but which are all the more crucial because their context is loaded with unambiguous references and connotations. The flying hat in *Miller's Crossing* recalls the René Magritte bowler hat that lives a life beyond its normal role of protecting the intellectual centre of its wearer. 'Le bouchon d'épouvante' was the title Magritte gave to a bowler he exhibited in 1966 inside a glass case, and in his 1930 painting 'Dream Key' he depicts another bowler hat with the words 'la Neige' (the snow) written underneath. The role of a hat in a Coen film is to create a spiritual link between the characters and suggest a higher order — as does the snow in *Fargo*.

Any Coen film is packed with cultural references, and Magritte, for his part, quoted directly from the cinema — his bowler hat was a homage to the early Chaplin. Likewise, another symbolic element that appears in a Coen film which is possibly crucial and possibly meaningless refers back to surrealist art — the package that appears on the writer's desk at the end of *Barton Fink*. The viewer believes there's a severed head inside, but there may just as well be nothing in there at all. The package motif plays a central role in the work of Marcel Duchamp (his 'Box in a Valise', for example), but it can also be compared to the drawers of Salvador Dalí, which in turn evoke Freud's interpretation of dreams. *The Hudsucker Proxy* also pays homage to surrealism and the avant-garde filmmaker Maya Deren — before Amy Archer makes the acquaintance of the clock-keeper Moses, she is lured by the illicit attraction of a keyhole in a sequence which recalls Deren's *Meshes of the Afternoon* (1943) (in which the Freudian image of the key plays a central role), particularly in its use of lighting. The sequence ends with a close-up of Jennifer Jason Leigh which, in its composition, is very similar to the door handle scene in Disney's version of *Alice in Wonderland* (1951). Of course, the fundamental hollow symbol in *The Hudsucker Proxy* is Norville Barnes' carefully preserved sketch of a circle... more of which later.

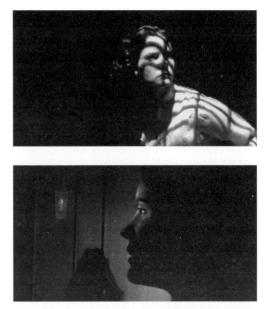

Amy in Wonderland

An empty sign: the Barnesian circle

'Cartoon figures': Norville Barnes (Tim Robbins) with Amy Archer (Jennifer Jason Leigh)…

Emotion and distance

There were few critics who didn't make an issue of the artificiality of what was commonly seen as a sort of cinema by numbers, and most also expressed disappointment over the lack of emotional involvement the film inspired. The idea that this might have been intentional — that the coded references might, through the loss of any ambiguity, enable the viewer to maintain a certain emotional distance — appeared incompatible with the expectations generated by a Hollywood motion picture. 'The juggling with old models becomes nothing more than an end in itself,' complained Carla Rhode in the *Tagesspiegel* newspaper. 'Jennifer Jason Leigh's irritating reporter and Paul Newman's cigar-puffing executive' are 'more like cartoon figures than real people'. Critic Verena Lueken accurately noted that the Coens' world had

always been synthetic, and 'its point of reference the cinema, not life,' but she then laments the lack of emotions in such a synthetic world, as though this were not a natural consequence: 'And Tim Robbins, who is similar to a Sturges hero upon whom greatness is thrust, appears to be a mixture of Gary Cooper, Cary Grant and Jimmy Stewart. What is missing is feelings. They behave as though they were in a comic strip.'

The storyboard, which we might see as the score for the Coens' movies, is, of course, nothing other than that. Derogatory comparison with the comic strip, which is still seen by conservative cultural critics as a synonym for a lack of emotion, shows just how far the cinema still is from being integrated into the historically established canon of the arts. Nobody would even think of insisting on the creation of emotion as the utmost goal of the theatre. And who would demand it from a piece of contemporary music? Only Hollywood

…and with Sidney Mussburger (Paul Newman)

is expected to apply what the film critics of the Frankfurt School long ago warned about — the palette of big emotions. The cinema is still expected to achieve what modern painters or writers no longer want to deal with.

Pia Horlacher believes the film comes under the category of 'Hollywood post-structuralism', that is, it shows 'how much vague stuff is being produced in other areas of the artistic (non-) debate on the chaos of post-modernity,' and that the aesthetic to be found in *The Hudsucker Proxy* was 'about as nourishing as a *nouvelle cuisine* dish that immediately makes you want to visit the hot dog stand round the corner'.

For Michael Althen it isn't just the skyscrapers in the film that are made of cardboard, but also the feelings. There is a metaphor that perhaps gives us a clue about where the Coens got their ideas from: 'Though it's only a paper moon / Hanging in from a cardboard sky...' goes the 1920s hit Peter Bogdanovich took the title for his film *Paper Moon* (1973) from. In this movie the paper moon in the paper sky is contrasted with the sincerity and the honesty of the feelings which the moon represents — we are expected to know that it is cardboard, but should at the same time let ourselves be seduced by what lies behind it. This is the rule that governs the type of film criticism which knows all about the artificiality of the medium but still wants to enjoy its emotional charge. Santa Claus might not be real, but what he stands for is.

This was the message sent out by *Miracle on 34th Street* (1947, dir. George Seaton), one of the few romantic social dramas not referred to in *The Hudsucker Proxy,* and it is one that would make the Coens smile. All of the Coens' films play with the public's expectations, but here, in their first venture into a genre that is by definition committed to romantic ideals, the trusting public treats any doubters like spoilsports and doesn't respond well to irreverence.

The Coens have no desire to train their public to be

The Coens as spoilsports: 'feelings made of cardboard'

better or cleverer people. Their emotional coldness links them to Paul Verhoeven's *Total Recall* (1990), a much less artistically oriented product, and to David Lynch's mythologies of the trivial. The distinctive elements that make up *The Hudsucker Proxy* cannot really be seen as simulacra, however — a simulacrum fulfils its role independently of the lack of authenticity of whatever has brought it about. Washing up liquid may well bring lemon freshness, but it manages to do so without containing any real lemon whatsoever. And besides, the Coens would only dismiss it as cheap perfume...

If they do use a cinematic set piece, like the scene featuring the two buddies who provide a running commentary on behalf of the viewer to Amy Archer's bid to chat up Barnes in a café, then they don't do so merely to profit from the emotional charge of such a set-up. They are more interested in the memory they expect to find in their viewer's consciousness, a memory so familiar it becomes almost a code, shorthand for a feeling, which the viewer will greet with pleasure. It is precisely this gratification that the Coens deny their audience.

David Lynch tends to invert the existing codes of a reference by changing the context. Roy Orbison's song 'In Dreams' may once have evoked a pleasant reverie, but the encounter with the sandman it describes becomes nightmarish once we have seen the horrific torture scene the song accompanies in Lynch's *Blue Velvet* (1986). This scene continues to affect us even years later — wherever in the world we happen to be when we hear the Orbison song again, we are aware that its now traumatic emotional charge is firmly established in the subconscious. While Lynch's associations leave the repositories of collective memory susceptible to viruses, the Coens content themselves with clicking on the icons on the surface.

It is interesting to note, within the context of cinema history, that *The Hudsucker Proxy* was the film that opened the Cannes film festival in the year that the top prizes went to a film that pushed the deconstruction of classic models to the extreme — Quentin Tarantino's *Pulp Fiction* (1994). Joel and Ethan Coen handle their aesthetic material (set pieces from screwball, social and romantic comedies) with the same reserve with which Peter Greenaway approaches his influences from art history, served up as deceptively opulent tableaux, as merely externally appetising still life, which often proves unpalatable on consumption. Like bad lovers, the Coens ensure that every moment of rapture is followed by a sudden, disorienting disillusionment, and in so doing almost casually dissect the functionality of the classic Hollywood film — as in architectural deconstructivism, a cleverly thought-out structure is part of the equation.

The Hudsucker Proxy, The Big Clock

Even the main setting, the Hudsucker building, is taken from an almost mythical film noir of the 1940s, *The Big Clock* (1948, dir. John Farrow). Moses, the black clock-keeper who is also the film's narrator, is a variation on the black role models who lived outside white society in the cinema of the 1930s and 1940s. This character is similar to Disney's Uncle Remus in *Song of the South* (1946), although the Coens have managed to get rid of any racist implications (while his characteristic speech and inexplicably good nature clearly belong to the cinematic cliché), but Moses is also given a philosophical depth that recalls one of the few positive black figures of this era — Rex Ingram's character in Frank Borzage's *Moonrise* (1948).

The film's formal structure also successfully revives past stylistic devices. One sequence, which can be seen as a virtuoso film within a film, tells the story of the

Street ballet: the start of a success story

On the trail of *Citizen Kane*: extreme depth of focus

Cinema by numbers: *Mr Deeds Goes To Town* (Gary Cooper, Jean Arthur), *Mr Smith Goes To Washington* (James Stewart), *Meet John Doe* (Barbara Stanwyck, Gary Cooper, James Gleason)

hula hoop from its beginning as a rough draft, through its time languishing unsold on shop shelves, to its eventual runaway success. In early sound films such devices, which are linked to the montage art of the late 1920s, were used to convey complex developments at lightning speed. Colour in *The Hudsucker Proxy* is generally muted, but the colours of the 1950s begin to appear while the bright hoops are waiting to be sold in the shops. This sequence fits in to the rest of the film as a Technicolor sequence would in a black and white movie. When a kid picks up a hoop that has been thrown out by a disgruntled shopkeeper and casually begins his impressive performance, it sparks a spec-tacular street ballet of the kind seen in MGM musicals, and the speedy rhythm of the sequence is matched by an equally racy score. And then, as if this were not enough, the Coens insert yet another element — a mock newsreel of the type that, after Orson Welles' *Citizen Kane* (1941), is seen in many films of the 1940s, and the extreme depth of focus Deakins uses to portray the offices and corridors of the Hudsucker building is also reminiscent of Welles' seminal movie.

Deconstructing Capra

Perhaps the clearest references in *The Hudsucker Proxy*, as regards content, are to the films of Frank Capra. It is the use of these identifiable elements, forcibly removed from their original moral motivation, that actually angered Capra fans. The film the Coens draw most deeply on is Capra's *Mr Deeds Goes To Town* (1936), featuring Gary Cooper as a country boy who inherits a fortune. When he goes to New York to collect his inheritance, a woman journalist embarks on a campaign to make him look ridiculous. Jean Arthur plays the reporter who makes the hero's acquaintance as if by chance — the hero, unaware of her unscrupulous motivation, falls in love with her and she eventually reciprocates. When Deeds learns of her deceit, he loses all interest in life. The Coens even swiped the idea of having the hero's opponents try (unsuccessfully) to have him certified. And they also adapted the Jean Arthur figure (changing her name to Archer), although they did invest their own reporter with some characteristics from the Rosalind Russell character in Howard Hawks' *His Girl Friday* (1940). The Coens took their idea for a 'useful idiot' being manipulated by dark forces from another Capra picture, *Mr Smith Goes To Washington* (1939). And from *Meet John Doe* comes the framing device

Racy reporters: Jennifer Jason Leigh in
The Hudsucker Proxy and Rosalind
Russell in *His Girl Friday*

of beginning the whole story with the main character on
the roof of a skyscraper.

While Capra heroes are always propelled by noble
motives, their transformations in the Coen film are set
at zero — a zero which appears as a circle on a piece of
paper. Even if the famous hula hoop is Norville Barnes'
creation, its value can hardly be compared with Mr
Deeds' honourable intervention on behalf of farmers
impoverished by economic crisis. It is also significant

that the circle has traditionally been a sign of whole-
ness and endlessness. High and low, as so often in the
work of Joel and Ethan Coen, come together within
the smallest space.

A zero: Barnes and his invention

The trick of separating the reference from its original moral value does more than draw attention to
Capra's unshakeable morality. Because the Coens are
primarily interested in the mechanics of the social
comedy, an apparatus that is as functional as the clock-
work mechanism in the Hudsucker building, they rob
it of any centre that might give it meaning. What might
have been a Capra character becomes, at best, a Preston Sturges character, a figure distinctly lacking in
superhuman ethical qualities who becomes a hero
purely because of external circumstances.

In Sturges' *Christmas in July* (1940) an irritating
clerk, a forebearer of Norville Barnes, is tricked by his
exasperated colleagues into believing the lousy advertising slogan he dreamed up for a contest has won him

An attached moral: Moses stops time, and Mr Hudsucker gives good advice

$25,000. He learns the truth only when he has already splashed out the money on credit. The Coens may not refer explicitly to this film, but they do use a similar rags-to-riches theme. Although the Sturges character fits into the Capra-esque liberal value system, his creative achievement is marginal and consists of nothing more than the creation of a non-sense text. Even this idea finds expression in the Coen film, enriched, of course, by a historical irony (we know today what success the hula hoop achieved). In Capra films, useless inventions are reserved for oddball minor characters such as Donald Meek in *You Can't Take It With You* (1938), who proudly presents a case with protruding fleecy rabbit ears.

The Hudsucker Proxy is not, however, entirely lacking in morality, even if this is expressed in the innocuous intonation of irony — Mr Hudsucker's death leap has clearly landed him in a better world, as can be seen from his last letter, the blue letter he has his former messenger Norville Barnes read out loud when he returns as an angel. Like his model, the angel in Capra's *It's a Wonderful Life* (1946), he uses his new form of existence to deliver some good advice to the mortals he has left behind. The letter's real addressee, Norville Barnes, listens to him in a state of suspended animation while his own death leap is temporarily interrupted by a broom handle which the divine figure of the clock-keeper has provisionally rammed into the gearbox of time. The circular narrative structure thus corresponds to Norville Barnes's circular sketch. The Coens proudly exhibit their formal skill, the symmetry and balance of their construction and the ambivalence of their content, but one should not see their apparent disregard for emotional involvement as a weakness. On the contrary, by attaching a moral to their film they expose the artificiality of even Capra's plots.

Appropriation may have been a prevalent, postmodern artistic device in the 1980s (there was even an entire genre known as 'appropriation art'), but it is definitely not an invention of this era. Capra himself knew how to make ironic use of quotations from other films. In his *You Can't Take It With You,* the hustle and bustle of the strange inhabitants of a house that is earmarked for demolition is accompanied by the tune 'Whistle While You Work' from *Snow White* (1937) — a hit film released just a short time before. And when Peter Bogdanovich made what was the first of several successful revivals of the screwball comedy, he well knew whose idea he was using. He got a fright during the auditions for *What's Up Doc?* (1972) — the plot of which was based on Howard Hawks' *Bringing Up Baby* (1938) — when he got a call from Hawks himself, who had just read the script. The veteran director was, however, merely calling to give him his blessing, but before doing so he growled: 'You stole the dinosaur. You're not stealing the leopard, too.' (*Howard Hawks — American Artist*).

Ward Bond and James Stewart in *It's A Wonderful Life*

Cary Grant and Katherine Hepburn in *Bringing Up Baby*

More is more

The Hudsucker Proxy, although its script was written in the mid-1980s, was only produced at a time when numerous film-makers started to revive various types of comedies that had their origins in the 1930s. Among the films they produced, only *Groundhog Day* (1993, dir. Harold Ramis) could come anywhere near the success of the fairytale romantic comedy *Pretty*

Woman (1990, dir. Garry Marshall). The interesting social comedies made by Andrew Bergman, who originally gained a reputation with a dissertation on the subject, such as *It Could Happen To You* (1994) and *Striptease* (1996), sank just as quickly as Stephen Frears' homage to Preston Sturges, *Accidental Hero* (1992). Seen in this context, *The Hudsucker Proxy* is by far the most multi-layered and suggestive of the wave of films. It is also the only example of a detached treatment of the ethical values of the social comedy, which in films such as *Pretty Woman* are displayed in largely unrefracted form.

It was the author Rainald Goetz who spoke of the wise man who discovered that more, and not less, is more. This post-modern credo could not be more elegant. Joel and Ethan Coen offer us this more without any false promises and without the ethical obligation of emotional involvement as the price for the pleasure the film gives us. 'We wanted everything to be big,' production designer Dennis Gassner said in the film's publicity notes. 'We wanted Mussburger's office to be like Mussolini's. The table in the conference room is based on a photo from the 1950s. It was so long that it had to be delivered in five separate pieces and assembled in the studio. We transformed a really long room with a ninety metre long corridor into the mailroom, which looks like it could have been designed by Albert Speer... We made 350,000 letters and packages for people like Norville to handle.'

More is more. The World Trade Centre is architecturally no more important than the Empire State Building — but it is higher. Norville Barnes's fall is forty-four floors long, but the Coens' god-like clock-keeper Moses feels the need to be absolutely accurate about its scale: 'Forty-five, if you count the mezzanine.' ∎

Fargo

Minneapolis car dealer Jerry Lundegaard (William H. Macy) engages in some decidedly criminal dealings in an attempt to resolve his pressing financial problems. He hooks up with two gangsters in Fargo and gives them a brand new car as down payment for kidnapping his wife (Kristin Rudrüd) and extracting a ransom from her rich father Wade (Harve Presnell). Jerry tells the hoods that the ransom will be $80,000, to be split down the middle between them. A simple plan, but it doesn't work. Jerry wants to call off the kidnap when it looks like his father-in-law might provide the funding for a $750,000 parking lot project, but, of course, he has no way to get in touch with the gangsters. They stick to the plan and arrive at his house and, after a tumultuous few minutes which end with Jerry's terrified wife entangling herself in a shower curtain and tumbling down the stairs, carry out the abduction. Jerry, meanwhile, learns that his father-in-law never intended to loan him the money after all, but plans to take over the car park project himself instead.

The kidnappers are driving along a lonely highway at night when they are stopped by police because they don't have proper number plates on their new car. Carl (Steve Buscemi) tries in vain to bribe the lone patrolman, and the taciturn Gaear (Peter Stormare) resolves the situation by shooting the cop in the head, then kills two youngsters who happen to be driving by.

The heroine moves into action the next morning. Marge (Frances McDormand), Brainerd's pregnant police chief, examines the scene of the blood bath and quickly draws some conclusions — the killer's car was a new Sierra, probably with dealer plates. She establishes that a car without official number plates recently checked into the Blue Ox motel near Brainerd, where the kidnappers stayed after they left Fargo and picked up a couple of women. These women tell Marge that the men were on their way to Minneapolis. A check on the telephone calls made there from the motel leads her to previously convicted car mechanic Shep (Steven Reevis), who works in Lundegaard's firm, and who put Jerry in touch with the two gangsters in the first place.

Back in town, Jerry persuades his father-in-law not to contact the police. He also explains that he alone is allowed to negotiate with the kidnappers who, he says, are demanding a million dollars. Wade, however, insists on handing the money over himself. The kidnappers, by now holed up in an isolated log cabin by a lake, have phoned Jerry to tell him that they want to keep the entire $80,000 to compensate for the three people they had to kill in Brainerd.

Plot developments now come thick and fast. Shep tracks down Carl, finds him in bed with a hooker, and beats him up. Carl, shaken, demands immediate payment from Jerry. A pistol-packing Wade sets off to deliver the money and meets Carl in a parking lot, but the confrontation leaves Wade dead and Carl with a minor

The kidnappers and their victim: Gaear (Peter Stormare), Carl (Steve Buscemi) and Jean Lundegaard (Kristin Rudrüd)

The opponents: William H. Macy as Jerry Lundegaard and Frances McDormand as Marge Gunderson

bullet wound to the face. Panicked, he grabs the money and runs, killing the parking attendant as he leaves.

In the meantime, a night porter has given the police a major clue — he recently heard a man, who he thought lived somewhere near the lake, boasting about killing someone. Carl, expecting to come away with $80,000, decides to stash the 'extra' $920,000 dollars that he found in the suitcase. He buries it somewhere in the snowy wastes, clumsily marking the spot with an ice scraper, and returns to the cabin in the wood, where Gaear has murdered Lundegaard's wife. Because Carl insists that he should be the one to keep

the car, Gaear kills him too.

Marge visits Lundegaard again to ask him if a tan Sierra has gone missing from his fleet, but Jerry flees during the interrogation. Marge finally finds the Sierra at the cabin by the lake and arrests Gaear, whom she finds stuffing Carl's leg into a wood chipper. She puts him in the back of her car and, as they drive to prison, reconstructs events before asking: 'For what? For a little bit of money. There's more to life than a little bit of money, you know. Don't you know that? And here you are, and it's a beautiful day.' Lundegaard is later arrested in a motel. At the end of the film we see

Marge in bed with her husband Norm (John Carroll Lynch). The television is on. Norm, a landscape painter, tells his wife that his painting of a mallard duck has been chosen to figure on the three-cent stamp (he had been hoping for the twenty-nine-cent stamp). Marge says: 'I'm proud of you.' And then: 'Two more months.'

◆

Fact and fiction

A caption at the beginning of the film tells us we are about to see a true story. Names have been changed, but 'out of respect for the dead, the rest has been told exactly as it occurred', and the words are supposed to authenticate the images. Not even a documentary film, at the end of the twentieth century, would dare to declare its authenticity so naïvely or so unabashedly. Anyone who has seen one or two Coen movies knows that they are genre films which echo other genre films — artificial products, replete with cross-reference and self-reflection. And suddenly we are offered a true story, faithfully reconstructed? Is it a trap? Or perhaps an ironic rhetorical figure which affirms its artificiality by the very way they profess its veracity?

This playful uncertainty is, however, only a side effect of the real intention. The more or less fake claim serves a mundane purpose that has to do with economy of narrative. By declaring the events to be true, the Coens could, as Joel said in an interview, include 'narrative escapades and digressions that the public would not have accepted in a classic thriller. *Fargo* doesn't fit into any genre, so we had to warn the public in the opening credits. How else could we get away with having the heroine appear for the first time half-way through the film?'.

So the claim is a trick to close a credibility gap. *Fargo* does indeed expect its viewers to swallow all sorts of peculiarities as it hops between different genres — it

Marge and Norm (John Carroll Lynch) at their favourite activity: eating

moves from thriller to comedy, a form of post-Western, a tale of the grotesque and a Minnesota version of *Little House on the Prairie* (the Coens grew up in Minnesota, and it is hardly surprising that the heroine Marge is one of the most sympathetic characters in their cinematic cosmos). The constructed reality acts as an aid to the fiction in which the gangsters don't behave like normal movie gangsters, but just as clumsily as 'real' people. The murders resemble real murders more than they do murders in thrillers. And the essential element of any thriller, namely suspense, is largely missing.

The 'true story' claim catapults us right into the middle of Coen County, that curious place where the simple, the straightforward, and the commonplace sit with the complicated, the enigmatic, and the distorted. Even the title of the film is misleading. The North

Dakota town of Fargo is the place where Lundegaard first meets with the two hoods, but it is not where the main events of the plot take place, nor does it have any symbolic function. It is an interchangeable name. This is one of the techniques the Coens use to achieve the strangeness that is perhaps *Fargo*'s most striking characteristic. Hierarchy, the order of things, is invert- ed. A detail becomes the most important element, and what is normally regarded as important is told merely in passing.

Thus, the thing we are most likely to remember about Marge is that right from when we first see her, she eats almost non-stop. The first thing she asks when she gets to Minneapolis is where she can get a decent bite to eat. And food plays a large part in her relation- ship with her husband — we see them eating together, we see him bringing her food and we frequently see the pair talking about food. Thus the normal, the common- place moves into the foreground, and thrill, suspense, sensation and action become secondary. The murder of the car park attendant, whom Carl kills as he flees with the suitcase full of dollars, is shown only elliptically. We see what comes before and what comes after, but the act itself remains invisible. A further example: Mike, an old acquaintance of Marge, phones up late at night because he has seen her on television. We thus learn *en passant* that the Coens have omitted a scene that forms an integral part of nearly all recent police thrillers — the police chief briefing the television reporters.

Violence and impotence

Coen County seems, if compared with mainstream cinema, somehow out of place and time, both familiar and alien. Or, as Ethan Coen puts it: 'We grew up in America, and we tell American stories in American settings within American frames of refer- ence. Perhaps our way of reflecting our system is more comprehensible to non-Americans because they already see the system as something alien.'

Violence here always has connotations of male helplessness (unlike in genre cinema or, for example, in *Pulp Fiction* (1994, dir. Quentin Tarantino), a movie which many critics used as a reference). The situations the characters face are simply too complex for them to cope with. The more they try, the more they screw up. In this respect, *Fargo* functions like a comedy in which the characters' plans are always thwarted. Violence is their vain attempt to gain the sovereignty they lack in even the most banal of situations. Carl, for example, goes to a parking lot to steal a number plate (much too late, as ever). As he leaves

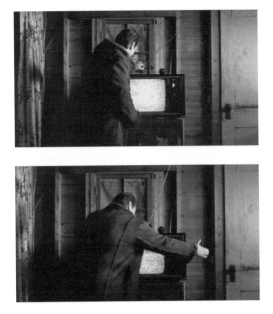

A contrary child: Carl battles with the television

he explains to the attendant that he has changed his mind and does not want to park there after all, but the attendant insists on his four dollars, provoking Carl and verbally abusing him. Carl exacts a bloody revenge for his humiliation just a short time later when he shoots dead a (different) parking attendant after he has taken the ransom money from Wade.

Outcasts, gangsters, those who operate outside of society, are defined in popular culture by their violence, by their ability to kill. But because the outlaw has transgressed, because he has broken the rules to which we are subject, he is someone with whom we often identify, even when he's a bad guy. His violence tells us that he has the power to break the rules, but in Coen films, violence is a sign of incompetence, of impotence, of restriction. In this respect, *Fargo* is a tale of the grotesque. The first three murders are the result of stupidity. Carl failed to put on the number plates, and not because he simply forgot to but because, as he says, he 'never does that'. The gangsters are repeatedly frustrated by objects that seem to have a will of

More slapstick than action: the kidnap scene

their own, and they fall apart because their self-image constantly collides with an unruly reality in which not even the television works. Carl never fails to react with a rage that gets him absolutely nowhere, like an ill-tempered child.

Violence in *Fargo* often seems like a domestic accident. The Coens depict Jean Lundegaard's kidnap as a combination of clumsiness and coincidence. Jean bites Gaear's hand and then flees up the stairs to the bathroom — the hoods follow her, but when they find the room empty and the window open, Carl rushes back downstairs again. Gaear, who is now only interested in finding some ointment for his wound, rummages in the bathroom cupboard and by chance spots Jean cowering behind the shower curtain. Jean panics, gets herself caught up in the curtain and stumbles down the staircase, watched by a bemused Gaear who has not yet laid a finger on her. This sequence is more like the orgies of destruction found in Laurel and Hardy pictures than an action scene from a thriller.

Gaear, the silent killer, murders people without batting an eyelid, but even this inscrutable figure is the source of his own undoing. Towards the end of the film he waits in the cabin for his accomplice to return. He sits and watches a soap opera on television and is obviously moved by what he sees — a woman telling her boyfriend that she is pregnant. Something approaching emotion stirs on Gaear's face — the first and only time this happens in the entire movie. Gaear sees the arrival of Carl, confused and bleeding, as an interruption, and kills him. Reality as a disruption of the cheap dreams of popular culture — we have already seen this motif in the kidnapping scene. Before the kidnappers arrive, Jean is watching a daytime cooking programme. She spots one of the hooded gangsters about to smash his way through the French windows and into the house, but it takes her a moment to grasp that this isn't just another television show. The bourgeois and the criminal share the same dull, fascinated gaze at the box. In such instances the Coens show themselves as not so much critics of a society that is amusing itself to death than as skilful Swiftean satirists.

A war between two families

The plot could also be related like this: the bourgeois world produces irreconcilable contradictions which lead to crime and destruction, but the policewoman solves the case and more or less straightens things out. Jerry, the commercially incompetent son-in-law, faces one humiliation after another. He's like a schoolboy who is always worried about getting caught cheating again. Jerry's impotence is matched by the comparative omnipotence, self-assurance and success which his father-in-law Wade takes for granted as an integral part of his nature. Jerry is sales manager in his father-in-law's business, and within Jerry's family unit it is Wade who calls the tune, even criticising the couple's lax attitude towards their son, who sits taciturnly in front of the box and stays home for supper only when he feels like it. Jerry's coup is thus an attempt to take that part of the family fortune which is legally refused him. The only role that Jerry can play within the patriarchal system is that of the loser. His criminal project is a sort of belated Oedipal revolt.

Jerry is not, however, merely the wayward 'son' — he is also the unhappy employee caught up in a system of soul-destroying dependency. It is this that leads him to betray his own position in society. This is the first time he has tried to take control — and he fails.

The father-in-law represents not only economic and family power, but also the American pioneer background. He is a self-made man who takes everything in

Cheap dreams: Carl as intruder – twice

Two kinds of family: Jerry and his father-in-law Wade (Harve Presnell); the Gundersons

hand (a characteristic that will eventually be his downfall), a man of action through and through, self-righteous, always resolute, never doubting. We might like to think of him when we see the enormous statue (outwardly impressive, but probably made of papier-mâché) that stands at the entrance to the town of Brainerd. The statue is of the giant Paul Bunyan, a figure from American mythology, striding through the landscape with his axe and his blue ox. It was his mighty footprints that created Minnesota's 11,000 lakes, according to the tale. In this place of legend the Coens evoke the pioneer myth, a myth more appropriate here in the Midwest than elsewhere. And just as the imposing figure of Paul Bunyan has his origins in a story, so too could the bloody finale form part of a nasty, violent fairytale.

Alongside the father-in-law's association with the pioneer myth, we may link the Lundegaard world with American history and the violent conquest of the

country. The statue of Bunyan that towers above
Brainerd is, to a certain extent, representative of two
different things: 'The yob Gaear becomes more and
more like the statue of the woodcutter Bunyan as the
film progresses. The killer shows himself to be a superfluous variation on the pioneer who robbed the land of
its innocence,' wrote Hans Schifferle, and this pioneer,
symbolised by the Bunyan statue is both the killer at
the bottom and the businessman at the top of society.

Fargo is the story of a war between different kinds
of household. The Lundegaards represent the misery
of the patriarchal family. They are associated with
commerce, with the world of business into which
Jerry, try as he might, cannot gain legitimate access.
There rages here a war over money and power, a war
which reaches into all areas of society, poisoning
private life, which is also waged with criminal means.
The female is a mere object in this world. Jerry plays
out his Oedipal struggle by kidnapping the daughter

A tragic figure: Jerry finds
his dead father-in-law

of the patriarch. This struggle is so gruelling and so central that it makes Jerry neglect even the most elementary of his own paternal duties — he forgets to tell his son that his mother has been kidnapped.

On the other hand, we see the sheltered, steady, almost unchanging and thoroughly contented world of Marge Gunderson and her husband. The Gunderson world, in contrast to the Lundegaard world in which Oedipal conflict inevitably leads to disaster, is a femininely oriented society. Marge goes out into the world while her husband Norm stays at home and cooks for her. The Lundegaard world is talkative and urbane, focused on verbal exchange and the deception of customers, something else Jerry fails to carry off, but the Gundersons are characterised by a rural mode of communication shaped by agriculture and nature. The farmer's work is concrete, material, its horizon is the biological cycle, the annual recurrence of the same elements. This basic experience enables people to develop

No panic: Minnesotans in conversation

the trust that is necessary to form simple, straightforward social relations, relations which need few words and which can survive without those rituals of self-assertion with which the free, deracinated individual has learnt to confirm his identity. Norm is a landscape painter who tries to be as naturalistic as possible when he paints wild ducks, and who likes to go fishing, and Marge's pregnancy is another indication that they are firmly in sync with the natural world.

This agrarian outlook is mirrored in the Minnesota dialect that atmospherically sets the tone in *Fargo*. It seems that this dialect, which comes from the state's Scandinavian immigrants, has no provision for speaking quickly, no possibility of panic and no means to express sensation or excitement. The lengthy 'Yaaahs', Marge's

'Oh, jeez', and Jerry's 'What the heck' are typical. The rest of America regards Minnesotans as backwoodsmen, as a brusque lot who have an unusual understanding of what constitutes friendliness. 'Minnesota nice' is the name ironically given to their subdued way of speaking. Interestingly, statistics say that Minnesotans are less likely to take part in television talk and game shows than citizens of any other states.

The Coens concentrated the sympathetic aspects of the Minnesotan in Marge, and the peculiarities in Jerry. The brothers portray this milieu — their own homeland — without any condescension, and only hypersensitive provincials could take exception. Thus, Jerry Lundegaard is not merely a wretched, grovelling, overbearing *petit bourgeois* man. He often appears as a genuinely tragic figure, whose downfall is as much his own fault as it is caused by external circumstances. The only truly satirical character is his wife Jean, a caricature of the American housewife, whose life seems to revolve around calling her father 'dad' and her spouse 'hon', and telling her son not to curse. The Coens refuse to let her develop — in the neurotic, patriarchal Lundegaard world she is allowed to function only as a MacGuffin, to serve as an impetus for the plot.

Marge Gunderson, laconically portrayed by Frances McDormand, is the exact opposite of what we expect in a heroine in an American thriller. She is stolid, her speech is slow, and 'Oh, jeez' is all she manages to say when confronted with one of the numerous strange events that mark the film. Even her vulnerable, inflexible body is the opposite of the usual police heroine body. 'We wanted,' said Joel Coen, 'to turn the cliché of the macho cop on its head. We found a pregnant policewoman in a parka to be much more interesting from a human point of view'. But all this is, of course, merely a ploy, a smokescreen to hide the fact that she does her job just as efficiently, logically and stubbornly as, say, the apparently absent-minded Peter Falk in *Columbo*.

The scene featuring the most playful treatment of horror comes at the end of the film. Marge catches the killer Gaear as he is disposing of Carl's body. Gaear stares at her, perplexed, as the wood chipper drones deafeningly and drowns out her words. Then, with one hand on her cocked pistol, she briefly touches the sheriff's star on her cap to make it clear to the uncomprehending murderer what the story is.

Marge moves within a world of ritualised social relations and communication. In her first scene she is woken early in the morning, and a short dialogue ensues with her husband in which he offers to fix her some eggs and she feebly declines. A sleepy Norm says he does not mind getting up. Not necessary, replies Marge. And thus it continues back and forward, until we see them both sitting at the breakfast table. The offering and refusing obviously forms part of a game with clearly defined rules — a lengthy exchange of meaningless phrases that fits in with the Minnesotan stereotype. Their way of speaking is a sign of their provinciality, but it also indicates an unshakeable composure. Even Marge's trademark stoic gaze at the most awful murder scenes is rooted in rural Minnesota.

Perhaps the strangest scene in the entire film (and one which any traditional Hollywood producer would immediately have cut) is also a reflection on the relationship between home, marriage and the world. Marge meets up with Mike (Steve Park), an old school friend, in Minneapolis. The reunion, which Mike has clearly mistaken for a date, ends in disaster. When Marge rejects his advances, a tearful Mike tells how his wife Linda died of leukaemia, and Marge is dismayed. The next day, however, she finds out by chance that Linda, whom Mike had been practically stalking for a while, is alive and in the best of health. 'Yaaah, that's a surprise,' says Marge, unmoved. And somehow it doesn't seem at all surprising to her that out there, in the modern world beyond Brainerd, marriages can exist as bizarre fictions.

The snowy wastes:
the human being as alien

Images of the family and of marriage impact on one another in *Fargo*, images that could not be more different or represent more contrary social milieux. As in many John Ford Westerns, there is an archetypal, pre-industrial, rural 'community' in which a harmonious order prevails. Against this is set an urban 'society' in which money and status are the ultimate goals. But the analogy with Ford's anti-modern images of the community ends when the Coens fit out their home with a false bottom, as we shall see.

Fargo as post-Western

If the title *Fargo* actually means something — aside from indicating the lack of importance the Coens invest in meaning — then perhaps we should examine its association with Wells Fargo, the stagecoach company that figured in numerous Westerns seeking to portray and celebrate the civilisation of the West. The fact that a native American — Shep, who put Jerry in touch with the gangsters — features among *Fargo*'s characters is perhaps a minor reference to Western lore. Coen County is, in *Fargo* at least, a specific US region populated by American people and myths.

The movie begins with a white screen. We see a car in the distance and realise that this is not a pure, unsullied frame, but a picture — an endless, flat, snow-covered landscape. *Fargo*, if seen as a descendant of the Western, depicts a region that still has not been conquered. In this landscape, which appears to have emerged out of nothing, there is nothing to be conquered. A never-ending sky vaults over a featureless white waste, and somewhere in between a car or a person is lost. In this chilly emptiness, the symbols of civilisation and of man's dominance over nature disappear. Humans are alien to this landscape, and become like intruders. This very first image evokes a myth of purity, which cannot be conceived of without guilt, and with the white comes the red, the blood, which later spurts out of the wood chipper, staining the snow.

The use of white in *Fargo* recalls Sergio Corbucci's famous white Western, *Il Grande Silenzio* (1968), which, like many late Westerns, told of the end of the pioneer myth. Corbucci's pioneers are transformed into outlaws who are killed by bounty hunters hired by the law and the banks. *Fargo*'s story may be different, but its themes are the same.

We could read *Fargo* as a sort of 'feminist Western'. In many classic films of the genre, women, generally from the East Coast, come as teachers to try to bring law and education — civilisation, in other words — to the West. Marge in *Fargo* to some extent combines the civilising mission of these women with that outstanding virtue of the male Westerner — the ability to do a job well and not to waste many words. The men, in contrast, stumble through the film like violent, regressive fools. They lack the fundamental insight without which life in Coen films is guaranteed to be a failure: don't try

Bizarre comedy: the finale

to do what you simply can't do. Things go wrong as early as the first scene in which Jerry meets the gangsters. Jerry arrives late (just as he will later arrive too late at the spot where the ransom is handed over). Carl, nervous as ever, wants to know why he can't just ask the father-in-law for the money directly, and Jerry furrows his brow and tries to explain that this is not the place to get into this. Carl acts like somebody who is merely playing at being a gangster. 'We don't debate,' he keeps saying — but he does. Jerry, the rebellious bourgeois son, and Carl, the regressive criminal, behave like mirror images of each other, continually trying to talk their way out of things, but their lies are too obvious and serve only to drag them deeper into disaster.

Fargo is laced, from its first to its last image, with an ambiguity upon which every attempt to find unequivocality founders. The first image — the caption — promises authenticity, while the last propels the heroine's understatement into the realm of the ridiculous. Marge (who, we may assume, has achieved some fame through her television exposure) has solved seven murders as well as single-handedly capturing one of the killers, and we now see her expressing her admiration for Norm because his drawing has been chosen to feature on the three-cent stamp. Such exaggerations tell us that we should not take their behavioural patterns too seriously.

Ruptures are also manifested through confusing changes in perspective. In a key scene, we see Jerry in a high-rise

building, on the executive floor of his father-in-law's company. Wade has just made it clear that he will not finance his project. The pair have a brief argument, which seals Jerry's fate, and when it is over he looks downwards in dejection. The next shot shows the view from the window onto the snow-white parking lot. It is like a stylised photo. Then we see a figure walking towards a car. It is Jerry, whom we are now seeing from above as though through his own eyes. Such moments, in which the subjective gaze (Jerry looks down) suddenly becomes 'objective', undermine our trust in the film's images. The irony in this scene is, to a certain extent, stylistic.

The Coens even risk a little peek into the abyss which may perhaps lie underneath Marge's apparently rock-solid marriage. Sitting in her office, Marge and Norm are chatting, once again, about food. We are then given a very brief, deliberate glimpse inside a paper bag containing a thoroughly revolting ball of worms which Norm plans to use as bait. A disturbing juxtaposition of the bizarre and the routine coming together but failing to correspond with the idyllic image of seasoned, modest married bliss. Maybe the friendly boredom of this marriage serves only to drive away the horror that America's past and present history have in store. Perhaps Brainerd is not so far from Twin Peaks after all. ■

The Big Lebowski

Atumbleweed drifts across the desert, through the streets of Los Angeles and on into the Pacific Ocean, as a powerful, virile voice announces the story of a hero of the 1990s, 'quite possibly the laziest man in Los Angeles County'. The man in question appears, dressed in bathrobe, slippers and sunglasses, buying a carton of milk in a supermarket. Ageing hippy Jeff 'The Dude' Lebowski (Jeff Bridges) then returns to his decrepit apartment to find two heavies waiting for him. They say they have come to recover debts his wife has run up before shoving the decidedly unmarried Dude's head down the toilet bowl to show they mean business. One of them pees on the threadbare rug in the hallway. After the credits have rolled we find the Dude at a bowling alley with his buddies Walter (John Goodman) and Donny (Steve Buscemi). Walter, a Vietnam veteran, explains that Dude has clearly been mistaken for the well-known philanthropist Jeff Lebowski, and advises him to seek financial compensation from his namesake. Dude attempts to do so, but the irascible philanthropist rejects his claims and shows him to the door with the words: 'Get a job, sir!' Dude nevertheless swipes an expensive rug on his way out of the man's mansion, and as he passes the pool meets Lebowski's very young and very blonde wife Bunny (Tara Reid), and a German nihilist (Peter Stormare).

A short time later, Dude gets a telephone call telling him that the other Jeff Lebowski wants to see him. Bunny has been kidnapped and Dude has been chosen to hand over the million-dollar ransom, whereupon Walter comes up with a plan to steal the money, replacing it with dirty underwear. Of course, when the time comes they mess up the handover by throwing away the wrong briefcase. They go bowling again, and emerge from the bowling alley to discover that Dude's car, along with the case supposedly containing the million dollars, has been stolen. Dude is trying to make a statement to two police officers in his apartment when he gets a call from Maude Lebowski (Julianne Moore), the philanthropist's daughter and latter-day Fluxus artist. He goes to her studio where she fills him in on Bunny's background as a former porn actress who has probably set up her own kidnap. Dude heads back home, mulling it over, but is intercepted on his doorstep and bundled into the back of a stretch limo. Old Lebowski wants to know where his money is. Dude comes out with the fake kidnap theory, and Lebowski responds by showing him a severed toe, with distinctive green nail polish that suggests it once formed an integral part of Bunny's foot.

Dude is relaxing in the bathtub after a bewildering day when three black-clad, heavily accented nihilists force their way into his apartment. They want money, and to underline the seriousness of their demand, they throw a vicious marmot into the tub next to the horrified Dude. The next day, the police tell Dude they have recovered his car, so he goes to pick it up and, on his way home, notices that he is being followed by a Volkswagen Beetle. Accidentally dropping his smoking joint into his lap, he panics, and drives into a trashcan. He then spots an enigmatic piece of paper on the back seat of his car which may be a much-needed clue. Walter finds out that the piece of paper (actually mistake-riddled homework) belongs to a boy called Larry, so they pick up Donny and call in on young Larry at home. The visit is fruitless, however. A short time later the two men who had previously threatened Dude (and peed on his rug) abduct him and take him to the house of porn film producer Jackie Treehorn (Ben Gazarra). Treehorn wants to know where Bunny is, because she owes him money. Dude's drink is spiked, and when he comes to he finds himself in Malibu police station, where a cop by the name of Kohl works him over.

He finally returns to his devastated apartment to find Maude, who has come to seduce him. In bed she coolly informs him that she has only slept with him because she wants to have a baby, and mentions in passing that the Lebowski fortune is tied up in a trust and her father only has access to a tiny portion. Whereupon Dude alerts Walter. Before he arrives, Dude spots the Beetle parked in front of his house, and grabs hold of the driver, who explains that he is trying to find a runaway called Bunny Knudsen. Back at the Lebowski mansion it emerges that Bunny has returned home safely. Both Lebowskis accuse each other of having stolen the million dollars, which in fact never existed, and Walter becomes violent toward the wheelchair-bound elder Lebowski. Later that evening, Dude's car is set on fire in front of the bowling alley, and the three nihilists repeat their demands for money. Walter stands up to them and a brawl ensues, during which Donny dies of a heart attack. Dude and Walter store his ashes in a coffee jar before solemnly scattering them to the wind. In the final scene, the cowboy narrator appears for the second time in the bowling alley, takes a seat at the bar, and delivers a brief commentary before taking his leave.   ◆

Narrative futures

In the half-light, a battered old tumbleweed catches the eye as the wind blows it across the desert, while a voice roughened by alcohol and cigarettes draws us into the realm of legends. 'What is a hero? He's the man for his time and place,' says the Westerner, the lonesome cowboy we know from the cinema and from advertisements. The voice is so anachronistic, the character so surreal, that when he turns up in the flesh in the middle of *The Big Lebowski* we might be forgiven for thinking that it is the tumbleweed doing the narrating, and not the nameless cowboy (he is listed as The Stranger in the film credits). In Lars Gustafsson's novel *Bernard Foy's Third Castling* the many-voiced narrator turns out to be a swarm of bees inside the bleached skull of a former customs inspector. We might well expect something similar from the Coen brothers. The cowboy has, after all, no more affinity with the events of *The Big Lebowski* than Barton Fink would have with the life and times of the people of *Fargo*.

The narrator is a man of straw, a fiction within the fiction, and Sam Elliott, who plays the character, looks like he has just walked off the set of *Tombstone* (1993, dir. George P. Cosmatos), where he played Virgil Earp, and into *The Big Lebowski* without even bothering to change his clothes. He is not an omniscient narrator, meditating benevolently on the doings of his protégés, nor is he a cunning mastermind, pulling the strings and gradually allowing the viewer to get an overview of what is going on. The cowboy's voice puts the events at an ironic arm's length, and the more he is supposed to carry out his function of ordering the narrative, the more his role unravels. His maxim about 'the way the whole darn human comedy keeps perpetuating itself down through the generations' at the end of the movie looks very like a last-ditch bid to bestow at least some sort of meaning on the nonsense of the story, but the narrator is in essence another red herring in a whole

'Quite possibly the laziest man in Los Angeles County': Jeff Bridges as 'Dude' Lebowski

series of them.

The gulf between the pathos of the narrator's words and the appearance of the Dude shuffling along has a similar effect to Nicolas Cage's voiceover in *Raising Arizona*, which points up a stark contrast between the elaborate language of the narrator and the rather modest intellectual abilities and slangy speech of the character Cage actually plays in the film. The Coens nearly always apply both meanings of the word 'pathetic' — emotional and ridiculous. The characters in *The Big Lebowski* could not be more indifferent to 'their' narrator. Half-way through the film, the cowboy sits next to Dude at the bar and tells him: 'I like your style.' At first, Dude barely takes any notice of him, then gives him a surly look, indicating that he regards him as no more than a tiresome interloper, before saying: 'I dig your style, too, man — that whole cowboy thing.' Good advice, such as Woody Allen got from his superego Humphrey Bogart in *Play It Again, Sam* (1971, dir. Herbert Ross), is superfluous. A cowboy in a bowling alley is a pretty useless thing.

As we can see at the end of the film, such a narrator is the perfect pawn in a zero sum narrative game, in which each participant draws on the imaginary million but never has to put any real money on the table to fuel the greed and trigger the action. The million dollars is another fiction within the fiction. The intricacies and impenetrability of the plot are a parody of the plot twists of so many films noir or contemporary cop movies. The Coens, keeping the straightest faces, take the most heterogeneous set pieces and weld them together. Digressions and false leads undermine the rigid logic of a plot in which every element has a function, and every gear must dovetail with the next. All the gags, all the narrative mischief in *The Big Lebowski* develop their own timing, delaying the progress of the narrative and muddying its resolution. And, in a comic, anarchic sort of way, they make it clear that all the characters are running after pipe dreams, chasing a zero that is just as empty and yet just as significant as the circle Norville Barnes draws in *The Hudsucker Proxy* when he sketches out his plan for the hula hoop.

The biggest bluff of all consists of taking a pile of trivialities, mistaken identities and unfortunate misunderstandings and turning them into something resembling

A place of refuge: Dude, Walter (John Goodman) and Donny (Steve Buscemi) in the bowling alley

a plot. The plot's coherence is really only a matter of form. It meets the standards of causal development in that it exposes this logic as a mere product of coincidence. We don't need to worry our heads too much about how little Larry's homework found its way onto the back seat of Dude's car, and this episode shouldn't be seen as a hole in the plot, nor as a structural defect which one can triumphantly blame on the screenplay. The follow-up scene, in which the three bowling buddies call on Larry and his parents, is perhaps nothing more complicated than an opportunity to gleefully present the viewer with the sight of Larry's wheezing father encased in an iron lung in the living room, and of Walter smashing up the red sports car he mistakenly takes as proof that Larry has indeed stolen and spent the million dollars.

The Big Lebowski adopts the tone of the light-hearted comedy right from the start. It makes the absurd plausible and makes narrative slapstick of the constant stumbling along the path of an orderly story. It has none of the dark overtones of *Fargo* or *Barton Fink,* and the abyss that it occasionally allows us to glimpse is not terribly deep. Its affinity with the comic book is as unmistakable as that of *Raising Arizona. The Big Lebowski* never gets oppressive enough to feel the need to resort to comic relief, it just keeps piling on the gags.

This associative sort of narrative requires great compositional effort. It constantly demands little gags and visual stimuli which can stand alone, without moving the plot on at all, but are not allowed to lead the viewer completely astray. The delaying function of these miniatures is a delicate balancing act, but it is an exercise in which the Coens have considerable experience. They have already shown what rarely gets shown in the cinema, in *Blood Simple* or in *Fargo*, for instance. They have illustrated just how difficult it can be to kill someone, and they have had fun showing how pathetically their heroes behave in situations that are merely routine in genre films. The Coens are not interested in the perfect crime. They are mistake freaks who mercilessly expose their characters' amateurism and transform it from an annoying adjunct into a central element of the plot. Coen County is not the best, but the most impossible of all possible worlds.

If plot elements are often no more than red herrings, then it is necessary to have one place that we can be sure of, a sort of centre of gravity. The bowling alley in *The Big Lebowski* is a place of refuge to which the narrative regularly returns after its episodes of turmoil. The bright neon stars that dot the outside wall of the long, flat building are first seen in the opening credits, and they also appear towards the end when the camera rises up after Donny's death and the screen slowly darkens. They are the guiding stars that lead lost souls back home. The game of bowling is not an existential metaphor, but simply a sport that does not require its participants to be hip — it epitomises the provincial at play. The Coens revel in the game's accessories and rituals just as much as in its players' deadly seriousness. Walter, who at one point draws a gun on a fellow player until he marks a zero on his scorecard (for having put his foot over the line), adopts a rigid perfectionism as his way of dealing with the flawed external world. And disturbingly inappropriate attention is paid to Jesus

Jesus (John Turturro), the narcissistic
super-bowler

(John Turturro), the champion bowler who dresses in
purple and pink outfits and likes to perform narcissistic
little dances with his bowling ball. 'That creep can bowl,
man,' says Dude. 'But he's a pervert,' adds Walter. The
bucket seats of the bowling alley are to the three friends
what the Doric temple was to the ancient philosophers.
This is the navel of the world, a place where you can
catch up on the latest news, a place where a quote from
Lenin is no more unusual than a chat about the next

Throwbacks: Dude and Walter, a textbook Vietnam vet

tournament. It is no coincidence that Walter responds to almost every situation life throws at him with the words: 'Let's go bowlin',' and it even triumphs effortlessly over politics — a picture of Nixon bowling hangs on a wall in Dude's apartment. The photo, just like Dude's view of the world, needs a good dusting off.

Chandler, bowling balls and a flying carpet

Coen County, that peculiar landscape peopled by amateur heroes, bloody incidents, macabre situations and absurd dialogue, has always been a pastiche. This can be seen not only in the historical trilogy that the Coens made between 1990 and 1994, but also in the collection of anachronisms that give *The Big Lebowski* its texture. Here we know that we are in the 1990s not only because the narrator explicitly says so but also because we see George Bush on television warning that he will not stand for the Iraqi invasion of Kuwait. However, we are also in a peculiar time warp where the 1970s are struggling under the weight of the 1960s, and where the pop culture icons of the recent past are shot through with allusions to the literary noir of the 1940s.

The Big Lebowski is secretly a period piece, a mocking obituary of an undaunted survivor of an era he refuses to leave. The numerous joints that Dude smokes, with the help of a pair of tweezers if necessary, have helped preserve the sweet haze of youth in his head, the hippy hedonism and the 'take it easy, man' philosophy. Walter's crew cut, his combat jacket and his weapons fetish make him a throwback too, but to a different way of life. His character draws as much on the demobbed and war-traumatised men of the film noir as on the *Taxi Driver*/Vietnam movie types. Walter earns his living as a security expert (Sobchack Security), wears his trauma like a badge, and is occasionally afflicted by bouts of political correctness. When the Dude refers to the chap who peed on his rug as a 'Chinaman', Walter points out that 'Chinaman is not the preferred nomenclature. Asian-American, please'.

The Big Lebowski's round of chronologically displaced figures is completed by the figure of the elder Lebowski's daughter Maude. Like a Fluxus art zombie she swings through the room on a rope spraying paint. 'My art has been commended as strongly vaginal,' she explains to a nonplussed Dude. Amongst her vinyl collection we glimpse Kraftwerk's infamous 'Autobahn', and were she not so tough and single-minded we might regard her as another hopeless nostalgia case. Maude can be compared to the provincial policewoman Marge in *Fargo*, though, in that in both films it is a woman who is the only character with an overview of the situation and a sure understanding of her own capabilities. In a decade in which the 1960s and 1970s almost simultaneously return as parodies of themselves, this patchwork of attitudes and ambience is the Coens' look back over the popular culture of the 1970s, the decade they grew up in.

With a large dose of irony, a few sarcastic sideswipes and some astonishment that these people can still exist, the Coens deploy their characters, labelling them. 'Lookin' Out My Backdoor', by Creedence Clearwater Revival, Dude's favourite band, blares out of his

A Fluxus art zombie:
Maude (Julianne Moore)

car radio, and the Dude himself bears quite a resemblance to the Fogerty brothers. The house of porn producer Jackie Treehorn exudes the discreet charm of the seventies in much the same way as the clip from one of his films Maude shows a moderately interested Dude, and the exotic party going on in Treehorn's garden shows that even the sexual revolution has its Stakhanovites. Anyone who has seen Paul Thomas Anderson's *Boogie Nights* (1997), a film about the porn industry set in the San Fernando valley of the 1970s, will feel right at home in this environment. And the Coens' trawl through various milieux is also, of course, a report by two field researchers who have come to Los Angeles to examine a society where certain character types and behaviour patterns continue to thrive when they have all but died out elsewhere. *The Big Lebowski*, said Joel Coen, was in this respect just as specific to LA as *Fargo* was to the Midwest.

The influences on this composition are a little more complicated, however. Pulp novels and film noir have long served as indispensable ingredients for Coen films, even when the allusions and quotes are not so conspicuous as in *Blood Simple* or *Miller's Crossing*. *The Big Lebowski*'s recapitulation of Chandler doesn't need any quotation marks. It delves repeatedly into the heart of the master's prose and, regardless of the comic use it is put to, contains a genuine homage to the literary narrative techniques which are far more important to the Coens than any Hollywood conventions.

The old Lebowski in his wheelchair recalls General Sternwood in *The Big Sleep* (1946, dir. Howard Hawks), while his wife and daughter are reminiscent of the two Sternwood daughters, and Knudsen — Bunny's maiden name — is the name of Eddie Mars' wife in the same film. The private eye on the trail of Dude (himself a hippy version of Philip Marlowe) has apparently come straight out of Chandler's novel *The High Window*. And the plot's meanderings again recall *The Big Sleep*. Hawks telegraphed Chandler while he was working on the film to ask who really did shoot Sternwood's chauffeur, to which Chandler reportedly replied: 'How should I know? You figure it out.'

General Sternwood (Charles Waldron) and his daughters (Lauren Bacall, Martha Vickers) in *The Big Sleep*

Like Chandler before them, the Coen brothers make use of a very large cast, whose peculiarities they use to transform their material into manifold masquerades. The pair of brutal rug molesters at the start of the film are thugs whose real purpose is to serve as a catalyst. A case of mistaken identity, of the sort that would hardly be tolerated outside of Coen County, leads them to set the mechanism of the story in motion.

The three leather-clad German nihilists are loosely associated with Bunny, even if their supposed kidnap-

The eternal hippy: lethargically true to himself

ping of her is done independently, but their ideological trappings have nothing whatsoever to do with the logic of the plot. Bunny, as it turns out, simply forgot to mention that she was taking a little trip to Palm Springs ('her' famous severed toe actually belonged to a female nihilist). And, to add another little flourish to this stereotypical bimbo, this wandering blonde joke, the Coens have her hail from their home state of Minnesota.

The hero integrates the mortal remains of the private eye into the Coen concept of men who vastly overestimate their own abilities. Although on first sight he appears entirely different, Dude Lebowski is in fact a distant cousin of Barton Fink and of Jerry Lundegaard in *Fargo*. While Lundegaard believes he can pull off the biggest coup of his life by having his wife kidnapped, and Fink selflessly seeks to spread the gospel of the common man through his plays, Dude has lost nearly all of his ambition, and as soon as he does get round to having one again, he founders on his own incompetence. He is not quite such an innocent as Norville Barnes in *The Hudsucker Proxy*, but neither is he a particularly deep thinker. He listens raptly to the song of the whale or to tapes of bowling balls rolling down the alley, and is happy once he gets his daily dose of White

Russian, his favourite tipple, made from vodka and milk.

In the Dude the Coens have once again recycled the long since worn out concept of the anti-hero. The incorrigible hippy lacks the moral fibre and the autonomy that distinguished the original Marlowe and his later reincarnations. Constancy, chivalry and integrity do not form part of his repertoire. He remains true to himself only because of his lethargy, and he lives from hand to mouth. He nearly gives the game away when he says 'we' while on the phone to old Lebowski as he drives with Walter to deliver the ransom, and tries to talk his way out by saying that he meant the 'royal we', an expression he has just picked up from Maude Lebowski. When the two ruffians come to his house to try to recover Bunny's debts, he tells them he's obviously single — the toilet seat is up. Even his nickname is almost programmatic — 'dude' means 'man' but it also means the type of city dweller tourist that visits a 'dude ranch', like the New York office workers in the film *City Slickers* (1991, dir. Ron Underwood).

The Dude is yet another Coen man who doesn't want to grow up, and who is not always tuned into reality, an Oedipal latecomer who finds women perturbing and is happy to bend to their will, and who is occasionally struck by fear of castration. The marmot which the nihilists drop into Dude's bathtub symbolises this fear, as do the nihilists themselves, who appear in the second dream sequence and threaten Dude with vastly oversized scissors. Jeff Bridges endows Dude with the necessary lethargy, sporting his leisure wear with just the right degree of sloppy grandeur. Dude is an uncomplicated soul for whom the world is always set to rights as soon as he hears the ice cubes rattle in his glass of White Russian, and who looks as convincing with a mobile telephone as an extraterrestrial with a bowling ball. Is he The Big Lebowski or is it his namesake? The Coens let the viewer decide.

Dude is a prime specimen of the hidden anthro-

Castration fears: the German nihilist, Dude and the marmot

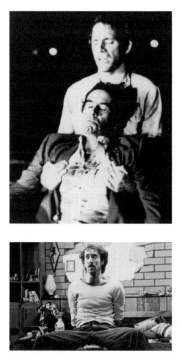

Hidden anthropology — the heroes of Coen County: Ray in *Blood Simple*, Hi in *Raising Arizona*, Tom Reagan in *Miller's Crossing*, Barton Fink…

pology that prevails in Coen County. Almost the entire population is made up of dummies, fools and, as the Coens say, dopes. The male heroes are generally hopelessly overstretched, but don't realise it. They are constantly faced with situations for which their physical and intellectual capabilities are insufficient. Or, as with Tom Reagan in *Miller's Crossing*, they achieve their aims only to realise that they are the victim of their own cunning. Even Ray in *Blood Simple* has, with the murder of his lover's husband, taken on more than he can handle. The awfulness of his act is added to by the awfulness of his incompetence.

It is from the grotesque discrepancy between the plan and its execution, between the viewer's expectation and the unexpected realisation of the expected, that the absurd comedy of Coen County arises. Its inhabitants often resemble walking, masculine nightmares in which the most simple of things will always go wrong and the tough guy will always turn out to be a useless idiot. In the Coen universe, only a fool like Norville Barnes can achieve more than was expected of him.

The Big Lebowski's other male characters also more or less correspond to this type. John Goodman's Walter operates with a very limited repertoire. He is a textbook Vietnam vet, whose rhetoric comes straight from the jungle and whose funeral oration for Donny honours him as though he had died in combat on the battle field and not from a heart attack in a car park. David Huddleston, as the second Lebowski, is the latest addition to a memorable series of loud, fat men that storm their way through Coen movies and whose impotence is at its most obvious when they are at their most bombastic: 'By God, sir, I will not abide another toe,' he screams at Dude. But the would-be tycoon has to live on an allowance, and he miserably fails to turn the imaginary million dollars into a real one.

Take it easy

Because the film is a comedy, we can accept its purely silly bits and its ventures into bad taste. We can place the conversation with the funeral director concerning the price of an urn in this category, as well as the scene where Walter scatters Donny's ashes into the Pacific and into Dude's face. Walter's attack on old Lebowski also fits in here. He pulls him out of his wheelchair with the words: 'I've seen a lot of spinals, Dude, and this guy's a fake', only to find that when he lets go the old man crumples to the floor. And perhaps the running gag that Walter can neither bowl nor drive a car on the Sabbath — which eventually leads Dude to remind him that he is a Polish Catholic who only converted to Judaism for his (now ex-) wife's sake — does wear a little bit thin. But these corny jokes help lubricate the engine of the plot — we laugh without remorse and without any lasting side effects.

The film's two dream sequences, where the Dude's mind processes the strange things he has seen, are no less playful or self-referential. The lazy Dude takes off on a flying carpet, which provides an opportunity for a night-time, bird's-eye view of Los Angeles, and then suddenly plummets, supplying the pretext for the spectacular swooping shot that the Coens have indulged in since *Blood Simple*, where the camera slides along the bar and moves carefully over the head of a sleeping customer. The hapless Dude is squashed by a bowling ball and then, along with the viewer, gets a chance to experience life from the perspective of a ball as he shoots helplessly down the lane toward the pins. Like the doggie flashback, the bowling-point-of-view shot enters cinematic history. The 'dramatic necessity' of this sequence is, of course, hardly worth discussing — it is yet another of many red herrings.

...Norville Barnes in *The Hudsucker Proxy*, Jerry Lundegaard in *Fargo* and Jeff Lebowski

The same goes for the second dream sequence, which might also be considered a step towards the first bowling musical in film history. Again, it is a distorted reflection of Dude's reality. He dreams that he is the star of a Treehorn production called *Gutterballs*. Dressed in a worker's overalls (and looking neater than he ever does in real life), he courts a Teutonic Maude who is kitted out with breastplate, helmet and horns. His erotic fantasy is indulged as he drifts like a bowling ball between rows of women's parted legs, but the castrating nihilists put a sharp end to his reverie. The visual extravagance here is quite astonishing, but not as compelling as the trip down the waste disposal pipes in *Barton Fink*. It's the price paid for the decision to push the comic tone to the fullest extent, but better one gag or gimmick too many than one too few.

These extravaganzas could be said to be neutral as regards the situational comedy of the dialogue or the plot. They neither spoil their effect nor do they provide any drive that may be lacking. Roger Deakins' camera gives the dream sequences a glossy finish just as efficiently as it introduces a note of homeliness into the neon light of the bowling alley or manages to capture the dingy, sloppy nature of the resident in its portrayal of Dude's apartment. *The Big Lebowski* has neither a dominant colour, like the white of *Fargo*, nor a limited and strictly nuanced palette of browns such as in *Miller's Crossing*, and it is, overall, the least stylised view of Coen County. But such objections do not detract from its sophistication or from the speculative gains made from its narrative futures. If, after *Fargo*, you feel shortchanged, then you might find solace in Dude's philosophy — take it easy. And our unemployed cowboy reminds us that 'it's good knowing he's out there, the Dude, taking it easy for all of us sinners'.

The Big Lebowski has, in its best moments, the grace of a flying carpet. It is impossible to predict what will come after this film. The sequence of *The Hudsucker Proxy*, *Fargo*, and *The Big Lebowski* provides no clue as to where the next trip will lead. In Coen County, there's a surprise lurking around every corner. ■

GAMES. RULES. VIOLATIONS.
Looking for a trail in Coen County

*I must create a system
Or be enslav'd by another man's*
William Blake, 'Jerusalem'

1

The Coens make films like other people make hula hoops — you know, for kids. At least, that's what they say. And they'll be damned if they'll get into a discussion of their methods. It's like the letter that Edgar Allan Poe leaves hidden on the table amongst the other mail — the simple in the obvious, which triggers such a complicated search for this very reason.The Coens' interviews and press conferences are full of false trails and more or less incomprehensible jokes, and you could stock a library with the books they supposedly haven't read (the Coens don't like to leave traces). Their films, they say, are no more than a vehicle for some very personal fun, but has there ever been a philosophical system, an aesthetic method that was anything else? Christianity, or Marxism, or pointillism, for example. Not to mention film criticism.

2

Whenever I come out of a Coen film, I find I have a strange, useless feeling of tenderness. I believe it's just possible to like people, even if they are hiding behind clichés, even if they are mean or desperate, even if, and maybe even because, they are wearing masks — at least, until I meet some real human beings. This feeling comes over me despite the fact that I have just waded through a cinematic stream of blood, sweat and tears, despite the fact that I have just been watching people who are inevitably too dumb, too corrupt and too fearful to prevent the worst. Despite the fact that I have just been in a place that has never claimed to represent the 'real' world. Despite the fact that I have in my head the memory of a hundred reviews condemning the 'soullessness', the 'coldness' and the 'mechanical brilliance' of these films. And despite the fact that I heard the Coens' laughter in the background — the film-makers mocking, for example, the 'banality of the good'.

Tenderness, then, but not optimism, and definitely not forgiveness. We like people who are beyond hope, who always get themselves and other people into trouble. Characters who are caught between their own family saga and the demands of a society that wants winners but at the same time despises winners, which pretends to like losers but at the same time despises losers. Liking people is one of the most pleasant feelings the cinema can generate. It isn't as intense as lust, fear, laughter, belonging, sentimentality or being in the know, but it is more lasting.

We just might like the people in the films of Italian neo-realism, for instance, if they were not obviously trying so hard to be liked, as when, for example, Cesare Zavattini so obstinately confuses his methods with reality. The Coens don't fall into this trap. Their characters aren't in the least concerned about whether you like them or not. In real life you wouldn't want to sit next to them on the bus, and you would go out of your way to avoid these unsympathetic, egotistic, pompous fools. But you can see them differently when they are larger than life, up there on an enormous screen. There you have the freedom to observe them with a look so intense that it would earn you a punch in the eye in real life.

They are never people who have anything particular to prove. Ostensibly basing *Fargo* on a true story is merely a ruse to prepare us for any cracks in the narrative structure. Characters in Coen films stare helplessly at their own lives and at themselves because they don't know whether they are the victim of stupid coincidence or of powerful metaphor. By extension, all Coen films are based on true stories in so far as they don't contain anything exemplary, like the bourgeois novel, and they don't mythologise their content.

True/untrue/true: *Fargo*

What we do see are certain things that undoubtedly belong to a living, biological system developing in both time and space, and we observe these things so closely that it is as if we are examining them through a microscope — a technique that is perhaps best compared to the *nouveau roman*. And we try to put together all the pieces, while at the same time musing over how what is observed changes by the very fact of being observed.

The images, movements and people in Coen films 'know' that they are objects observed by a camera, and they react to this by alternating between their symbolic and their representative nature. One moment they behave in the irrational, unique, but conditioned manner any 'real people' would, and the next they are purely cinematic fantasy figures who can only behave as mere shadows of life within a given system of signs, within a text.

In the cinema, at least, we don't have to fall for the chimera of the difference between the true and the untrue. Nor are we required to differentiate between what does and does not have a soul. The authentic and the synthetic circle around each other in a way that contradicts the classical hierarchy which ranks the 'real' before the 'counterfeit', which places life before art.

'I'm playing,' says the bourgeois individual. 'No, you are being played!' replies his double. 'According to which rules?' asks a third. 'I shall find out,' says the bourgeois individual in his temporary state of revolt (a state which exists predominantly within the realm of art), 'by breaking the rules'.

The Coen film viewer is, on the one hand, like a child who is not at all surprised that an object can behave like a human being, an image like the thing it is representing, and the thing it is representing like an image, a symbol like a sign, or a sign like an icon. And he is also like an old man who is far removed from the objects of his passion, the passion whose choice of targets and methods was both more free and more determined than was foreseen in the greatest bourgeois myth of them all — the biography.

But what is a biography? 'The game that I was playing,' says the optimistic bourgeois individual. 'Rubbish,' replies his pessimistic double. 'It is the game that was played with you'. — 'But who drew up the rules? And where are they written down?' — *'That is your biography — the vain search for the rules.'* And that, beginning with the heroes of Franz Kafka's books, is precisely the comic tragedy of the young bourgeois individual. He cannot find the text that contains the rules. It is not the games, nor the rules, nor the violations of the rules, but the desperate and futile hunt for the text containing the rules which constitutes his life, or his non-life.

Nowhere else but in the polyphony of cinema can this meta-biography of the disintegration of characters who are forced to play but have no idea what rules govern their game be so truthfully expressed. It is as if we are there in the midst of things and can sense the despair ourselves. At least in the films of Alfred Hitchcock we can save ourselves with an act we can actually understand by carrying it out, or take shelter in a moral-romantic pose which allows us to see the impossibility of understanding the rules as part of our own drama, as in the novels of Dashiell Hammett and Raymond Chandler. Or if we at least had the truth of passion, as though obsession could interfere with the rules of an otherwise beautiful sacrifice, as in the works of James M. Cain and their many cinematic interpretations. In all of this the aesthetic-moral creation, the work of art, constantly threatens to escape its creators.

The authors can no longer trust their creations, and worse, the creations can no longer trust their authors. This process started when the first human being began to doubt God's authorship, and continues with ever more rebellions against the authors of our own biographies, against fathers, against society, against logic, against usefulness. A process that ends with the odd feeling that we are both author and creation, endlessly rewritten. This comically awful move into the interior, into the body, into the fear of an ambiguous state of not-being-created and not-being-born, has been designated post-modernism. An aesthetic that doesn't labour under the linear negation of modernism (where each text appears to exist only to be entirely and radically overwritten by the next), but in which texts and semiotic systems are layered over one another, the simple and the complex, the old and the new, the physical and the abstract.

This is how the films of Joel and Ethan Coen 'function', outside of the Oedipal myth of author, text and life, of being and expression, of body and spirit, soul and biography. They don't trade in the game itself, but rather in the deadly search for the rules.

3

Back to tenderness. Where in the world does it come from? I have just seen a Coen film, a film that professes to belong to a genre — a gangster film, a comedy, a police film; and a genre film tolerates all sorts of feelings, but not tenderness. It stands in the way of problem solving and wish fulfilment. Think about your dreams, for instance. You might remember lust, fear, violence or weirdness, but tenderness? Don't try and tell me that people dream of tenderness. Tenderness is a complicated, demanding and contradictory feeling. You have to work hard to be able to let it suddenly take hold of you. It is not a feeling for the faint-hearted.

Film is the art of regression (and we look at it from one side or the other according to whether we want to emphasise 'art' or 'regression'), but if it is to be any more than run-of-the-mill, it must go further than this. It has to lead to realisation or to tenderness — if there is any difference between these two things other than one convolution of the brain or another.

Tenderness? Pah! Didn't this film sarcastically destroy everything that makes up the world in which its characters live, all the things I finally decided I liked? A Coen film is quite radical in its destruction of all that its inhabitants cling to, and it makes it quite clear that they deserve what they get. Besides, they aren't real people, not even shadows or dreams of real people, but outlines, sketches, phantasms. Nevertheless, they are living traces of that which constitutes real people.

The film I've just seen was about two different ways of either ruining yourself or making a fool of yourself, or both at the same time. The first way is to play by the rules, and the second is not to play by the rules. Something as simple as a moral is not on offer here. At the same time, though, the film is nothing other than a long, complicated process of reflection, similar to what rabbis call 'clarification' — an examination of the texts until they reveal whatever help they can give, and which also leads on into all other areas of life to offer resolution of moral questions. And on to the point at which there is nothing left to say, because everything comes out of the texts (ie the screen images) themselves, and even film criticism could keep its mouth shut if it wasn't charged with the arduous task of giving the text a consciousness, the consciousness a language, and the language a story.

It is said that there are no 'messages' in the films of the Coen brothers, but I don't believe in soulless or non-moral art, and I don't think art can exist that doesn't go beyond itself or its material. These films deal with my favourite theme, which is that in order to be able to love people you have to hate the society in which they live. Of course, it is no longer so easy to separate the two — if it ever was.

Two ways of ruining yourself or making a fool of yourself: Tom Reagan in *Miller's Crossing*, Barton Fink…

4

The Coen brothers' movies are American, as opposed to Hollywood, films, while someone like Jim Jarmusch, for example, makes films *about* America. American films are also, of course, films about us in so far as they are films about capitalism. What is seductive about the Coens is the fact that their films are about people who live in a capitalist system, and also about how people can't really be fulfilled by life within that capitalist system — not for

...Norville Barnes in *The Hudsucker Proxy*, Jerry Lundegaard in *Fargo*

good or for bad, and not by its corruption, its success, or its desires. They cannot be classed as anti-capitalist films, but they do go a lot further than the movies of, say, Frank Capra or the films of neo-realism or political modernism.

It may well be correct to view *The Hudsucker Proxy* as a Capra story peopled by Preston Sturges characters in a Fritz Lang setting, as critic John Harkness did in *Sight & Sound*. It is difficult to imagine more varied influences, and these interferences alone create an aesthetic-moral force. If we go along with Harkness' theory, we have one creator who

Tastelessness instead of redemption: *Raising Arizona's* happy ending

believes in the healing powers of the individual against society, another who allows the individual to survive only as an 'author' rebelling against society and a third who portrays society as a pitiless ornament which gives the individual no chance. Or we could put it this way: we have the shattering of illusion in Capra; the mirroring of illusion in Sturges' happy endings, characterised by the fact that the public misjudges the hero as much as the hero has misjudged the public; and the disintegration of fate through *mise en scène* in Lang's films.

The fairytale doesn't come to the man to save him, as in Capra's films, but to devour him and then spit him out. The fairytale exists, and it is beautiful, but it brings neither redemption nor explanation. *Raising Arizona*'s happy ending, for example, consists of nothing more than the hero's reconciliation with the untruthfulness of his dream fulfilment, while we might actually view its simultaneous reconciliation and distancing as regressive and tasteless.

What happens in Coen films is similar to the musical technique of sampling. Things are brought together that do not necessarily belong together, and the compositional accomplishment of this impossibility overcomes the veracity and originality of invention. The dynamism of a Coen film comes from the transgression of various aesthetic-moral systems. One of the projects the brothers currently have in development is a movie called *Cuba Libre* (based on a novel by Elmore Leonard), described as a combination of *Butch Cassidy and the Sundance Kid* (1969, dir. George Roy Hill) and *The English Patient* (1996, dir. Anthony Minghella)... in other words, a typical Coen film, complete with the usual dreams and illusions — as well as a story full of big, enigmatic feelings, in which each character can try to become his own legend or discover his innermost self.

Within this collision of ideas we can learn how to read one dream through another. Bitterness, frivolity and naïveté trip over each other, dreams reveal the nightmares which encircle them and vice versa. If you don't believe that sampling can be creative and surprising, then you won't have lost anything by going to see a Coen film.

This linking of sources and references to film history as well as contemporary movements never fully succeeds. The contradictions remain and this is why the Coens' films have on occasion been described as 'empty', as though it were simply a case of pulling another white rabbit out of the hat. The off-the-wall coupling of a sentimental baby film — a genre that was much in vogue when the Coens were working on *Raising Arizona* — with the utterly amoral kinetic energy of a Roadrunner cartoon is as unlikely a combination as the cross between gangster film and philosophical-aesthetic essay on hats that is *Miller's Crossing*. In European art history we learned to appreciate such techniques as employed towards the end of the Surrealist period, and then adapted them to advance the narrative as well as the fine arts. Fine art used a true representation of things, things which were in themselves real but had a thoroughly unreal relationship to each other. The cinema, however, has always shied away from the use of such techniques, and shown itself to be a particularly conservative medium, perhaps precisely because it is so conscious of its freedom. The cinema's mythical and psychological narrative methods permit the use of such unsettling juxtapositions only in dream sequences or as a representation of the demonic presence of the here-after (as in horror films, for example). But even more scandalous is the mixing of codes, the blending of readable signs with those which can only take on meaning when seen in relation to others, combining abstraction (the refusal of representability) and Surrealism (the unleashing of representation).

It was the post-modern film that made these two methods of going beyond ideal representation in the image appropriate for the cinema. Practically nowhere else is this union of aesthetic methods so stringently linked to the liberation of theme as in the films of the Coen brothers. It is also possible — and this, along with the technique of cinematic sampling, is a second peculiarity of the Coen aesthetic — that the theme repeats itself in the form.

It is a form of release that goes beyond modernist freedom through negation (in which only a radical anti-aesthetic can oppose the all-powerful Hollywood aesthetic) and it is a liberation of motifs that are as stranded in the structures of high culture as they are in mass culture. This not only brings together the popular Surrealism of wish fulfilment in entertainment and intellectual abstraction in art, but also the collective subconscious of genres and the deliberate intent of the author.

The same process is reflected once again by the Coens' films in the critical discussion of the 'blasphemous' violation of an aesthetic-moral order. It is the same resistance with which the critics seek to defend the authority of the masters, the self-sufficiency of the text and the authentic in art against the breakdown of borders between lower and higher forms — the resistance which Coen heroes sooner or later experience when they come up against the power of the father. In the centre of the story, in the centre of the aesthetic method, in the centre of the critical debate, we find — and this is the third element of Coen films — the violation of order, the infringement of an (unwritten) rule, the breaking of a taboo.

By reproaching the Coens for their 'soulless cinema of quotations' which is no more than 'an end in itself', critics are, it would seem, placing themselves on the side of assailed authority in this Oedipal drama. The established order is still very willingly defended in all its falseness against the truth of the details (the whole body of the father, to use an amusing image from Freud and Marx, is defended against the progressive, or even cannibalistic, tendencies of the sons to divide). It's so much easier if cinema functions as a mythical-emotional unit, providing either the security of self-explanatory signs or an entirely rational, tasteful illustration of what has in any case already been thought.

The eternal youth: Ethan (left) and Joel Coen (right) on the set of *Barton Fink*

The Coens' cinema, and that of a few other representatives of the 'post-modern film', violates the order of the world as we would like to see it. The fact that they are brothers gives the Coens a peculiarly childlike aura (as it does for other brother teams in the cinema), and the Coens naturally foster this image as they see fit . The idea of brothers who do not split up and who fashion their fantasy worlds together is in itself the violation of a taboo. They are revolts against the idea of the self and against the principle of unambiguity — I know what I'm talking about... I never had a brother.

The Coens complete rather than merely reflect each other. Sam Raimi, their friend and co-writer, says that Joel is the more visual of the pair, and Ethan the more literary, but that is also a way of establishing the type of hierarchy questioned in their films. It is the hierarchy of the literary and the visual code which we might see as the basis for the culture which we are in the process of leaving behind, the culture of the Christian West.

'In our partnership,' says Joel Coen, 'I am nominally the director and Ethan the producer, and we are both listed as authors. But our work is a lot more mixed than you would think from the credits. We could be listed jointly in the credits for all these functions, but my standard answer to that is that I'm bigger than he is. But seriously, what we do is of equal importance.' We might then use the term 'stereo directing' to describe how the Coens operate. It is a term which very clearly and pragmatically describes their working methods and which perhaps touches on the core of their work — perception in a virtual space which is formed by the influence of very different impulses.

5

The Coens are from a solid, middle class background and were brought up in suburban Minneapolis. Both their parents were college teachers, and Joel and Ethan seemed predestined for life as typical 'Jewish intellectuals' — a cliché they like to play with, but which they also seek to distance themselves from. In any case, they arrived in the film business with a much broader education than many other figures of the post-New-Hollywood generation. Cinema for them has more of a centrifugal than a centripetal force. It is simply the form most suited to expressing what they want to express, but it is not, as it is for François Truffaut or Martin Scorsese, for instance, 'life'. And it is definitely not sacred.

Joel says their parents were 'not exactly overjoyed with our decision to become film-makers, but they came round to the idea'. Which meant, among other things, that they saw fit to contribute to the financing of *Blood Simple* — a fact which could be grudgingly held against the Coen brothers. Their history conspicuously lacks the delay, suffering and sacrifice so popular in the arts. It's almost as if they were handed their opportunities on a plate, and success was, it would appear, taken for granted — not the type of main-stream success that can only be followed by downfall, but a focused success that comes within a very restricted framework. The Coens were always the architects of their own artistic achievements.

Of course, it wasn't quite that simple. They knew right from the start that they didn't simply want to make films, they wanted to make independent films. The route they took may not have been a trial by fire, but it was, and is, very far from being the inevitable result of a cool, calculated plan. Joel learnt the basics of film-making by editing cheap horror films, and he and his brother later began writing scripts together in their spare time. The first screenplay they saw pro-duced — *Crimewave,* directed by Sam Raimi (with whom the brothers remain in constant contact) — is a flamboyant experiment containing what might be regarded as the unstructured primary core of Coenism. But it is also a film that didn't make enough money to lead to even temporary financial indepen-dence. The Coens chose to make *Blood Simple* as an independent production to avoid the rigmarole of working for the studios and also because they feared — presumably correctly — that their work would be interfered with.

All in all, *Blood Simple* took four years to make, and during this time everyone involved had to take on other jobs to keep their heads above water. Joel had never directed before, Ethan had never produced, and cinematographer Barry Sonnenfeld — who has since had considerable success as a director — says he had never even looked through the viewfinder of a 35mm camera until then. The threesome produced a three minute long trailer first, which they showed to poten-tial financial backers, and it took them eight months to scrape together the $1.5 million budget. Maybe the Coens don't know what hunger is, and they didn't exactly have to step over drunks on their way to school, but they do know the price of artistic freedom.

The rest, as they say, is history. *Blood Simple* was a popular success at the New York and Toronto film festivals, and both *Time* magazine and *The Washington Post* listed it among their top ten films of the year in 1985, but the critics were largely divided. On one side were those who saw the movie as innovative, with commercial potential, and on the other were the independent film purists who saw it as the Coens' strategic bid to have their cake and eat it, and to bluff the public with a 'vacant curiosity' (Elliott Stein).

It was after *Raising Arizona* and *Miller's Crossing* that the Coens were really 'discovered' in Europe. *Cahiers du Cinéma* critics admired their mix of irony, poetry and drama, the playing with established forms, the transgressions and the more surreal elements. The brothers' biggest European success came in 1991 when *Barton Fink* was awarded the Palme d'Or, best director and best actor (John Turturro) awards at Cannes. If the Coens were the answer to a contemporary dilemma facing film culture, then this was the case in Europe above all, where few harboured any real hope for a revitalisation of the 'modern' cinema. For *Fargo*, which also scooped two Oscars, the Coens took the best director award at Cannes a second time.

The Coens occupy a particularly ambivalent position in the ranks of those post-modern film-makers who refuse to see any difference between genre and auteur films, or between high and popular culture. Their movies cannot be so unequivocally classed as 'art' as the films of David Lynch, nor do they have the cult status of the works of Quentin Tarantino. Their films initially appear more accessible to mainstream viewers than the works of other American 'post-modernists', but on closer inspection they turn out to be more complex and even more intellectual.

Only a film culture which seeks to break down the borders between commercial and independent or art house films could lead to an acceptance of their work that would assure them a place in the middle of the box-office scale, at least (although even this wouldn't be enough to bring a costly, offbeat film like *The Hudsucker Proxy*, produced by Joel Silver for Warner and Polygram, into the profit zone).

It could be argued that strategic chutzpah is the Coens' aesthetic equipment, and part of that strategy is to change narrative tone and genre from film to film. Their first fully-realised project was *Blood Simple*, a hard-as-nails thriller, and they moved directly on to make what *Los Angeles Magazine* described as a cross between Buñuel's *Un chien andalou* (1928) and Laurel and Hardy — the comedy *Raising Arizona*, again with cinematography by Barry Sonnenfeld (who adopted a sort of lightweight, de-intellectualised Coenistic approach to his work as a director). And thus developed what came to be known as the Coen style — a wilful mixture of violence, humour and sophistication within the framework of a range of different genres. *Raising Arizona*'s $5 million budget was far from enough to bring it into the block-buster category, but it was sufficient to open the door to greater things.

Each new film is an experiment for the Coens. Their internal development is matched by an external discontinuity in both genre and theme: 'We have a rough idea of how the design will look and where the camera will be. But we don't think about how we can give our films a particular look. We're not trying to establish a style, we're not interested in having any sort of continuity from one film to the next.' This state-ment is false, however, at least as far as the specifics are concerned. The Coens do not start with a 'rough idea' of what they want to achieve — they work from a multi-layered storyboard that details each individual scene and every single camera movement, and is their most important aid after the screenplay.

Which is why it is unimportant which of them is the 'real' director, because the film exists long before it is shot, and the actors aren't given the slightest

The storyboard for the scene in *Fargo* where Gaear kills Carl

chance of becoming co-authors. All they can hope for is to find their niche within the Coen system and make the most of it. (Several of their regular actors, such as John Turturro, John Goodman and Frances McDormand, are at their best in a Coen film.) Or they can remain brittle, visual creatures of surface (like Paul Newman in *The Hudsucker Proxy*), which is not necessarily a bad thing. Only where their movement and expressions are concerned do they have a little bit of freedom.

'We aren't despots,' say the Coens, but they readily admit that they are not particularly taken with the 'filmed acting class' methods of John Cassavetes. 'The technical aspects of film-making,' explains Joel Coen, 'are always overestimated. If a film works in your head, then it will work when you get the cameraman, the actors and the special effects people to make it.'

Sam Raimi might be able to explain why the Coens have never quite managed to conquer the mainstream: 'They're not interested in money beyond what they need for their next production.' After *Fargo,* which marked their return to moderately budgeted features, a new way for Coen ideas to infiltrate the mainstream seemed possible. There were plans to turn *Fargo* into a TV series, and Kathy Bates was already working on a pilot episode, but the project was quickly dropped, because on closer inspection the Coens' images seemed less and less compatible with the mainstream, despite their cult status. Their place is on the edge, not at the centre.

It can be a long wait between Coen films, and the brothers' scripts develop slowly. The screenplay for *Miller's Crossing* was begun before *Raising Arizona,* for example, but was put on hold because they couldn't make it go where they wanted, and they spent a total of three years working on it. The Coens' is more than just a working method — it is a programme. The material determines the dimension of the product, not the authors and not the apparatus.

'Heil Hitler!': the fascist murderer as killer cowboy

The Coens, like a few other American directors who are held in high esteem in Europe, find themselves in a precarious position between independence and integration into the system (and their films naturally reflect this situation). But, thanks to their multiple roles as writer, director and producer, they do have the privilege of being able to control their projects right down to the final cut, even when they're working for the major film companies.

6

The fact that discontinuity is an integral part of the Coens' working method doesn't mean that their themes or techniques can't be described, and without taking away the mystery behind the autarchy. *Barton Fink* above all pretends to give us an answer to the question of its aesthetic methods since it would be difficult not to read a model, a form of self-portrait, into this figure of the author arriving at the film factory. The cowardly artist in the strange hotel meets a demon, wrestler Charlie Meadows, actually German murderer Karl Mundt (who shoots the cops while crying 'Heil Hitler!'). Behind the treatment of a writer's block lurks the collective memory of a Jewish story. This is perhaps the most absurd, the most blasphemous and arguably the most coherent evocation of the Holocaust — the Hollywood

Ghosts from a dark past: *Raising Arizona, Blood Simple, The Hudsucker Proxy*

return of the fascist murderer as killer cowboy.

We might choose to see this allusion to fascist Germany as yet another of *Barton Fink's* false leads, a frivolous game with the collective imagination, or another, particularly bloody, example of a Coen 'private joke'. But if we bear in mind that there are very direct statements in most of their films about American society and politics (even if these can't be classed as unambivalent 'messages'), then we can appreciate the fascist killer, who operates in the very heart of the dream factory and assumes the bizarre role of both midwife and teacher for the mythical birth of the artist, as rather more than just a link between abstraction and Surrealism.

This idea of a historical mythology, which lies beneath a familial mythology which in turn hides behind an individual mythology, is reinforced and given weight by another project. The Coens, like many film-makers who have created their 'own world', have within their 'world' an imaginary film which they will never make but which influences everything they produce (such as Fellini's *The Voyage of Giuseppe Matorna* or David Lynch's *Ronnie Rocket*). It is a film about Adolf Hitler, that is, Adolf Schickelgruber, whose grandparents would have emigrated to the United States of America. The Coens' Adolf would have grown up in Glendale, California, and would have worked as an agent in the film industry.

Without this encounter with the spectre of fascism neither the biography nor the dream factory can exist. The figure of the fascist murderer in *Barton Fink*, who has so many stories to tell if only someone would listen to them, is mirrored in several other Coen films. There is the mad biker in *Raising Arizona*, the bloated private detective in *Blood Simple*, or the white enemy of the black clock-keeper in *The Hudsucker Proxy* — all familiar ghosts from a dark past.

So, being 'creative' means confronting demons, guilt and death, and then being cheated out of the fruits of your labour. Barton is courted as long as he hasn't handed in any work, and is derided and silenced as soon he does so. *Barton Fink* is a particularly pernicious description of the relationship between aesthetic creation and societal (or familial) power. Its success lies, paradoxically, in the recognition of its impossibility. *Barton Fink* succeeds where Barton Fink must fail, because the film, unlike its hero, accepts that there is no unambiguous or direct way to arrive at a 'true' statement. Barton is punished by writer's block not least because he believes that he himself is master of his imagination, while the Coens for their part are content to develop their fantasies within the framework they have chosen.

Fortunately, the Coens worked through any idea of self-redemption through art in *Barton Fink,* and the films they made next were all the sharper for it — *The Hudsucker Proxy* as a deconstruction of the vertical, masculine structure of the world, and *Fargo* as a deconstruction of the horizontal, feminine opposite. Like *Barton Fink*, these films are also about people's attempts to become 'authors', attempts which fail because, among other things, it is so very difficult to listen to others and hear anything apart from yourself.

Gunfire creating patterns of light: *Blood Simple*

Acts of violence in Coen films are very similar to creative, aesthetic processes, a fact which can be seen particularly clearly in *Blood Simple*, where each death is like a work of art, with gunplay creating hypnotically pretty patterns of light.

In keeping with the post-modern aesthetic, Coen films don't simply tell a story (and the story within the story), they also tell of the genesis, the inspiration and the disintegration of the story. They achieve an almost unique form of aesthetic liberation not found in mainstream genre cinema or in art house movies. Their work on myth — and a story is nothing else but this — is limitless: the individual, the familial, the social, the historical and the transcendental are struck against each other to such an extent that the construct within them becomes visible. And it is not merely the construct of a film narrative, but the construct of reality itself. What all these films 'deal with' is the relationship between compulsion and freedom, and this takes place on different levels between the authors, the characters and the audience.

We could say that the Coens use film narrative not just as a vehicle for their private jokes, but also for the construction of images of experience, freeze-frames which trigger direct emotional processes precisely because they can never be completely resolved either in the genre myth or in the psyche of the characters. These moments of truth are so very effective because there is absolutely nothing there which attempts to be 'natural'. With each image, with each frame, we focus in tighter, but the more we see of a character's individual aspects, the more mysterious the whole person becomes.

The moment of awful self-recognition — fascinated and horrified, Barton stares at the bloodsucking mosquito (himself, his story, or art as a creature sucking blood from the flesh of life) on the back of the woman with whom he was writing a screenplay and with whom he has spent the night. Then he realises that she is dead. In *Fargo*, Norm brings his wife Marge her lunch, the usual fast food, and next to it are the writhing worms he plans to use for fishing (more self-images — bait for the big fish). Such scenes tell us that Coen films do not merely show experiments, but are in themselves experiments. If we try to define our feelings during such sequences, we quickly realise that this too has no beginning and no end. We have, at

Barton Fink: the moment of self-knowledge

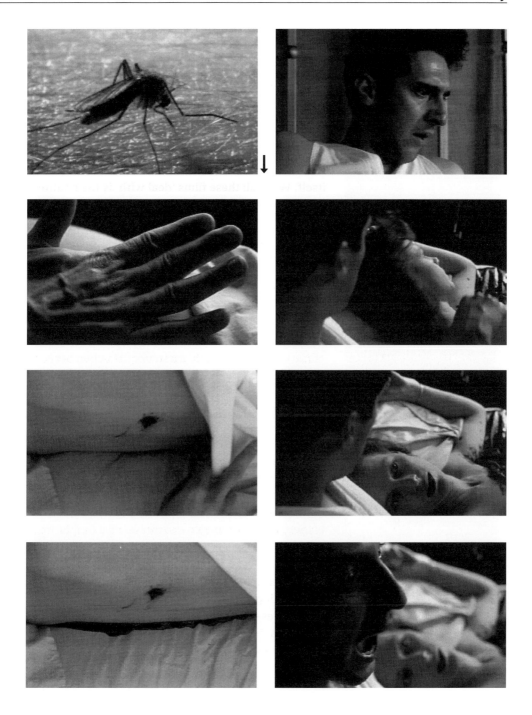

Authoritarian 'fathers': Marty in *Blood Simple*, Nathan Arizona in *Raising Arizona*, father-in-law Wade in *Fargo*...

the very moment we failed to understand the characters on the screen, understood a little bit more about ourselves. Coen films are attempts to confront very private ghosts and by doing so create a general, aesthetic demonology.

Almost all Coen films are based around a showdown with such a demon, but they are also attempts to first evade the demon, then confront and overcome it. Evil exists in Coen films in three very different forms. Firstly, in the very real form of power, power that is generally in the hands of fat, older men, power which is deeply rooted within society and whose continuation is guaranteed by capitalist exploitation and family order. Secondly, in the travails of young protagonists whose desire for something or other brings them into confrontation with the fat, older man. And thirdly, evil exists in the form of a very unreal, murderous projection, in wandering killers and monsters which come into being at the point where the power of the old man meets the desires of the young hero.

Terrible, damaging and damaged images are set against visions allowing a glimpse of happiness and liberation. There are places and signs in Coen films which point directly to paradise, but these images are opposed by a forbidding, stony, and above all unpredictable authority, an enigmatic father figure which even Kafka could not have bettered.

Just as the evil fathers' power and conflicting nature appear to be expressed by their names, so too is there in the young losers' monikers a hint of their weakness and their betrayal. A fink is a coward and a traitor, and a dangerously unbalanced lunatic may well be lurking behind Jerry Lundegaard's slowness. In any case, all the young heroes want something and can only get it by challenging paternal power. But they never get what they want, even if they end up killing the father for it.

A recurring feature in Coen films is the disturbed gaze at the authoritarian man. Barton Fink stares at

...Leo O'Bannion in *Miller's Crossing*

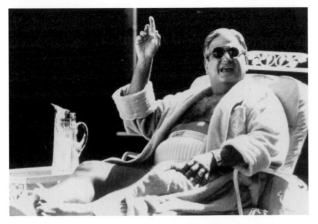

Jack Lipnick in *Barton Fink*

Sidney Mussburger in
The Hudsucker Proxy

Hollywood mogul Jack Lipnick. Jerry Lundegaard stares at his father-in-law. Tom Reagan stares at his Mafia godfather. Norville Barnes stares at the new Hudsucker boss. Hi stares at the world of the rich Arizona family and its head. The evil father figure haunts the Coen film universe — he is corpulent and he takes up a lot of space, but the hero is small and weedy and seems just as badly equipped for his Oedipal confrontation as any Kafka creation. The Coen leading man does, however, have one crucial advantage — he is an American.

The strange drama of the Coen film begins with a son forcing his way into the father's territory. Whether he knows it or not, like Oedipus he wants to steal the father's wife, wealth, image and fire (while all the time believing that he is only doing what is expected of him — trying to be successful, to be American). The paternal element — the space or the figure — has of course been anticipating this crime (perhaps has even encouraged it), as he knows all about the ambivalence of women, of power, of image and of fire. (In *Blood Simple* the husband knows that his employee is cuckolding him even before we have seen any adultery take place, and Barnes' fairytale success in *The Hudsucker Proxy* was instigated and manipulated by several rival 'fathers'.)

This is why they do more than merely threaten and plan, and why their conspiracies are all the harder to escape from, because of their powerful positions as bar owners, Hollywood moguls or business tycoons. Above all, they understand the art of deception. (The fact that we only *hear* Mayhew's worst fits of rage in *Barton Fink* makes us suspect that they could be just as 'real' for him as any performance).

The young man does not so much hope to defeat the father (he is often merely seeking affection and recognition) as to simply find his place in the world, but the rage he experiences as he goes through the second birth process leads to another end, to death.

Coen films always portray a sort of purgatory.

Then there is the strong woman. She comes in a variety of guises, some of them good and some bad, but she is always more directly in touch with the real things of life. The first 'disruption' that the Coens build into their narratives is the fact that the women do not conform to what is expected of them in the Oedipal game between father and son. In *Fargo*, the kidnapped woman, the woman who never really left the father, is mirrored by the policewoman who so badly wants her silently desperate husband to find happiness. It is because the Coen hero is caught between the evil father and the strong woman that he seeks to divide and mirror himself and ends up inhabiting fantastical parallel realities, where he meets his demons in new manifestations.

We could also view this story of the woman from another perspective, however. We could see her as being oppressed and abused by the father, with the son unable to save her. In *Barton Fink* this leads to her death, and in *Blood Simple* she ends up alone with the knife. Or — and this is perhaps the cruellest and the funniest fate of all — she ends up alone with her child and with her enormous longing for a happiness which the man can never give her. Love is a fundamentally inappropriate promise in Coen films, the real MacGuffin. How can a person who can't even become himself open up to someone else?

So, beyond the narrative of the films, we have a meta-narrative. This takes shape not so much in the form of a psychologically revealing private mythology but more as a methodical revision of fundamental (Western) narrative models. What happens if, within an Oedipally constructed narrative (and a film genre is just as suited to this as a fairytale), I change an important building block? What happens to the characters quickly becomes clear — they no longer understand one another. And the resultant misunderstandings are what keep the story going. Not the misunder-

It's the women who make things happen:
Abby in *Blood Simple*

Edwina in *Raising Arizona*

Verna in *Miller's Crossing*

Audrey in *Barton Fink*

Amy in *The Hudsucker Proxy*

Marge in *Fargo*

standings that bring about what has been pre-determined, but those which lead to irreparable disruptions till something else emerges — the impression of freedom.

Coen films continually shift their perspective. The author disintegrates, seeing both his sovereignty and his morality questioned. There is always a higher authority present, a very strange, wicked authority that is neither within the film nor outside it. It is an omnipresent institution, a voice and a look. We glimpse it in *Blood Simple*, for example, when the camera makes threatening movements that do not seem to be required by the action, or when we hear a heart beating but cannot see whose heart it is. We see it also in the acoustic flash forward when Barton Fink hears the roar of the ocean in the New York bar, which can be interpreted as a sort of commentary on the action; like the rustling of the leaves in *Miller's Crossing*, which appear to be laughing at the hero as he runs after his hat; or the slow, inevitable turning of the ventilator fan blades in *Blood Simple*.

The use of such 'irrational' perceptions, which go against the conventions of cinematic narrative, and the minor violations of the Aristotelian logic of the narrative unit (which the Coens, in contrast to Tarantino, make use of surreptitiously) have been classified by critics as 'empty' elements that serve only to create suspense or atmosphere. These strange noises, the roar of the ocean, the dog's panting, the rustling of the leaves, may well have another, compositional function, though. They appear to ridicule the hero, to show nature laughing at him (the roar of the ocean in *Barton Fink* is the mocking echo of the fatal pseudo-realism with which the author so impressed the New York critics — and from which the Coens seem to be distancing themselves). And, like the strange sounds in David Lynch films, they are transcendental noises as well, noises that come from an alien outside into which one is not yet realised.

We can also detect an empty or a 'black' transcendence in Joel and Ethan Coen's films — the negative presence of something that doesn't come from the characters whose tales are being told, or from the act of telling their stories, or from the perception of the audience. We could content ourselves with the conclusion that the Coens were destabilising art in an aesthetically cunning manner by introducing this rogue element (and in so doing were positively deceiving their public). And their handling of the acoustic in their films is not merely contrapuntal (as though they were the only ones to have both read and understood Eisenstein's book on montage in sound films) but also topographical.

If the camera refuses to let us establish where 'we' actually are — whether we are inside or outside the action, on this side or that side — then we are thrown into even deeper confusion by the use of sound. In *Blood Simple*, somebody makes a call from a telephone box on a busy road. He has to shout, but even then we still have trouble making out what he's saying above the roar of passing cars. On the other end of the line is a person whom we do not see, who speaks in what is little more than a whisper, but whom both we and the person making the call can understand perfectly. The fact that the voices overlap prevents us from telling ourselves that we are optically in one place and acoustically in another. We are everywhere and nowhere. This process of communication, to which we are witness, is in itself entirely irrational. Its irrationality is seen, for example, in *Miller's Crossing*, when the characters occasionally lapse into sequences of dialogue that have been taken directly from literary sources where the fate of the original speakers is entirely different to that of the characters who have now adopted them.

Transcendental noises and stolen, irrational dialogue are not just further disruptions of the aesthetic equation of emotional, rational and mythical narra-

The transcendental and the material:
The Hudsucker Proxy

tive. They go to make up a certain unity, revealing the presence of the 'higher' authority, whose aim seems to be to involve the characters and the text in a rather nasty game. And with that disappears whatever faith we might have had left in what we call 'destiny'. The intervention of the transcendental in *The Hudsucker Proxy*, with the return of Waring Hudsucker as a heavyweight angel, seems particularly precarious. It depends, to be precise, on the tenability of the broom handle jammed into the giant cogs of a clock. The relationship between the transcendental and the material is shown to be unhierarchical and absurd.

In Coen films a great deal of effort is put into establishing (narrative) order, but once it has been established, the transcendental intervenes with just as much effort (for the viewer also), only to become dependent on a ridiculously insignificant detail. (Perhaps this is an expression of childlike purity of imagination — stopping a clock is the same as stopping time.)

If it is true that the Coens developed their cinema aesthetic merely to be able to crack a few private jokes, then we shouldn't forget that these jokes are about things as fundamental as birth, death, religion and love.

7

Coen films positively encourage us to use words like 'post-modern' or 'manneristic' to describe them, and it might be useful to look at the origin of the term mannerism. It was originally applied to the techniques of a group of artists in sixteenth century Florence who sought to paint in the manner (in the *bella maniera*, to be exact) of Michelangelo, Raphael and Leonardo da Vinci, but out of their attempts to imitate and quote came a radical aesthetic revolt. They moved painting on from the clear perception of the world presented by established Renaissance artists to the ecstatic, organic and fragmentary movement of the baroque. Mannerism refuses to let its figures have a firm hold on anything. It diverts the gaze away from the centre and towards the periphery, and its spaces are fragmented and multi-dimensional. It wildly draws the viewer into the picture while refusing to surrender its topography or its boundaries. Instead of one central figure there are several equally important, and sometimes distorted, subjects, and there is a shocking contrast between light and dark. Light is not used for illumination, but for effect. Presenting an 'orderly' picture of the world is no longer the aim — the aim is to set the world in motion.

To describe the Coens' films as 'manneristic' is therefore not to cheapen them. They also draw very deeply upon the 'old masters', upon the rules of classic Hollywood films, in order to bring them into ecstatic, uncertain and multi-dimensional movement which no longer obeys the principle of order but that of experience. The richer, the more turbulent and the more grotesque the world becomes, the less easily can it be seen from a single perspective.

Just as space is broken down in mannerist paintings, so too does the mannerist, post-modern film break down the 'objective' narrative time of the traditional film along with the relation of the protagonist to his story.

Spatial composition in the mannerist painting is equivalent to the ordering of space and time through montage in the post-modern film. There is, for example, no 'average speed' in Coen films. The camera moves just as furiously in *Raising Arizona* as it does in Sam Raimi's *The Evil Dead* (1983) — and paradoxically draws (or even pushes) us into something which is far too dissonant and crazy for us to feel at ease with. In a famous and very alarming scene in *Vertigo* (1958), Hitchcock robs us of the certainty of our perception

Two ways of going mad: Abby in *Blood Simple*...

by using a triple reverse zoom (a zoom and a track in opposite directions at once). The Coens adopted this as their basic structural technique — the simultaneous use of stylistic devices that promise us trust, warmth and symbiosis and those that signal strangeness, cold and distance. One method of achieving this is the use of the relationship between narrative time and filmic information.

No less effective than *Raising Arizona*'s acceleration is *Fargo*'s deceleration, which seems so familiar to us at first because it appears to be drawn from the very essence of the characters. As the plot develops, however, we see in it a further manifestation of a transcendental authority. The clock might not be stopped here, but a different sort of time prevails, and what had initially inspired so much trust in us — are not

...and Barton Fink

'slow people' always 'good people'? — now seems ever more frightening and absurd.

An 'inner' narrative time emerges, just as in mannerist painting there is internal light and internal movement. Its role seems to be to win back some of the sympathy that has been lost through a counter-movement that is essentially anti-image (originally, the Reformation, along with a form of iconoclasm directed against imagery that was as mendacious as it was brutal; and now the cinematic modernists, along with a form of cinematic reduction in American independent film culture directed against Hollywood imagery that is as mendacious as it is false). To win back the passion and the tenderness of the gaze, the image places its own authority on the line with an enthusiasm that can only be described as counter-Reformatory.

Both mannerist painting and post-modern cinema claim not to order the world for us but to unfold its endless suggestiveness (which perhaps explains why the strongest criticism directed against Coen films — alongside the traditionalist complaint that they mix high and low culture — is that they do not aim to achieve cinematic enlightenment). If there is a proposition that has no validity in the Coen universe, then it is that of the being that determines consciousness, because instead of a 'consciousness' they present a *stream* of consciousness, of the sort we have seen in literature from James Joyce to Arno Schmidt. The hero of the mythic film narrative, of, say, a Western, 'does what he has to do'. The hero of a modern European film narrative does what his consciousness tells him to do. But the heroes of a Coen film are caught between action and consciousness, and it is almost irrelevant to question whether the characters of *Blood Simple* go mad because they have too little consciousness, or if Barton Fink goes round the bend because he has too much. Consciousness — including the consciousness of images — has become an open system. We see how images gestate their own consciousness, and we see also how consciousness in turn generates images.

The screen itself wants to disappear and become the theme, as in the works of El Greco. Just as space can stretch out into infinity and mystery only because it has become conscious of its own construction, so too does the character become aware of his inner riches only when he has understood that he is a representation. The character behaves 'manneristically' because he no longer wants to pretend to be 'natural' — 'manneristically' being a word that, not by coincidence, conveys the fact that the authoritarian character has something quite offensive and incomprehensible about him.

It is not only the characters in Coen films who are 'manneristic' (they are explained through themselves and draw everything in towards themselves, with the result that they fail to gain our sympathy) and therefore have to 'exaggerate' themselves. The construction of the images is also manneristic — they quote *la bella maniera* and give it another, second life, which comes from the inside instead of the outside.

The post-modern film, like mannerist art before it, has to deal with the relationship between reproduction and symbol, a dialogue that is necessarily coloured by both violence and pain. There is, firstly, a serious disruption of this relationship. The body is opened up through pain — mannerist artists were the first to understand that the martyr, through the symbolic necessity of the horror he goes through, experiences a subjective pain, which has something to do with the yearning gaze he directs towards the heavens. Cinema used to have no other way of showing violence except to break it down into its hot and cold elements, to look at it from the sadistic perspective of lust, from the cold curiosity that wants to see wounds on a body and from the symbiotic experience of fear. Neither Renaissance painting on the one hand nor Alfred Hitchcock on the other were able to entirely reconcile the internal and external aspects of pain.

There is injury: in *Blood Simple* the heroine pins the pursuer's hand to the window frame with a knife; in *Fargo* Carl is accidentally shot by the kidnapped woman's father and runs bleeding through the snow; in *Barton Fink* Charlie suffers a purulent discharge from his ear. We are hyper-realistically close to all these wounds, but they are at the same time purely symbolic.

There is pursuit: somebody sends a killer (or even better, two killers) after somebody else. In *Blood Simple* it is the husband who wants his cheating wife taken out of circulation (but ends up being killed himself). In *Raising Arizona* the rich businessman sends an evil biker (who ends up blown to pieces) after Hi, the petty criminal. In *Fargo* the husband hires two

Violations and symbols: *Blood Simple, Fargo, Barton Fink*

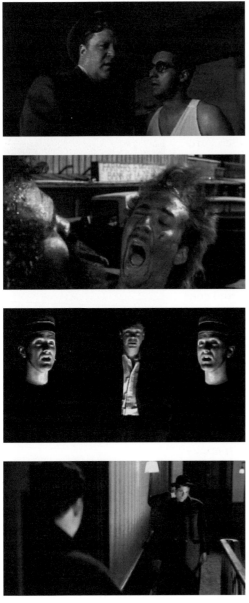

Negative reflections: *Barton Fink, Raising Arizona, The Hudsucker Proxy, Miller's Crossing*

hoods to kidnap his wife, but they turn out to be undisciplined killers. And in *The Hudsucker Proxy* there is the mysterious old man who paints signs and tries to prevent the clock being stopped. All these pursuits create kinetic energy (movement plus sympathy), but are at the same time purely symbolic.

And there is duality: in *Raising Arizona* and *Barton Fink* it is the crazy gangster couple, but all characters run into their mirror images. Barton Fink meets Karl Mundt, Hi meets the mad biker, Barnes meets the cheeky lift boy who will later be his nemesis, and Tom Reagan meets his (Jewish) gangster adversary. This is both a plot device and, certainly, the basic theological problem: I am me. The first alarming step toward consciousness. And: I am somebody else. The second alarming step. (This is, if we allow ourselves a digression into the European history of ideas, the confrontation between the Hoelderlin being, who feels the God within himself, and the Kafka being, who begins an interior monologue because he is afraid of the power of the principle).

And isn't the man who is split between his I and his not-I forever beholden to the myth of the 'whole woman'? Only masculine meta-beings have difficulty in being both Gods and men, both image and reality. This is also the case in mannerism — the divided man and the reflected woman construct the world differently.

This stems from the different 'roles'

they play. It is the women who make things happen: the journalist in *The Hudsucker Proxy*, the police-woman in *Fargo*, Hi's cop wife in *Raising Arizona*. The women's trajectories are straight, but the men tend to go round in circles. Hi, for example, is torn from his cycle of crime and incarceration by a flash, and Barton Fink spends many days trying to change a single sentence. 'Early morning. The traffic is audible,' becomes 'It is too early for us to hear traffic'. Perception or non-perception. What presents itself here as immobility is actually the most intractable contradiction. Not only does Barton want to delay his beginning/awakening/birth with this sentence, but he also wants to hinder his progress through the text, and he therefore kills the woman (his writing partner) who can save him.

Barton Fink: perception/non-perception

Perhaps we are coming to a new understanding of mannerism in the cinema. In the seemingly anti-rational and even anti-enlightenment refusal of the text in the unleashed image only the revolt against its Oedipal power can overcome all possible instances of censorship and self-censorship. Barton Fink is the programmatic representative of all the Coen heroes who engage in the struggle between text and image. They want to write whilst they are being depicted, and thus we see the link — and a very post-modern one it is too — between age-old, immutable Greek mythology and the constant motion of particle physics. We also attempt to describe a construction principle, where point and line become area, a whole greater than the sum of the parts.

We could, if we were to look at the movies as choreography, say that the men in Coen films only move around themselves, and inevitably end up going nowhere. They begin with desires and end up with desperation, but the women move in a straight line, even if it is an entirely offbeat and insubordinate path. (Thus Frances McDormand's route from *Blood Simple* to *Fargo* is both peculiar and obvious — she must live,

regardless of whether she can understand the men's madness or not.)

Power always has a literal architecture. We see this in the Hudsucker skyscraper and, in the other films, in the outer and inner circles. Any given character wants to move from the edge to the heart of this structure in order to find the answer to an important question ('Do I belong here?'), and ends up getting thrown out. It is as though someone has been putting enormous effort into opening a door which turns out to be no more than a façade and which had been open for quite some time anyway. This person eventually finds himself outside again because the architecture of power is no more than a sham, a mystification, the inner consciousness — the fear of the doorkeeper. Coen heroes are descendants of Josef K — they are full of presumption, they pretend to be who they are not, and they sleep with the cook in their vain bid to get into the castle. We don't know if they are really 'condemned' or if they have merely dreamed the verdict because they have condemned themselves.

Both these possibilities come together at the moment of refused self-recognition that comes in almost every Coen film. The hero's judgement in *The Hudsucker Proxy* is passed at the moment when he fails to recognise himself in the presumptuous lift boy. Because the simplest of things become incredibly difficult in this world, people have to rage within the world of their dreams — the image from *Crimewave* of the row of doors which are thrown open and closed, doors which don't actually separate an outside from an inside, is repeated in ever more subtle form.

We cannot say that the world remains unchanged by the empty frenzy of Coen heroes, though. We watch as it rebuilds itself, as it revolts, as it adapts its mechanisms and mixes the earthly with the transcendental.

The dream has a different meaning in a Coen film than it might do elsewhere. The dream within the

Reagan's dream in *Miller's Crossing*

Frances McDormand: from *Blood Simple* to *Fargo*

dream is a direct derivation of the truth — Hi sees himself as a biker monster, Tom Reagan dreams about his hat being blown off his head. In their dreams, Coen heroes go beyond their dream-like state, predicting how they will become real people, but the actual deed that might fulfil their predictions — the hesitation of the murderer before the murder, for instance — is then stripped of its meaning.

Here we have a further principle of the mannerist/post-modern structure — the disintegration of the clear order of consciousness and plot and objective space, and even of the linear nature of time. The Coens are, as we have already said, extremely restrained in their use of non-linear narrative elements, but we never come away from any of their films with the impression that an and-then construction is missing. The terrible slowness of the lift operator in *Barton Fink* may seem to tell the hero (and us) that he is in a 'real' place, but it also anticipates the non-linear direction of the narrative, just as the restless speed of the lift boy in *The Hudsucker Proxy* anticipates the fact that the hero will be overtaken by his own story.

8

oen heroes are at first sight naïve idealists who are thrown into a situation which forces them to confront violence and corruption (but who nevertheless appear to hang on to their naïveté). Barton Fink and Norville Barnes arrive in the city just like Jefferson Smith or John Doe, but they behave differently. We watch as they are infected by power, as they become corrupt. There are people like Barton Fink or Tom Reagan who think they are smarter than the system, and who fall victim to it for this very reason. The threatening father figure and his environ-

Sweating in the mailroom: Barnes in *The Hudsucker Proxy*

ment, which we have come to know as a fixed component of the Coen film meta-story, is to be understood as representative of an institution — the Mafia, big business, the welcome of a bar, Hollywood. The hero rises within this institution, as an 'advisor' in *Miller's Crossing*, as an employee in *Blood Simple*, as a son-in-law in *Fargo*, but sooner or later comes the moment when he can go no further. He realises that he is not really 'inside', and he hasn't penetrated the circles of real power. (The Hudsucker building, for example, sucks our hero into its viscera and lets him sweat there until he climbs up to the head before eventually being spat out again.)

Of course, they all start out with big ideas. They plot murders, start a family, think the hula hoop might become a craze, or want to write a play. The problem with Coen heroes is that they don't seem to be entirely of this world. They are like children who have not been properly prepared for the life they are thrust into. It would be extremely difficult to try to make them responsible for what they do, particularly as what they actually do is generally not what they planned to do. The tenderness we feel for these men (the women are another story), who do little besides

From the realm of the dead:
Steve Buscemi as the zombie bellboy in
Barton Fink

screw things up, stems therefore from many different things: it is a tenderness towards born losers, towards children who are forced to make adult decisions, towards dreamers and, finally, towards people who are as 'normal' as me or you. And, because tenderness feeds on so many different, even contradictory sources, the Coens don't have to worry too much about nourishing it themselves.

The men are helpless and confused. The more they think they are taking their lives in hand, the more certain is their demise. The more they speak, the less they are understood. Even their names suggest that their dreams are ridiculous — Hi McDunnough, Barton Fink, the Snopes brothers in *Raising Arizona*, Crush and Coddish in *Crimewave*. Just as they have no choice but to confront their demons, so too is there inevitably a big idea at the centre of their legend, or, more precisely, the embryo of an act of creation (a screenplay, a child's toy, a picture of a bird for a three-cent stamp).

These people are continually losing their grip on reality. They are transformed into pursuers, into unreal zombies like the staff at the Earle Hotel in *Barton Fink*; they cannot 'read' the world in which they move. This is why they can't recognise either dangers or opportunities. They aren't, unlike Candide, unshakeable optimists living in a hell which they think is 'the best of all possible worlds,' but children who have been locked away, and have never been able to build up trust.

This is why they are unaware of their own ability to cause disasters and unable to deal with the destructive potential of the people with whom they come into contact. Barton Fink doesn't see the evil in Charlie, nor does Marge in *Fargo* understand how someone could commit murder for a few banknotes.

Coen heroes are different from Capra's because they can't achieve either the dignity of self-sufficiency or the security of the group. They differ also in that they cannot become the subject of their stories. They don't act — they react. They are controlled and manipulated, but this control and manipulation doesn't obey any real order. Only the breakdown of character and narrative are orchestrated.

The reason for the loneliness and despair that we find in the Coen cosmos is seen most clearly in their craziest films: the gangster couple in *Raising Arizona* confess that their mother did not breast-feed them, and the terrible biker killer has the words 'Mother didn't love me' tattooed on his body. And thus ensues a largely hysterical film in which two big kids frantically try to put together a family by stealing the baby they could not have themselves (and their construction of the family represents the creations other Coen heroes 'invent' to help establish their own identity). It is also a renewed attempt to break open a myth from the inside, in this case that of the outlaw family who sanctify themselves through the imperturbability of their will, as in Steven Spielberg's *The Sugarland Express* (1974), for example.

Instead of defending its natural strength against the absurd superior power of society, the holy family in *Raising Arizona* turns out to be an invention, an attempt at socialisation, a further bid to reach the inner circle of society. There is always transgression, however, and not only when women slip into police uniforms — Edwina turns into Ed, and life in *Fargo* clearly 'functions' only because Marge has developed enough masculine and feminine impulses for two, and later three, people. Ultimately, *Fargo*'s family idyll is as false as that in *Raising Arizona*, and neither the melodramatic (the meeting with the old friend who invents a tragic story about his marriage) nor the Gothic (the murderer's punishment in another family saga) reflection can change anything.

The heroes therefore suffer doubly — firstly under the absurd rule of old men, fossilised board members in *The Hudsucker Proxy* or clownlike rulers in *Barton*

Fink, and secondly through rejection by their mothers. The women suffer because of the men's inability to deal with their pain. This double tragedy is, of course, also comic, because it cannot comply with the Oedipal myth. The dream of the family, as illustrated at the end of *Raising Arizona*, must therefore always prove to be a chimera.

The Coens go beyond the failed construction of the family to examine an even more fundamental process — birth (and not merely as part of a private mythology, but as the result of a mannerist, post-modern composition of text and image. Identity, which is no longer available in the form of the bourgeois biography, must be pursued beyond all boundaries). *Barton Fink*, for example, is not merely about the trouble an author has in giving birth to a text, but also about the trouble a text has in giving birth to an author.

The hotel in this film is a living organism, a womb — it is warm and damp, it sheds its skin and it is dark. It is the Earle, the early, which is haunted by the ear that doesn't listen (which returns through Goodman's aches) and by the master of ceremonies (the shadow of past power). Barton is in a truly embryonic state here, which makes his ambivalence about his environment entirely understandable, as the fear of being born is the natural state of the foetus.

The mother, in the form of Audrey, must be taken away from the father, from the model, from the destructive superego. She must die so that Fink can live, in the inevitable Oedipal drama already unfolding in the womb — the first thing Barton hears are sounds from neighbouring rooms that evoke sexual intercourse. It is the woman from the picture who is waiting for him at the end, after he has undergone his real birth. This birth has been able to take place only through trauma, a trauma in which the woman/mother/body disappears and the father/power condemns him. He must live but is not allowed to be an author (a truly awful judgement).

In *Raising Arizona* the Snopes brothers' breakout from jail is depicted as a sort of difficult birth. How does one come to be born? The film offers us a whole catalogue of possibilities — the capitalist technique that produces the Arizona quints; the dirty, violent process which brings forth the Snopes; the incarnation of a dream that gives life to the mad biker; and kidnapping, the approach favoured by the McDunnoughs. Every type of birth is possible (and we see birth in many other forms in other Coen films), but none is complete. With the incomplete birth begins the process of the ever more comic acceleration that invariably leads to loss of life.

Birth is central to *Fargo,* where the heavily pregnant woman fights for a better world for her child. The people she meets are terrible parents, and the trace of blood across the snow is like an umbilical cord that signifies the fear of being born into a cold and violent world. And then there is the staggering scene where Gaear is sitting in the hut and watching some idiotic serial on television, featuring a girl talking about her pregnancy. Gaear is moved by her words, then Carl comes in, bleeding, wakes him from his reverie and further irks him by demanding the car. Gaear reacts by murdering him — the act is given an air of fratricide because of the soap actress's words — and stuffs him, into the wood chipper, in a macabre inversion of birth. One leg is still protruding when Marge turns up and arrests him.

Why has this murder taken place? Because Carl wants more than he is entitled to? Because Carl wants to leave him? Because Gaear is a man and does not have the mysterious power of the pregnant woman? He doesn't answer when Marge asks him if he thinks life is just about money (a question she is also asking for her unborn child). But perhaps Marge has not fully understood the real cause of his violence — it was never 'just' a question of money.

If only her life would return to its everyday banality, to a husband called Norm, a landscape painter whose work is to be published on the cheapest stamp on the market (the three-cent stamp, the number of the family, and not the twenty-nine-cent stamp,which doesn't actually exist). Three-cent stamps are always handy, though, says Marge. The family is exactly what is needed to compensate for the disorder of the world, for the world's lack of redemption — and here another circle is complete. Norm's painting is of a bird — an image traditionally associated with freedom, happiness or death.

The Big Lebowski is also a 'birth' film. A pair of gangsters, those favourite Coen characters, turn up at the hero's home and stick his head down the toilet as a (totally undeserved) punishment. All the signature elements of the Coen's earlier films reappear here. There is the kidnap attempt, the doppelgänger, the Oedipal abduction of the woman from the paternal space, the homage to the Western, the botched coup, the narrator as deceiver and even the Volkswagen Beetle from *Blood Simple*. As we watch the hero, we see a person who is becoming somebody else — somebody he may always, unwittingly, have been.

Images of birth in Coen films are matched by images of death. The fall from the window in *The Hudsucker Proxy* represents both birth and death. Barnes and Hudsucker go from the bottom to the top and, once they have made it up there, leave the building and all it represents by jumping out of the window. Despite the peculiarities that arise from the use of deconstructed myth and the cinematic stream of consciousness, Coen films provide very precise images of society. They do so by describing the spaces and the overlap between the individual consciousness and the stream of collective images and texts; between the functioning (or non-functioning) of familial and social relationships of power and violence, communication and deception.

9

The 'tenderness' of Coen films stems not from the approximation of biography in the actor (the first cinematic reality) nor from the argument driving the story (the second reality). It comes rather from the form of representation itself (a third cinematic reality). This begins with apparently simple things. The fact that the characters are given so much time to develop, for example, and that they always reveal things about themselves that seem to have nothing to do with the main plot. It continues in the Coens' balance of intimacy and distance. The camera 'plays' with the characters (a game that is by its nature precarious) and in doing so gets behind their masks, and seeks to endow them with both dignity and a reservoir of opacity.

The tenderness also stems from the fact that these films avoid elevation just as much as humiliation. The Coens are, of course, not the only film-makers who avoid presenting a clear-cut struggle between good and bad, but they differ in that they turn the disintegration of this dichotomy into a theme. It is precisely the dismantling of the central character that brings him closer to us — in this respect, sympathy (which the Coens have always denied themselves) is the opposite of tenderness. What they put in its place is the meticulous construction and description of those very elements which we tend to disregard in everyday life (if only to avoid becoming demented). But if we spend long enough looking at a garden, a suburban estate, the rear of a car or a bar, then a sort of structural madness emerges that is enjoyable because this is, after all, the cinema. Thus, we have a realism of the second order.

'They are probably so hyper-realistic,' says Joel Coen in his usual off-hand manner, 'that they have nothing at all to do with reality.' And more precisely: 'The films have less to do with reality than with what people think is reality.' Or, to put it another way, they approach reality by means of their hyper-perception. As in the films of David Lynch, the aim is not merely to show the abyss behind the smooth surface, but to reveal the surface itself as abyss. The Coens put so much pressure on their characters right from the start that they have no chance of taking evasive action or considering which particular window between their internal and external lives they should try to keep closed.

Tenderness in a synthetic world, a world in which the protagonists don't seek to become real people, like other film characters, or to escape from the realm of shadows, of repetitions, of quotations and imitations. Coen characters are, it seems to me, fully aware that they are ghostly creatures. They operate within a world of shadows, a world made up of references, echoes and interpretation, which is also defined by experiences of claustrophobia and emptiness (the fundamentals of fear) an emptiness that is glimpsed in the endless canyons between the skyscrapers in *The Hudsucker Proxy*, the snow in *Fargo*, the slow-motion drop of water in *Blood Simple* or the infinite darkness of the whispering wood in *Miller's Crossing*.

Coen heroes are dream creatures who have not been born (but who may, like Barton Fink or Norville Barnes, go through the dramatic equivalent of the birth process). They encounter demons who enable them to embark on their second lives, and they encounter the 'empty sign' that is obviously closely linked to their desire to be born (the package in *Barton Fink*, whose contents we are never shown; the page with the circle drawn on it in *The Hudsucker Proxy*; the hat in *Miller's Crossing*). Unlike the classic Hitchcock MacGuffin, these empty signs are not catalysts but symbols of a complete standstill, appearing instead of what the traditional cinema presents as a 'moral'. *The Big Lebowski*'s plot centres on a million dollars that do not exist — the reverse of the zero in *The Hudsucker*

Proxy that brings in millions for Norville Barnes (entirely 'realistic' given the virtualisation of money in highly-developed capitalist systems).

All these empty signs are, in a simple, unobtrusive way, quite Freudian in their evocation of the concealed and the concealer, of the cyclical return, of birth.

A sign that signifies nothing, which comes to signify everything through the use that is made of it. The way the Coens use empty space, and not only in *The Hudsucker Proxy*, has its roots in fascist ideology (set designer Dennis Gassner said he got some of his ideas directly from German and Italian fascism, or at least from its echoes in American architecture). It is no wonder, then, that in Coen films there is no difference between a sign that is empty and a sign that is not.

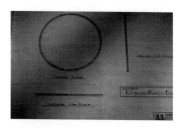

This is certainly a sarcastic comment on Western pragmatism — the Knight of the Round Table is devastated when he finds out that all his friends have been killed in their search for the Holy Grail and that the Grail itself is a worthless object that can be replaced by any other object; and the Hitchcock hero has been able to use the empty sign as a key to the subconscious. Even after all this the American comes along and tries to capitalise on it, but it will not become capital, opening itself up again simply as meaning.

Or to put it more simply: a Coen film presents us with a liberation of the MacGuffin. And the more closely we watch the more clearly we see the MacGuffin — which, as in Hitchcock films, is an apparently unimportant object or message, such as Miss Froy's song in *The Lady Vanishes* (1938) — spread out among the flesh of the narrative. In fact, what we have is the negation of the MacGuffin.

Signs for everything and nothing: *Barton Fink, The Hudsucker Proxy, Miller's Crossing, Blood Simple*

In *Blood Simple*, Abby's unloved husband gives her a small pistol with a mother-of-pearl handle as a present on their first wedding anniversary. She leaves him because she is afraid she might one day be unable to resist the temptation to point it at him, but then the weapon begins to follow her like a curse, and she ends up shooting him with it after all (or at least she thinks she has, whereas in fact the real murderer was his envoy, his doppelgänger). This magic object, rather than behaving like a good MacGuffin should and serving as an impetus for the plot, is instead used to bring death and to signify feminine power. Instead of emptying itself, this object/sign is brimming with meaning, which is also why there is no Hitchcockian disappearance, merely the final misunderstood use.

The empty space (as the distance that an object or person has to fall, a snow field, a stylishly under-furnished office, as darkness) may ultimately also be an element of the narrative itself. The hyper-reality with which detail is observed (independently of its relationship to the whole) itself creates empty spaces within the narrative which we experience both as a threat and as a new freedom. These are not so much false trails that the Coens are laying as trails that do not necessarily lead to the centre of events (to the myths, the references, the models), but possibly to one of the stories within the story within the story.

The crime story in *Fargo*, for example, is made up of numerous other stories whose narrative centres lie elsewhere. And each dramatic element itself contradicts its function: the exposition (the projection of the kidnap plan and the presentation of the participants) because the heroine does not appear here and because she is part of the disruption, not of the intrigue; the intensification (the murder on the highway and the arrival of the police) because it is the beginning of the deceleration of the plot; the climax (the encounter between Marge and Jerry) because it involves people who for various reasons are unsuited to either a violent or an intellectual confrontation; the retardation (which, among other things, gives us insights into Marge and Jerry's domestic life) because it almost makes us forget the suspense that was previously created; and finally the resolution (the capture of the remaining villain) which leads more to the break-up than the drawing together of the internal and external conflicts. The resolution in a Coen film is the sum total of its deceptions and misunderstandings. Or, to come back to Peter Körte's formulation, the narrative is made up of a whole heap of diversionary tactics.

The classic configuration of hero, sidekick, villain and minor character is also lacking here. While Tarantino fascinates us with convoluted tales in the centre of the plot, the Coens lure us with threads which can branch out endlessly in all sorts of directions. In a strange episode in *Fargo*, for example, Mike tells a tragic story about the marriage that he never had — a story that has nothing to do with the plot, and just a little bit to do with the person, but which has a lot to do with the structure of the narrative, because *Fargo* is firstly a crime film, secondly a post-modern game with genre elements and thirdly a portrayal of despair. It is a despair that appears all the more terrible because it is silent, a despair that is at its worst in Marge's husband because there is no apparent reason for its existence.

Empty spaces: *The Hudsucker Proxy, Fargo, Miller's Crossing*

Coen films teach us to watch and to listen very carefully. There is nothing in them that doesn't have an important part to play in the plot, even if it does so in an unexpected way. We are often on the point of forgetting something when the fiendishly clever construct catches us out.

Barton Fink is almost didactic. The fat neighbour with the infected ear comes into Barton's room and says he could tell him, the author who has written plays that are supposedly true to life, a whole pile of stories. Barton, instead of listening, merely blusters about the

reality of the common man, and we immediately see this as a sideswipe at the author who claims to write about life but is really only interested in himself. After a while, however, we find out that we haven't been listening or watching properly either, that we have contented ourselves too easily with a cinematic convention. The neighbour's 'You don't listen' is directed at us too. (Perhaps 'realism' is just another word for a particular method of making perception easy.)

Coen films take the time to make sure everything shown is essential, and although they are full of surprises, they never try to trick the viewer. The deception lies in the audience and in the characters, not in the medium. This is one of the side effects of the 'deconstructive' logic with which the Coens approach their material. Everything is reduced to a skeleton before being put back together again.

The heroes' stories run in a straight line, apart from the disruptions already mentioned, but the background is not necessarily governed by the rules of Newton's cosmos. In *Barton Fink* the hero leaves behind the 'thundering' applause that greeted his first play to go to a bar where suddenly the roar of the ocean can be heard. It is Hollywood, the West Coast, that is beckoning to him, and it is also an anticipation of the film's final scene, where Barton has entered a picture of the sea, trapped and liberated, a picture that may be waiting to be washed away by the waves itself.

10

Branching out: *Fargo*

All Coen films are films about the home. They are not played out all over a large, generic American city, but depict a very specific place — or the tension between two different places whose peculiarities initially seem to be there to add local colour, giving a little more definition (and often irony) to the characters. It becomes clear that place is an integral part of the plot. The films tell stories which feel as if they could only have taken place in the particular part of the world they are set in — *Blood Simple* is inextricably linked to Texas, for example, and the hillbillies from the Phoenix area are no less lovingly portrayed in *Raising Arizona*. It is another manifestation of the tenderness of Coen films that they do not wheel out backwoodsmen and post-pioneers merely to denounce them.

It is not the 'reality' of these places which emerges but their clichés, which are, by their very nature, more real than reality. And the people who live in them have, in the end, no other choice.

These places are also one hundred per cent film sets. They are not in Texas but in the film noir, not in the big city but in the world of Frank Capra. They are places, like *Miller's Crossing*, which lie at the crossroads between Fritz Lang and Howard Hawks, or somewhere between Preston Sturges and George Cukor.

Place becomes a stage in Coen films, and time cannot be archaeologically determined. We find ourselves existing in different times at once. We are in the present (into which one political 'message' or another may extend), in another epoch of pop mythology, which expresses itself through fashions or signs, and finally we are in the idealised cinematic era of the 1930s and 1940s.

This simultaneous definition and fragmentation of fairytale material in time and space is continued in the presentation of language. The Texan drawl of the voiceover in *Blood Simple* is difficult to understand even for an American, and in *Fargo* the locals' undramatic, slow and apparently aimless speech pattern — with their innumerable 'yaahs' — seems to be no more than cute clumsiness, but we come to see it as the expression of a very specific experience and mentality (which will in the end, perhaps by coincidence, perhaps not, be the characteristic that enables them to deal with evil when it breaks into their world).

At the beginning, there is always a wish, and often not a very big wish. A wish for the place in society to which one is entitled (*The Hudsucker Proxy*), for a baby to make up a happy family (*Raising Arizona*), a body of work that you can be proud of (*Barton Fink*), money to fund your own projects (*Fargo*). But these little human wishes trigger unholy catastrophes. What is it that requires them to be answered with such terrible demons and blood baths?

Perhaps it is their limitlessness, their excessiveness. If you are looking for a job, are you not also dreaming the American dream, the dream of rising from dishwasher (or messenger boy) to millionaire? Is not every small-time gangster seeking to kill the boss and become top dog himself? The dismantling of myth in Coen films is not merely an aesthetic revolt, it is an experiment with the American dream, with the dream of capitalism, the dream of moving from one social situation to another.

The fact that several figures remain enigmatic, particularly as there is no traditional flashback to explain everything, is hard enough to take on board. When everything is said about them that can possibly be said within the narrative and using the means that cinema provides, it leaves us with the simple fact that nothing turns out as it was meant to, not a destiny being fulfilled. But the unexpected does not invalidate the rule, it merely rumbles around inside it before confirming it again in an indirect way — the violation *is* the rule. Norville Barnes is chosen to be the sucker who will lead a profitable company into ruin, but ends up doing the very opposite. Barton Fink writes himself into silence. Tom Reagan uses the rules of gangland to stage his own demise.

Objects behave in a similar manner to the people in Coen films. On first sight they appear highly stylised, as if part of a meta-design, but on closer inspection they are seen to stick incredibly closely to their remit. It is a commonplace that people need more and more signs to make it clear to themselves and to others who or what they are, but in real life we do not dare do this, or else we lose the personal within the general. We create a space in which almost all signs are legible and where art finds a place inside a frame, just like the pictures in Coen films of the bathing beauty, for example, or Nixon bowling.

Spaces in Coen films are more than mere reflections of characters and situations. Indeed, it is hard to know whether the space or the person is more alive. Again and again the Coens, like Fellini and David Lynch, lead us into strange spaces that are halfway between the living and the dead, between the body and the architecture. In *Barton Fink* there is the hotel room which sweats its own skin off the walls and which eventually banishes Barton into the only image that is has apart from itself. Did this hotel room exist before Barton Fink?

Coen spaces thus define themselves through what they allude to. They point in this direction, remind us of that, quote from something else, but none of the signs that are related to them function within a poetic or a logical system. It isn't simply a case of the contradiction between the authentic and the synthetic, though. Each Coen space is a sort of living work of art which also behaves like one — it invites and repulses, it provokes a hundred and one explanations but in the end remains autonomous, tautological, enigmatic. It has, quite literally, abolished reality.

In what we might call the sorcerer's apprentice films of the Coens, there are all the elements of the classic Hollywood movie, but they don't abide by the rules (the lexicon stays the same, but the grammar changes). They behave like toys that come to life after dark. The production of meaning in art is quite a difficult affair, and even more difficult is the production of non-meaning. Film can, of course, use montage to kill

Modest ambitions: *The Hudsucker Proxy*

The Earle hotel room — did it exist before *Barton Fink?*

meaning (a late variation on the montage of attractions — instead of building a concept through montage, it is used to destroy one).

It may find itself in a race with the production of meaning in the head of the viewer, where the plot twist becomes an aesthetic weapon, just as it can happen that a MacGuffin can turn out to be the thing with the most important meaning within the entire semantic system, so too can a running gag take control over the direction of the plot and lead, for example, to a deadly outcome.

The behaviour of the signs might be a little nonsensical, but it is decidedly human. In *Miller's Crossing*, Tom Reagan is always losing his hat (a hat that makes him a gangster, or an actor playing a gangster, or a descendant of the real American, or the right man, or a man who follows the rules, or an outsider, or a man who wants to cover his fear, or a man who can order his thoughts). By the end of the film he still has his hat but has nothing else — and he has certainly lost whatever it was that his hat stood for.

In *The Hudsucker Proxy* there is the circle on a piece of paper that Tim Robbins carries around with him and shows everyone as though they should be able to catch on immediately — 'You know, for kids.'

Only his innocent face stops us from seeing this as an obscene joke (and we could argue that our hero is born through the hula hoop, an object whose use is a fairly ambiguous ritual), and it is absolutely right that his cheerful rival seeks to copy his success by inventing the flexible straw. The joke here is not so much in the semiotic-psychological subtext but in the sheer obviousness. The hula hoop is an invention that is both inspired and idiotic, the most simple thing in the world, but also something that could only function in a tremendously complicated society.

11

L anguage behaves just like the people and the objects. At first, it appears to be merely a caricatured description of the strangeness of the people who use it, but it soon takes on its own life, meanders through the film and suddenly becomes mysterious and poetic. It could be argued that in each of their films the Coens develop a new and sometimes intoxicating secret language, a new opera of the spoken word, where what is spoken forms the libretto.

A place inside a frame: *Blood Simple, Barton Fink, Fargo*

The fact that even Americans could barely 'understand' the slang in *Miller's Crossing* (the question is whether at this level of language there is actually anything to be understood) is on the one hand proof of ethnographic exactitude, but it is also a pretext for playing with the sounds and rhythms of speech until they join with the images to form not only their own poetry but also their own poetics. The same principle is at work in *Fargo*, in which the very undramatic, Scandinavian slowness and the lengthy 'yaahs' seem to be a mild form of satire, but a point is soon reached at which language, people, objects, spaces and movements begin to become independent, to develop their own system.

Coen films are worlds full of rules which nobody abides by. The fatal mistake that many of their heroes and bad guys make is that they think they are the only ones who don't stick to them. Because nobody, or almost nobody, follows the rules, there emerges a meta-rule of deception and coincidence. The sign and the environment make up two languages in this world, relating not only to the actual speech, but even more so to that which is in essence most typically American — the action, or indeed, the violent action.

Most people don't stick to the rules because the rules contain so many contradictions. *Fargo*'s Jerry Lundegaard only wants to achieve the success (at least by his own standards) which his family demands of him, but which it simultaneously denies him the means of achieving. Barton Fink only wants to play the role of the 'writer in Hollywood', but his efforts founder with the very mogul who had hailed him as a genius and now literally condemns him to nothingness. Just as the sign becomes alive, or at least becomes a product, so too does the game come to life — a crazy, chaotic life that is merely a retardation of its real meaning... the bowling game.

There is nothing funnier than watching someone trying to tell a joke but failing to pull it off. This meta-joke is to be seen throughout the films of the Coen brothers. Each character is trying to tell his own story, but the others keep getting in the way, and even when they don't, he manages to screw things up himself, causing the others to stare at him with cold curiosity. It is precisely here that people's unfulfilled dreams emerge. Their comic acts and non-acts are gestures of revolt against their lives, gestures which lose nothing of their force even if they must fall into a moral offside trap or lead to nothing. Coen films are about people who cannot come to terms with what is.

Coen films teem with people, like Tom Reagan in *Miller's Crossing*, who only experience other people's stories, and people who cannot even do that properly,

like Barton Fink. There is much to remind us of Kafka in
Coen films: the judgement, the metamorphosis, the
inability to cross a 'forbidden' threshold, and, not least,
the punitive, misunderstood, threatening (even when it
seeks to do good) paternal authority. This figure frequently takes the form of a corpulent man (who perhaps wants to transform himself into a circle or a bowling ball), and, despite its comic aspects, always seems
ominous because we never know if the other threatening elements are creations of its evil imagination or if
they came from the hero's fear of the father figure.

It would be quite straightforward to establish a
meta-structure, a story behind the story, in a Coen
film: an insecure, almost childlike man wants to
become 'I'. He is opposed by a paternal authority, a
paternal architecture, a paternal imagination. This
has the effect of both spurring him into action and lur-
ing him into the spaces of power and of betrayal. The
closer the hero comes to the father-imago, the more
complex and enigmatic it becomes. It may even send
out its deadly demons. If the hero succeeds in killing
the father, it is achieved at a terrible cost. The hero
must also always ask himself whether the woman is in
cahoots with the father or whether she can be his
accomplice. Worse: the woman always reveals the
secret of the relationship, and uncovers the futility of
the struggle between the 'father' and the 'son', but she
is also interested in occupying the protected space.
She demands of the man that he grow up without
killing the father. Unfortunately, she is not as simple
as a bowling ball.

All this is not a psychoanalytic but a mythical solution. And we are not looking at a Coen family neurosis
but at something intrinsic to bourgeois society and its
phantasms, from William Shakespeare to Dashiell
Hammett. What the hero has to confront are the
phantoms of the exacting, masculine authority which
uses violence and cunning in a bid to prevent him
from achieving his identity. It is guilt, a guilt which

must be expiated, that produces the process itself. Each Coen hero begins life, at least within the context of his world and his genre, entirely pure.

This is why the secondary figures (who are always related) seem to form part of a special Coen *commedia dell'arte*. There is the absurd brother pair — Crush and Coddish, Hi's former cellmates, the amateur criminals Carl and Gaear, and even Barton Fink and Charlie, *aka* Karl Mundt, could fall into this category. There is the fat, brutal killer — the detective in *Blood Simple*, Karl Mundt, or the biker in *Raising Arizona*. And there is the man with the money — the furniture tycoon Nathan Arizona, Jerry Lundegaard's father-in-law, the Hollywood mogul, the bar owner in *Blood Simple*, the Mafia boss in *Miller's Crossing*, and the company director in *The Hudsucker Proxy*.

Each of the above embodies an aspect of power or an aspect of its dysfunction. But even the 'man with the money' causes catastrophes and is clearly characterised by not insignificant impulses of self-destruction. And in the midst of all this staggers the naïve loser — Candide, but also Josef K — whose purity we can perhaps no longer believe in, quite apart from the fact that he is not immune to the powers of corruption. His biggest problem is that he must react right from the start. Everything around him is speeding up, and he is the one person who is least likely to have an overview of the whole chain of cause and effect.

The Coens' *commedia dell'arte* doesn't end with the recurring figures or the internal structure, however. There are also recurring masks, dialogues and scenes that run through their movies — feet dragging across the floor, impossible verticals, the lighter with the monogram, a single car in the distance, or a clock that distorts time. The codes of the Coen cosmos establish their value through the strangeness of their familiarity (or the familiarity of their strangeness). They reappear, but mean something else. Even names are linked — Hudsucker is the name of the prison in

Crimewave and of the company in *The Hudsucker Proxy*, and in *Miller's Crossing* the building where the hero lives is called The Barton Arms.

And finally there is the motif of the doppelgänger, who may also be a usurper (symbolised in the recurring scene in which someone parks himself in someone else's space). The biker in *Raising Arizona* may well be Hi's doppelgänger, gangster Tom Reagan finds his in Bernie Birnbaum, and Jeff Lebowski's is to be found in the foreground of *The Big Lebowski*.

12

Thus, 'tenderness' would in the end be nothing more than a feeling manufactured through a certain aesthetic method: the balance of rapture and communion which is expressed through every cut, every change in perspective and every piece of dialogue, and which conveys concrete humanity and dreamlike (but also nightmarish) fairytales.

If you are a film-maker you can save your hero if he falls from a building by having the man in the clock tower stop time and then making a fat angel swing down to put everything right again. The condition is that, like the Coens, you have to prepare everything so exactly that however much the events surprise us, we still regard them as the only possible and consistent outcome. That we do not thereby gain any complete and arbitrary sovereignty we can see not only through the further development of events (in which things nearly go awry again) but also through the character who stops the clock. This figure is, and we had almost forgotten, also the narrator, and thus also rather like an author. But he is nevertheless attacked by a demon-like figure who wants to force time to start again, making the narrative continue within its 'prescribed' form. It would be hard to imagine a more

Commedia dell'arte: absurd pairs in *Crimewave*, *Raising Arizona* and *Fargo*

The final scenes: *Blood Simple, Raising Arizona, Miller's Crossing, Barton Fink, The Hudsucker Proxy, Fargo*

beautiful metaphor for an author fighting for one of his characters.

Tenderness thus emerges not only from the authors' treatment of their characters but also through the reflection of authorship they contain. All the protagonists in Coen films are, in fact, themselves 'authors'.

So it is not what the Coen films say that is the most important thing about them (though this is, of course, not to be underestimated), but what they set free. It is not the strenuous violation of the Oedipal aesthetic (in which one breaks a rule only so that one can establish a rule of one's own) but a game of the heart. In *The Ladies' Man* (1961, dir. Jerry Lewis), Jerry Lewis is cleaning a case containing large butterflies. He accidentally opens it and in no time the butterflies have all flown away. Jerry is thrown into despair, because they aren't even his butterflies, but then he has a brainwave. He puts his fingers in his mouth and whistles, and the butterflies fly back to their case. And this is how the Coens make their films.　■

Filmography

I. Directed/Produced

BLOOD SIMPLE (USA 1984)

Production: River Road/Circle Films. *Producer:* **Ethan Coen**. *Executive Producer:* Daniel F. Bacaner. *Associate Producer:* Mark Silverman. *Production Office Coordinator:* Alma Kutruff. *Location Manager:* Edith M. Clark.

Director: **Joel Coen**. *Assistant Director:* Deborah Reinisch, Steve Love, Shannon Wood. *Screenplay:* **Ethan Coen, Joel Coen**. *Script Supervisor:* Andreas Laven. *Cinematography:* Barry Sonnenfeld. *Music:* Carter Burwell. *Music Coordinator and Producer:* Murri Barber. *Editor:* Roderick Jaynes (aka **Ethan & Joel Coen**), Don Wiegmann, Peggy Connolly. *Production Design:* Jane Musky. *Lead Propmaker:* Robert A. Sturtevant. *Wardrobe Design:* Sara Medina-Pape. *Make-up:* Jean Ann Black. *Title Design:* Dan Perri. *Special Effects Coordinator:* Loren Bivens. *Special Effects Make-up:* Paul R. Smith. *Sound Mixer:* Lee Orloff. *Re-Recording Mixer:* Mel Zelniker. *Casting:* Julie Hughes, Barry Moss.

Special Thanks: Hilary Ney, Earl Miller, Ivan Bigley, Renaissance Pictures, Ron Seres, George Majesski.

Soundtrack: 'It's the Same Old Song' (written by Eddie Holland, Lamont Dozier & Brian Holland, performed by The Four Tops); 'Louie Louie' (written by Richard Berry, performed by Toots and the Maytals); 'The Lady in Red' (written by M. Dixon and A. Wrubel, performed by Xavier Cugat and his Orchestra); 'Rogaciano' (courtesy of Monitor Records); 'He'll Have to Go' (written by Joe Allison & Audrey Allison, performed by Joan Black); 'El Sueno' (written by Camilo Namen, performed by Johnny Ventura y su Combo); 'Anahi' (performed by Maria Luisa Buchino and her Llameros).

Cast: John Getz (Ray), Frances McDormand (Abby), Dan Hedaya (Julian Marty), M. Emmet Walsh (Private Detective Visser), Samm-Art Williams (Meurice), Deborah Neumann (Debra), Raquel Gavia (Landlady), Van Brooks (Man from Lubbock), Señor Marco (Mr Garcia), William Creamer (Old Cracker), Loren Bivens (Strip Bar Exhorter), Bob McAdams (Strip Bar Senator), Shannon Sedwick (Stripper), Nancy Ginger (Girl on Overlook), Rev. William Preston Robertson (Radio Evangelist), Holly Hunter (Voice on Answering Machine).

Format: 35mm, colour (DuArt). *Running Time:* 99 min. *US Release:* 18 January 1985.

RAISING ARIZONA (USA 1987)

Production: Circle Films. *Producer:* **Ethan Coen**. *Co-Producer:* Mark Silverman. *Executive Producer:* James Jacks. *Associate Producer:* Deborah Reinisch. *Production Manager:* Kevin Dowd. *Production Supervisor:* Alma Kutruff. *Location Manager:* David Pomier. *Post-Production Manager:* Andrew Sears.

Director: **Joel Coen**. *Assistant Director:* Deborah Reinisch, Kelly Van Horn. *Screenplay:* **Ethan Coen, Joel Coen**. *Script Supervisor:* Thomas Johnston. *Cinematography:* Barry Sonnenfeld. *Assistant Camera:* David M. Dunlap. *Camera Operator:* David M. Dunlap. *Steadicam Operator:* Stephan St. John. *Music:* Carter Burwell. *Music Engineering:* Sebastian Niessen. *Editor:* Michael R. Miller. *Associate Editor:* Arnold Glassman. *Production Design:* Jane Musky. *Art Director:* Harold Thrasher. *Set Decorator:* Robert Kracik. *Costume Design:* Richard Hornung. *Wardrobe Supervisor:* Stephan M Chudej. *Make-up:* Katherine James-Cosburn. *Hair:* Dan Frey. *Title Design:* Dan Perri. *Storyboards:* J. Todd Anderson. *Special Effects*

Coordinator: Peter Chesney. *Special Effects:* Image Engineering. *Production Sound Mixer:* Allan Byer. *Supervising Sound Editor:* Skip Lievsay. *Re-Recording Mixer:* Mel Zelniker. *Casting:* Donna Isaacson, John Lyons. *Stunt Coordinator:* Jery Hewitt. *Baby Wrangler:* Julie Asch. *Still Photographer:* Melinda Sue Gordon.

Special Thanks: Dick Bowers, Carol Porter, Dom Masters, Kurt Woolner, Susan Rose, Señor Greaser, John Raffo.

Soundtrack: 'Down in the Willow Garden' (by Charlie Munroe); 'Goofing-Off Suite' (by Pete Seeger); 'Girls, Do Not Wink' (courtesy Monitor Records); 'Home on the Range' (performed by Phil 'Dusty' Stockton).

Cast: Nicolas Cage (H.I.), Holly Hunter (Ed), Trey Wilson (Nathan Arizona Sr), John Goodman (Gale), William Forsythe (Evelle), Sam McMurray (Glen), Frances McDormand (Dot), Randall 'Tex' Cobb (Leonard Smalls), T.J. Kuhn Jr (Nathan Junior), Lynne Dumin Kitei (Florence Arizona), Peter Benedek (Prison Counselor), Charles 'Lew' Smith (Nice Old Grocery Man), Warren Keith (Younger FBI Agent), Henry Kendrick (Older FBI Agent), Sidney Dawson (Ear-Bending Cellmate), Richard Blake (Parole Board Chairman), Troy Nabors, Mary Seibel (Parole Board Members), John O'Donnal (Hayseed in the Pickup), Keith Jandacek (Whitey), Warren Forsythe (Minister), Ruben Young ('Trapped' Convict), Dennis Sullivan, Richard Alexander (Policemen in Arizona House), Rusty Lee (Feisty Hayseed), James Yeater (Fingerprint Technician), Bill Andres, Carver Barns (Reporters), Margaret H. McCormack (Unpainted Secretary), Bill Rocz (Newscaster), Mary F. Glenn (Payroll Cashier), Jeremy Babendure (Scamp with Squirt Gun), Bill Dobbins (Adoption Agent), Ralph Norton (Gynecologist), Henry Tank (Mopping Convict), Frank Outlaw (Supermarket Manager), Todd Michael Rodgers (Varsity Nathan Jr), M. Emmet Walsh (Machine Shop Ear-Bender), Robert Gray, Katie Thrasher, Derek Russell, Nicole Russell, Zachary Sanders, Noel Sanders (Glen and Dot's Kids), Cody Ranger, Jeremy Arendt, Ashley Hammon, Crystal Hiller, Olivia Hughes, Emily Malin, Melanie Malin, Craig McLaughlin, Adam Savageau, Benjamin Savageau, David Schneider, Michael Stewart (Arizona Quints), William Preston Robertson (Voice).

Format: 35mm (1:1,85), colour (DuArt), Dolby Stereo. *Running Time:* 94 min. *US Release:* March 1987.

MILLER'S CROSSING (USA 1989/1990)

Production: Circle Releasing. *Producer:* **Ethan Coen**. *Co-Producer:* Mark Silverman. *Executive Producer:* Ben Barenholtz. *Production Manager:* Alma Kuttruff. *Production Coordinator:* Terri Clemens. *Location Manager:* Amy Ness. *Post-Production Supervisor:* James DeMeaux. *Line Producer:* Graham Place.

Director: **Joel Coen**. *Assistant Director:* Gary Marcus, C.C. Barnes, Greg Jacobs. *Screenplay:* **Ethan Coen**, **Joel Coen**. *Script Supervisor:* Thomas Johnston. *Cinematography:*

Barry Sonnenfeld. *Assistant Camera:* Angelo DiGiacomo, Michael Chabronnet. *Camera Operator:* Barry Sonnenfeld. *Steadicam Operator:* Larry McConnkey. *Music:* Carter Burwell. *Music Editor:* Todd Kasow. *Editor:* Michael R. Miller. *Assistant Editor:* Michael Berenbaum, Anthony Grocki. *Production Design:* Dennis Gassner. *Art Director:* Leslie McDonald. *Set Design:* Kathleen McKernin. *Set Decorator:* Nancy Haigh. *Property Master:* Douglas Fox. *Costume Design:* Richard Hornung. *Wardrobe Supervisor:* Bonney Langfitt. *Set Costumer:* Barbara B. Baker. *Make-up:* Kathrine James. *Hair Stylist:* Cydney Cornell. *Storyboards:* J. Todd Anderson. *Special Effects Coordinator:* Peter Chesney. *Production Sound Mixer:* Allan Byer. *Supervising Sound Editor:* Skip Lievsay. *Re-Recording Mixer:* Lee Dichter. *Casting:* Donna Isaacson, John Lyons. *Stunt Coordinator:* Jery Hewitt. *Still Photographer:* Patti Perret.

Special Thanks: Señor Greaser, Stephanie Samuel and Tesa La Violette, Frank Toye, Kurt Woolner, Alex Albanese, Sue Ney and Hilary Ney.

Soundtrack: 'Decatur Street Tutti' (written and performed by Jabbo Smith); 'Come Back to Erin' (written by Claribel, performed by John McCormack); 'King Property Stomp' (by Ferdinand Morton, Sonny Burke & Sid Robin); 'Runnin' Wild' (by Joe Grey, Leo Wood & A. Harrington Gibbs); 'Goodnight, Sweetheart' (written by Rudy Vallee, Ray Noble, James Campbell & Reg Connelly, performed by Frank Patterson); 'Danny Boy' (performed by Frank Patterson).

Cast: Gabriel Byrne (Tom Reagan), Marcia Gay Harden (Verna), John Turturro (Bernie Bernbaum), Jon Polito (Johnny Caspar), J.E. Freeman (Eddie Dane), Albert Finney (Leo), Mike Starr (Frankie), Al Mancini (Tic-Tac), Richard Woods (Mayor Dale Levander), Thomas Toner (O'Doole), Steve Buscemi (Mink), Mario Todisco (Clarence 'Drop' Johnson), Olek Krupa (Tad), Michael Jeter (Adolph), Lanny Flaherty (Terry), Jeanette Kontomitras (Mrs Caspar), Louis Charles Mounicou (Johnny Caspar Jr), John McConnell (Cop — Brian), Danny Aiello (Cop — Delahanty), Helen Jolly (Screaming Lady), Hilda McLean (Landlady), Monte Starr, Don Picard (Gunmen in Leo's House), Salvatore H. Tornabene (Rug Daniels), Kevin Dearie (Street Urchin), Michael Badalucco (Caspar's Driver), Charles Ferrara (Caspar's Butler), Esteban Fernandez, George Fernandez (Caspar's Cousins), Charles Gunning (Hitman at Verna's), Dave Drinkx (Hitman #2), David Darlow (Lazarre's Messenger), Robert LaBrosse, Carl Rooney (Lazarre's Tough), Jack David Harris (Man with Pipe Bomb), Jery Hewitt (Son of Erin), Sam Raimi (Snickering Gunman), John Schnauder Jr (Cop with Bullhorn), Zolly Levin (Rabbi), Joey Ancona, Bill Raye (Boxers), William Preston Robertson (Voice), Frances McDormand (Secretary — uncredited).

Format: 35mm (1:1,85), colour (DuArt), Dolby SR. *Running Time:* 115 min. *US Release:* September 1990.

Effects Coordinator: Laurel Schneider. *Special Effects:* Robert L. Olmstead, Don Markel, Roy Goode, Tom Griep, Don Krause. *Special Make-up:* Rick Lazzarini. *Production Sound Mixer:* Allan Byer. *Supervising Sound Editor:* Skip Lievsay. *Re-Recording Mixer:* Lee Dichter. *Casting:* Donna Isaacson, John Lyons. *Stunt Coordinator:* Gary Jensen. *Choreographers:* Bill Landrum, Jacqui Landrum. *Still Photographer:* Melinda Sue Gordon.
Special Thanks: Señor Greazer, Jan Kelly, Rob Taub, Hilary Ney.
Soundtrack: 'For Sentimental Reasons' (by Edward Heymann, A. Sherman & A. Silver); 'Down South Camp Meeting' (by Irving Mills & F. Henderson).
Cast: John Turturro (Barton Fink), John Goodman (Charlie Meadows), Judy Davis (Audrey Taylor), Michael Lerner (Jack Lipnick), John Mahoney (W.P. Mayhew), Tony Shalhoub (Ben Geisler), Jon Polito (Lou Breeze), Steve Buscemi (Chet), David Warrilow (Garland Stanford), Richard Portnow (Detective Mastrionotti), Christopher Murney (Detective Deutsch), I.M. Hobson (Derek), Megen Fay (Poppy Carnaham), Lance Davis (Richard St. Claire), Harry Bugin (Pete), Anthony Gordon (Maitre D'), Jack Denbo (Stagehand), Max Grodénchik (Clapper Boy), Robert Beecher (Referee), Darwyn Swalve (Wrestler), Gayle Vance (Geisler's Secretary), Johnny Judkins (Sailor), Jana Marie Hupp (USO Girl), Isabelle Townsend (Beauty), William Preston Robertson (Voice).
Format: 35mm (1:1,66), colour (DuArt), Dolby Stereo. *Running Time:* 116 min. *Location:* Los Angeles. *US Release:* August 1991.

BARTON FINK (USA 1991)
Production: Circle Films. *Producer:* **Ethan Coen**. *Co-Producer:* Graham Place. *Executive Producer:* Ben Barenholtz, Ted Pedas, Jim Pedas, Bill Durkin. *Production Manager:* Alma Kuttruff. *Production Coordinator:* Judi Rosner. *Location Manager:* Amy Ness. *Post-Production Supervisor:* James D. Meaux. *Unit Manager:* Ron Neter.
Director: **Joel Coen**. *Assistant Director:* Joe Camp, Randall Newsome, Tom Gamble. *Screenplay:* **Ethan Coen, Joel Coen**. *Script Supervisor:* Thomas Johnston. *Cinematography:* Roger Deakins. *Assistant Camera:* Scott Andrew Ressler, Susan Pollack. *Steadicam Operator:* Mark O'Kane. *Music:* Carter Burwell. *Music Supervisor:* Sonny Kompanek. *Music Editor:* Todd Kasow. *Editor:* Roderick Jaynes (*aka* **Ethan & Joel Coen**). *Associate Editor:* Michael Berenbaum. *Production Design:* Dennis Gassner. *Art Director:* Leslie McDonald, Robert C. Goldstein. *Set Design:* Richard Fernandez. *Set Decorator:* Nancy Haigh. *Costume Design:* Richard Hornung. *Wardrobe Supervisor:* Laly Poore. *Set Dresser:* Leslie 'Tinker' Linville. *Make-up:* Jean Ann Black. *Hair Stylist:* Frida Aradottir. *Title Design:* Balsmeyer & Everett. *Storyboards:* J. Todd Anderson. *Special Effects Supervisor:* Robert Spurlock. *Special

THE HUDSUCKER PROXY (USA 1994)
Production: Silver Pictures/Working Title Films. *Producer:* **Ethan Coen**. *Co-Producer:* Graham Place. *Executive Producer:* Tim Bevan, Eric Fellner. *Associate Producer:* Mary Weisgerber. *Production Manager:* Alma Kuttruff, Gilly Ruben (2nd Unit). *Production Coordinators:* Holly Gent Palmo, Christy N. Gilmer (2nd Unit). *Location Coordinators:* Heidi Mehltretter, Kim Miller (Chicago).
Director: **Joel Coen**. *2nd Unit Director:* Sam Raimi. *Assistant Director:* Victor Malone, Sarah Addington, Vincent Palmo Jr. *Screenplay:* **Ethan Coen, Joel Coen**, Sam Raimi. *Script Supervisor:* Thomas Johnston. *Cinematography:* Roger Deakins. *Assistant Camera:* Robin Brown. *2nd Unit Photography:* Paul Elliot. *Steadicam Operator:* Frederick Raphael. *Music:* Carter Burwell. *Music Editor:* Todd Kasow. *Music Themes:* Aran Khachaturian. *Orchestrations:* Sonny Kompanek. *Editor:* Thom Noble. *Assistant Editor:* Tricia Cooke. *Production Design:* Dennis Gassner. *Art Director:* Leslie McDonald. *Set Design:* Tony Fanning, Gina Cranham, Richard Yanez. *Set Decorator:* Nancy Haigh. *Costume Design:* Richard Hornung. *Costume Supervisor:* Ellen Ryba. *Set Costumers:* Paige Augustine,

Claire Gaul, Tinker Linville, Linda Cathey, Kip Bartlett, Matthew Sullivan. *Make-up:* Lydia Milars. *Hair Design:* Cydney Cornell. *Graphic Design:* Eric Rosenberg. *Title Design:* Balsmeyer & Everett, Syzygy Digital Camera (Computer Graphics). *Storyboards:* J. Todd Anderson. *Visual Effects Photography:* Patrick Turner, Kim Foster Marks (Blue Screen Unit). *Visual Effects Producer/Supervisor:* Michael J. McAlister. *Visual Effects Co-Producer:* Kat Dillon. *Visual Effects Coordinator:* Chris Watts. *Digital Compositing:* The Computer Film Company. *Matte Paintings:* Mark Sullivan, Rich Cohen. *Digital Matte Images:* Industrial Light & Magic. *Mechanical Effects:* Peter M. Chesney. *Miniature Effects:* Stetson Visual Services, Mark Stetson, Robert Spurlock. *Chief Modelmaker:* Ian Hunter. *Model Design:* Chris Gorak. *Lead Model Electronics:* Erik Stohl. *Lead Model Mechanics:* Roy Goode. *Mechanical Effects:* Peter M. Chesney, Design FX Company (2nd Unit). *Production Sound Mixer:* Allan Byer. *Supervising Sound Editor:* Skip Lievsay. *Re-Recording Engineers:* Michael Barry, Lee Dichter. *Sound Re-Recordists:* Michael Barry, Lee Dichter. *Casting:* Donna Isaacson, John Lyons. *Stunt Coordinator:* Jery Hewitt. *Choreography:* Wesley Fata.

Special Thanks: North Carolina Film Office, Illinois Film Office, The Chicago Film Office, Early Halloween, Señor Greaser.

Soundtrack: 'Memories Are Made of This' (written by Terry Gilkyson, Richard Dehr & Frank Miller, performed by Peter Gallagher); 'In a Sentimental Mood' (by Duke Ellington); 'Flying Home' (written by Benny Goodman & Lionel Hampton, performed by Duke Ellington); 'Carmen' (written by Georges Bizet, performed by Grace Bumbry).

Cast: Tim Robbins (Norville Barnes), Jennifer Jason Leigh (Amy Archer), Paul Newman (Sidney J. Mussburger), Charles Dorning (Waring Hudsucker), John Mahoney (Chief), Jim True (Buzz), William Cobbs (Moses), Bruce Campbell (Smitty), Harry Bugin (Aloysius), John Seitz (Benny), Joe Grifasi (Lou), Roy Brocksmith, I.M. Hobson, John Scanlan, Jerome Dempsey, John Wylie, Gary Allen, Richard Woods, Peter McPherson (Board Members), David Byrd (Dr Hugo Bromfenbrenner), Christopher Darga (Mail Room Orienter), Patrick Cranshaw (Ancient Sorter), Robert Weil (Mail Room Boss), Mary Lou Rosato (Mussburger's Secretary), Ernie Sarracino (Luigi the Tailor), Eleanor Glockner (Mrs Mussburger), Kathleen Perkins (Mrs Braithwaite), Joseph Marcus (Sears Braithwaite of Bullard), Peter Gallagher (Vic Tenetta), Noble Willingham (Zebulon Cardoza), Barbara Ann Grimes (Mrs Cardoza), Thom Noble (Thorstenson Finlandson), Steve Buscemi (Beatnik Barman), William Duff-Griffin (Newsreel Scientist), Anna Nicole Smith (Za-Za), Pamela Everett (Dream Dancer), Arthur Bridges (The Hula Hoop Kid), Sam Raimi, John Cameron (Hudsucker

Brainstormers), Skipper Dune (Mr Grier), Jay Kapner (Mr Levin), Jon Polito (Mr Bumstead), Richard Whiting (Ancient Puzzler), Linda McCoy (Coffee Shop Waitress), Stan Adams (Emcee), John Goodman alias Karl Mundt (Newsreel Announcer), Joanne Pankow (Newsreel Secretary), Mario Todisco (Norville's Goon), Colin Fickes (Newsboy), Dick Sasso (Drunk in Alley), Jesse Brewer, Stan Lichtenstein, Ace O'Connell, Frank Jeffries, Philip Loch, Todd Alcott, Richard Schiff, Lou Criscuolo, Michael Earl Reid (Mailroom Screamers), Mike Starr, Willie Reale, Tom Toner, Dave Hagar, Harvey Meyer, David Fawcett (Newsroom Reporters), Jeff Still, Gil Pearson, David Massie, Peter Siragusa, Michael Houlihan, David Gould, Marc Garber, Mark Miller, Nelson George, Ed Lillard (Newsreel Reporters), Wentland Sandel, James Deuter, Rick Peeples, Cynthia Baker (New Year's Mob).

Format: 35mm (1:1,85), colour, Dolby Stereo SR. *Running Time:* 113 min. *US Release:* 11 March 1994.

FARGO (USA 1995/1996)

Production: PolyGram Filmed Entertainment/Working Title Films. *Producer:* **Ethan Coen**. *Executive Producer:* Tim Bevan, Eric Fellner. *Production Manager:* Gilly Ruben. *Production Coordinator:* Karen Ruth Getchell. *Location Manager:* Robert J. Graf. *Post-Production Supervisor:* Margaret Hayes. *Line Producer:* John Cameron.

Director: **Joel Coen**. *Assistant Director:* Michelangelo Csaba Bolla, James Allen Hensz, Brian O'Kelly, Donald Murphy. *Screenplay:* **Ethan Coen**, **Joel Coen**. *Script Supervisor:* T. Kukovinski. *Cinematography:* Roger Deakins. *Camera Operator:* Robin Brown. *Music:* Carter Burwell. *Music Editor:* Todd Kassow. *Associate Music Editor:* Shri Schwartz. *Editor:* Roderick Jaynes (*aka* **Ethan & Joel Coen**). *Assistant Editor:* Big Dave Diliberto. *Associate Editor:* Tricia Cooke. *Production Design:* Rick Heinrichs. *Art Director:* Thomas P. Wilkins. *Set Decorator:* Lauri Gaffin. *Costume Design:* Mary Zophres. *Costume Supervisor:* Sister Daniels. *Costumer:* Virginia Burton. *Key Make-up Artist:* John Blake. *Key Hairstylist:* Daniel Curet. *Graphic Design:* Bredford Richardson. *Title Design:* Balsmeyer & Everett. *Storyboards:* J. Todd Anderson. *Special Effects Coordinator:* Paul Murphy. *Special Effects Snowmaker:* Dieter Sturm, Yvonne Sturm. *Pyrotechnician:* Wilfried Caban. *Production Sound Mixer:* Allen Byer. *Supervising Sound Editor:* Skip Lievsay. *Re-Recording Mixers:* Michael Barry, Skip Lievsay. *Casting:* John Lyons. *Stunt Coordinator:* Jery Hewitt. *Still Photographer:* James Bridges, Michael Tackett.

Special Thanks: Malcom Ritchie, David Daugherty, Deana Elwell, Peter Graves, Mark Wolfe, Rick Finkelstein, Russel Schwartz, Aline Perry, Steward Till, Minnesota Film Board, North Dakota Film Commision, Julie Hartley, The Computer Film Company, Robert Hauptman and James Hauptman.

a film by
Joel & Ethan Coen

Fargo

a homespun murder story

Trooper), J. Todd Anderson (Victim in the Field), Michelle Suzanne LeDoux (Victim in Car), Frances McDormand (Marge Gunderson), John Carroll Lynch (Norm Gunderson), Bruce Bohne (Lou), Petra Boden (Cashier), Steve Park (Mike Yanagita), Wayne A. Evenson (Customer), Cliff Rakerd (Officer Olson), Jessica Shepherd (Hotel Clerk), Peter Schmitz (Airport Lot Attendant), Steve Shaefer (Mechanic), Michelle Hutchinson (Escort), David S. Lomax (Man in Hallway), José Feliciano (Himself), Don William Skahill (Night Parking Attendant), Bain Boehlke (Mr Mohra), Rose Stockton (Valerie), Robert Ozasky (Bismarck Cop #1), John Bandemer (Bismarck Cop #2), Don Wescott (Bark Beetle Narrator), Bruce Campbell (Actor in Soap Opera — uncredited)
Format: 35mm (1:1,85), colour (DuArt), Dolby Stereo SR Digital. *Running Time:* 98 min. *US Release:* 8 March 1996.

THE BIG LEBOWSKI (USA 1997/1998)

Production: PolyGram Filmed Entertainment/Working Title Films. *Producer:* **Ethan Coen.** *Co-Producer:* John Cameron. *Executive Producer:* Tim Bevan, Eric Fellner. *Production Manager:* John Cameron. *Production Co-ordinator:* Gregg Edler. *Production Supervisor:* Gilly Ruben. *Location Manager:* Robert Graf. *Post-Production Supervisor:* Charlie Vogel.
Director: **Joel Coen.** *First Assistant Director:* Jeff Rafner. *Second Assistant Director:* Conte Mark Matal. *Screenplay:* **Ethan Coen, Joel Coen.** *Script Supervisor:* T. Kukowinski. *Cinematography:* Roger Deakins. *First Assistant Camera:* Andy Harris. *Second Assistant Camera:* Adam Gilmore. *Camera Operator:* Ted Morris. *Music:* Carter Burwell. *Music Supervisor:* Happy Walters. *Music Coordinator:* Emilie Charlap. *Music Editor:* Todd Kasow. *Editor:* Roderick Jaynes (*aka* **Ethan & Joel Coen**), Tricia Cooke. *Assistant Editor:* Lisa Mozden, Alex Belth. *Associate Editor:* Big Dave Diliberto. *Production Design:* Rick Heinrichs. *Art Director:* John Dexter. *Set Design:* Mariko Braswell. *Set Decorator:* Chris Spellman. *Costume Design:* Mary Zophres. *Costume Supervisor:* Pam Withers. *Set Costumer:* Virginia Seffens-Burton. *Make-up Supervisor:* Jean Black. *Hair Stylist:* Daniel Curet. *Graphic Design:* Bradford Richardson. *Title Design:* Balsmeyer & Everett. *Designer:* Randall Balsmeyer. *Animation Producer:* Kathy Kelehan. *Computer Animators:* Daniel Leung, Amit Sethi, Matt McDonald, Gary Miller. *Visual Effects by:* The Computer Film Company. *Visual Effects Supervisor:* Gilly Ruben. *Visual Effects Producer:* Janet Yale. *Sound Mixer:* Allan Byer. *Re-Recording Mixers:* Michael Barry, Skip Lievsay. *Casting:* John Lyons. *Stunts:* Jennifer Lamb, Vince Deadrick Jr, Loyd Catlett. *Still Photographer:* Merrick Morton.
Special Thanks: Clay Rand, Brian Biles, Emil Moscowitz, Patrick Sheedy, Gary Spero, Liz Young, Señor Greaser.

Soundtrack: 'Do You Know the Way to San Jose' (by Burt Bacharach & Hal David); 'Up, Up and Away' (by Jimmy Webb); 'Tie a Yellow Ribbon Round the Old Oak Tree' (by Irwin Levine & L. Russel Brown); 'Sometimes in Winter' (by Stephan Katz); 'Feels So Good' (written and performed by Chuck Mangione); 'Big City' (written by Merle Haggard & Dean Holloway, performed by Merle Haggard); 'These Boots are Made for Walking' (written by Lee Hazelwood, performed by Boy George); 'Let's Find Each Other Tonight' (by José Feliciano); 'Jonny's Theme' (by Paul Anker & Jonny Carson).
Cast: William H. Macy (Jerry Lundegaard), Steve Buscemi (Carl Showalter), Peter Stormare (Gaear Grimsrud), Kristin Rudrüd (Jean Lundegaard), Harve Presnell (Wade Gustafson), Tony Denman (Scotty Lundegaard), Gary Houston (Irate Customer), Sally Wingert (Irate Customer's Wife), Kurt Schweickhardt (Car Salesman), Larissa Kokernot (Hooker #1), Melissa Peterman (Hooker #2), Steve Reevis (Shep Proudfoot), Warren Keith (Reilly Diefenbach), Steve Edelman (Morning Show Host), Sharon Anderson (Morning Show Hostess), Larry Brandenburg (Stan Grossman), James Gaulke (State

Soundtrack: 'The Man in Me' (written and performed by Bob Dylan); 'Ataypura' (witten by Moises Vivanco, performed by Yma Sumac); 'Branded' theme song (written by Alan Alch & Dominic Frontiere); 'Glück das mir verblieb' from the opera *Die tote Stadt* (written by Erich Wolfgang Korngold, performed by Ilona Steingruber, Anton Dermota & Austria State Radio Orchestra); 'Hotel California' (written by Don Henley, Glenn Frey & Don Felder, performed by The Gipsy Kings); 'Behave Yourself' (written by Booker T. Jones, Steve Cropper, Al Jackson, Jr & Lewie Steinberg, performed by Booker T. And The MGs); 'Dead Flowers' (written by Mick Jagger & Keith Richards, performed by Townes Van Zandt); 'Her Eyes Are a Blue Million Miles' (written by Don Vliet, performed by Captain Beefheart); 'I Got it Bad & That Ain't Good' (written by Duke Ellington & Paul Francis Webster, performed by Nina Simone); 'I Hate You' (written by Gary Burger, David Havlicek, Roger Johnston, Thomas E. Shaw & Larry Spangler, performed by Monks); 'Looking Out My Back Door' (written by John Fogerty, performed by Creedence Clearwater Revival); 'Mucha Muchacha' (written by Juan Garcia Esquivel, performed by Esquivel); 'Oye Como Va' (written by Tito Puente, performed by Santana); 'Piacere Sequence' (written and performed by Teo Uselli); 'Requiem in D Minor' (written by W.A. Mozart, performed by The Slovak Philharmonic Orchestra and Choir); 'Just Dropped In (To See What Condition My Condition Was In)' (written by Mickey Newbury, performed by Kenny Rogers & The First Edition); 'Lujon' (written and performed by Henry Mancini); 'My Mood Swings' (written by Elvis Costello & Cait O'Riordan, performed by Elvis Costello); 'Peaceful Easy Feelings' (written by Jack Tempchin, performed by The Eagles); 'Pictures at an Exhibition' (written by Modest Moussorgsky, performed by The Royal Concertgebouw Orchestra); 'Run Through the Jungle' (written by John Fogerty, performed by Creedence Clearwater Revival); 'Stamping Ground' (written by Louis Hardin, performed by Moondog); 'Tammy' (written by Ray Evans & Jay Livingston, performed by Debbie Reynolds); 'Tumbling Tumbleweeds' (written by Bob Nolan, performed by Sons of The Pioneers; 'Walking Songs' (written and performed by Meredith Monk); 'We Venerate Thy Cross' (performed by The Rustavi Choir); 'Standing on the Corner' (written by Frank Loesser, performed by Dean Martin); 'Traffic Boom' (written and performed by Piero Piccioni); 'Viva Las Vegas' (written by Doc Pomus & Mort Shuman, performed by Shawn Colvin, also performed by Big Johnson).

Cast: Jeff Bridges (The Dude), John Goodman (Walter Sobchak), Julianne Moore (Maude Lebowski), Steve Buscemi (Donny), David Huddleston (The Big Lebowski), Philip Seymour Hoffman (Brandt), Tara Reid (Bunny Lebowski), Philip Moon, Mark Pellegrino (Treehorn Thugs),

Peter Stormare (Uli), Flea (Kiefer), Torsten Voges (Franz), Jimmie Dale Gilmore (Smokey), Jack Kehler (Dude's Landlord), John Turturro (Jesus Quintana), James G. Hoosier (Quintana's Partner), Carlos Leon, Terrence Burton (Maude's Thugs), Richard Gant (Older Cop), Christian Clemenson (Younger Cop), Dom Irrera (Tony the Chauffeur), Gerard L'Heureux (Lebowski's Chauffeur), David Thewlis (Knox Harrington), Lu Elrod (Coffee Shop Waitress), Michael Gomez (Auto Circus Cop), Peter Siragusa (Gary the Bartender), Sam Elliott (The Stranger), Marshall Manesh (Doctor), Mary Bugin (Arthur Digby Sellers), Jesse Flanagan (Little Larry Sellers), Irene Olga Lopez (Pilar), Luis Colina (Corvette Owner), Ben Gazzara (Jackie Treehorn), Leon Russom (Malibu Police Chief), Ajgie Kirkland (Cab Driver), Jon Polito (Private Snoop), Aimee Mann (Nihilist Woman), Jerry Haleva (Saddam), Jennifer Lamb (Pancake Waitress), Warren David Keith (Funeral Director).

Format: 35mm (1:1,85), colour (Technicolor). *Running Time:* 113 min. *US Release:* 4 March 1998.

II. Screenplays

CRIMEWAVE (USA 1985)
aka Broken Hearts and Noses
Production: Renaissance Pictures/Columbia Pictures Corporation/Embassy Films. *Producer:* Robert G. Tapert. Co-Producer: Bruce Campbell. *Executive Producer:* Edward R. Pressman, Irvin Shapiro. *Associate Producer:* Cary Glieberman. *Production Coordinator:* Shalini Waren. *Location Manager:* Douglas McGeorge.
Director: Sam Raimi. *Assistant Director:* Claudia Sills, John Cameron. *Screenplay:* **Ethan Coen, Joel Coen**, Sam Raimi. *Script Supervisor:* Corinne Saaranen. *Cinematography:* Robert Primes. *Assistant Camera:* Ann Lukacs, Robert Rycroft. *2nd Unit Camera Assistant:* Tom Stackpoole. *2nd Unit Camera Operator:* Tom Campau. *Additional Photographer:* Eugene D. Shulgleit. *Music:* Arlon Ober, Joseph LoDuca (Jazz Music). *Music Editor:* Fred Aronow. *Music Consultants:* Joseph LoDuca. *Music Recordist:* Paul Ratajczak. *Editor:* Kathie Weaver. *Assistant Editor:* Craig Boyajian. *Art Director:* Gary Papierski. *Set Decorator:* Kimberly Thrasher. *Wardrobe:* Carol Haefner. *Make-up:* Deborah K. Larsen. *Hair Design:* Mary Lee Nelson. *Special Effects:* Martin Bresin. *Special Make-up Effects:* Roger White. *Production Sound Mixer:* Burr Huntington. *Re-Recording Mixer:* Don MacDougall. *Sound Effects Editor:* Dick Legrand. *Sound Designer:* David Lewis Yewdall. *Casting:* Barbara Claman. *Stunt Coordinator:* Rick Barker. *Choreographer:* Susan Labatt. *Still Photographer:* Jim Coe.
Soundtrack: 'Rialto' (by Joe LoDuca); 'We Go Together' (written by Arlon Ober, performed by Jonathon Beres &

Katie Yanai); 'Cherish' (by Terry Kirkman).
Cast: Louise Lasser (Helene Trend), Paul L. Smith (Faron Crush), Brion James (Arthur Coddish), Sheree J. Wilson (Nancy), Edward R. Pressman (Ernest Trend), Bruce Campbell (Renaldo 'The Heel'), Reed Birney (Vic Ajax), Richard Bright (Officer Brennan), Antonio Fargas (Blind Man), Hamid Dana (Donald Odegard), John Hardy (Mr Yarman), Emil Sitka (Colonel Rodgers), Hal Youngblood (Jack Elroy), Sean Farley (Jack Elroy Jr), Richard DeManincor (Officer Garvey), Carrie Hall-Schalter (Cheap Dish), Wiley Harker (Governor), Julius Harris (Hardened Convict), Ralph Drischell (Executioner), Robert Symonds (Guard #1), Patrick Stack (Guard #2), Philip A. Gillis (Priest), Bridget Hoffman, Anne Marie Gillis, Frances McDormand (Nuns), Carol Brinn (Old Woman), Matthew Taylor (Muscleman), Perry Mallette (Grizzled Veteran), Chuck Gaidica (Weatherman), Jimmie Launce (Announcer), Joseph French (Bandleader), Ted Raimi (Waiter), Dennis Chaitlin (Fat Waiter).
Format: 35mm, colour (Technicolor), Mono. *Running Time:* 83 min. *Location:* Detroit and Hollywood.

III. Miscellaneous

FEAR NO EVIL (USA 1981)
Director: Frank LaLoggia. *Screenplay:* Frank LaLoggia. *Cinematography:* Fred Goodich. *Music:* Frank LaLoggia. *Assistant Editor:* **Joel Coen**. *Special Effects:* John Eggett. *Production Sound Mixer:* Mary Jo Devenney.
Cast: Stefan Arngrim (Andrew Williams), Frank Birney, Elizabeth Hoffman, Kathleen Rowe McAllen, Richard Jay Silverthorn (Satan).
Format: 35mm, colour.

THE EVIL DEAD (USA 1982)
Production: New Line Cinema/Renaissance Pictures. *Producer:* Robert G. Tapert. *Executive Producer:* Bruce Campbell, Sam Raimi. *Director:* Sam Raimi. *Screenplay:* Sam Raimi. *Cinematography:* Tim Philo, Joshua M. Becker. *Music:* Joseph LoDuca. *Editor:* Edna Ruth Paul. *Assistant Editor:* **Joel Coen**. *Special Make-up Effects:* Tom Sullivan. *Production Sound Mixer:* Mel Zelniker. *Supervising Sound Editor:* Joe Masefield.
Cast: Bruce Campbell (Ashley J. 'Ash' Williams), Ellen Sandweiss (Cheryl), Hal Delrich (Scotty), Betsy Baker (Linda), Sarah York (Shelly), Philip A. Gillis, Dorothy Tapert, Cheryl Guttridge, Barbara Carey, David Horton, Wendall Thomas, Don Long, Stu Smith, Kurt Rauf, Ted Raimi, Ivan Raimi, Bill Vincent, Mary Beth Tapert, Scott Spiegel, John Cameron, Joanne Kruse, Gwen Cochanski, Debie Jarczewski (Fake Shemps), Sam Raimi (Fisherman on Side of Road/Voice of Evil Spirit), Robert G. Tapert (Local Yokel).
Format: 35mm, colour. *Running Time:* 85 min.

Joel Coen (right) in *Spies Like Us*.

SPIES LIKE US (USA 1985)
Production: Warner Bros. *Producer:* George Folsey Jr, Brian Grazer. *Executive Producer:* Bernie Brillstein. *Director:* John Landis. *Screenplay:* Dan Aykroyd, Lowell Ganz, Babaloo Mandel. *Cinematography:* Robert Paynter. *Music:* Elmer Bernstein. *Editor:* Malcolm Campbell. *Production Design:* Terry Ackland-Snow, Peter Murton. *Supervising Art Director:* Terry Ackland-Snow. *Costume Design:* Deborah Nadoolman. *Production Sound Mixer:* Ivan Sharrock.
Cast: Mark Stewart (Ace Tomato Courier), Sean Daniel (Ace Tomato Driver), Bruce Davison (Ruby), William Prince (Keyes), Steve Forrest (General Sline), Tom Hatten (General Miegs), Chevy Chase (Emmett Fitz-Hume), Jeff Harding (Fitz-Hume's Associate), Heidi Sorenson (Fitz-Hume's Supervisor), Stephen Hoye (Captain Hefling), Dan Aykroyd (Austin Millbarge), Margo Random (Reporter), Douglas Lambert (Reporter), Frank Oz (Test Monitor), Christopher Malcolm (Jumpmaster), Bernie Casey (Colonel Rhumbus), Terrance Conder (Soldier #1), Matt Frewer (Soldier #2), Jim Staahl (Bud Schnelker), James Daughton (Bob Hodges), Tony Cyrus (The Khan), Gusti Bogok (Dr La Fong), Charles McKeown (Jerry Hadley), Terry Gilliam (Dr Imhaus), Donna Dixon (Karen), Derek Meddings (Dr Stinson), Ray Harryhausen (Dr Marston), Robert Paynter (Dr Gill), Bob Hope (Himself), Gurdial Sira (The Khan's Brother), **Joel Coen** (Drive-In Security #1), Sam Raimi (Drive-In Security #2), Michael Apted (Ace Tomato Agent), B.B. King, Larry Cohen (Ace Tomato Agents) etc.
Format: 35mm, colour (Technicolor), Dolby. *Running Time:* 102 min.

p16. - Jacques Valot: Joel Coen, *Revue du Cinéma*, May 1990, p55 (biography, filmography). **(ger:)** Frank Schnelle: Tänze am Rande des Nichts – Über das Kino der Brüder Joel und Ethan Coen und ihren neuen Film FARGO, *epd Film*, Nov. 1996, p 21-26. - Stefan Lux: Geschichten aus dem Fegefeuer – Joel & Ethan Coen und ihre Filme, *film-dienst*, 21/1991, p4-6.

Bibliography

I. On Joel & Ethan Coen in general

Articles/Features/Profiles:

(eng:) David Ansen: The Coens – partners in crime, *Newsweek*, 21.1.85, p74-75. - Eric Breitbart: Leaving the seventies behind, *American Film*, May 1985, p46-51. - J. Clark: Strange bedfellows, *Premiere* (USA), April 1994, p61ff. - Manohla Dargis: Double vision, *The Village Voice*, 13.8.91, p55-56. - K. Ferguson: From two directions, *Film Monthly*, Feb. 1992, p14ff. - Marlaine Glicksman: Getting down to the bone, *Film Comment*, Sept./Oct. 1990, p34-45 (interview with John Turturro). - H.S. Hample: Filmographies, *Premiere* (USA), April 1994, p152 (biography/filmography). - D. Handelman: The brothers from another planet, *Rolling Stone*, 21.5.87, p59ff. - John Harkness: The sphinx without a riddle, *Sight & Sound*, Aug. 1994, p6-9. - Mark Horowitz: Coen Brothers A-Z, *Film Comment*, Sept./Oct. 1991, p27-32 (glossary of themes and influences in the films of Coens). - Janet Maslin: What is a new director? *New York Times*, 29.3.87, p17. - E. Pooley: Wrapped in America, *New York Magazine*, 23.3.87, p44-48. - J.H. Richardson: The Joel & Ethan story, *Premiere* (USA), Oct. 1990, p94ff. - William Preston Robertson: The Coen Brothers made easy, *Playboy* (USA), April 1994, p112ff. - Richard Schickel, J.C. Simpson: A three-espresso hallucination, *Time*, 26.8.91, p58-59. - R. Seidenberg: Out of NYU into independence, *New York Times*, 27.1.85, p17ff. - K. Sessums: Ethan and Joel Coen, *Interview*, April 1987, p96 (interview, profile). - B. Sharkey: Movies of their very own, *New York Times*, 8.7.90, p22ff. **(fr:)** Joel et Ethan Coen, *Avant-Scène du Cinéma*, Nov. 1991, p95. - Joel Coen, Ethan Coen: Notre acteur préféré, *Positif*, June 1994, p21-22 (profile of actor Harry Bugin). - Franck Garbarz: Petits drames de la solitude – FARGO dans l'œuvre des frères Coen, *Positif*, Sept. 1996, p9-11. - Laurence Giavarini: L'accouchement du cinéma, *Cahiers du Cinéma*, Oct. 1991, p41-44. - Laurence Giavarini: Joel et Ethan Coen, *Cahiers du Cinéma*, Dec. 1992, p85. - Iannis Katsahnias: Frères de sang, *Cahiers du Cinéma*, March 1991, p39. - Jacqueline Nacache: Ethan et Joel Coen, *Revue du Cinéma*, Sept. 1991, p58-62. - Nicolas Saada: Ethan et Joel Coen, *Cahiers du Cinéma*, May 1991,

Interviews with the Coens (general and on individual films):

(eng:) Geoff Andrew: Too weird for words, *Time Out*, 5.2.92, p18-21 (on BARTON FINK). - Geoff Andrew: Pros and Cons, *Time Out*, 15.5.96, p24-26 (on FARGO). - David Edelstein: Invasion of the baby snatchers, *American Film*, April 1987, p26-30, 56 (article and interview on RAISING ARIZONA). - Lizzie Francke: Hell freezes over, *Sight & Sound*, May 1996, p24-27 (on FARGO). - H. Hinson: Bloodlines, *Film Comment*, March/April 1985, p14-19 (article and interview with the Coens and Barry Sonnenfeld about BLOOD SIMPLE). - K. Sessums: Ethan and Joel Coen, *Interview*, April 1987, p96 (interview, profile). **(fr:)** Henri Béhar: Les frères Brothers en stéréo, *Le Monde*, 28.2.91. - Emmanuel Burdeau, Nicolas Saada: Les forces de L'ordre, *Cahiers du Cinéma*, Sept. 1996, p40-47, 49 (review and interview about FARGO). - Michel Ciment, Hubert Niogret: Entretien avec Joel et Ethan Coen, *Positif*, July/Aug. 1987, p61-65 (about literary and cinematic influences). - Michel Ciment, Hubert Niogret: Un rocher sur la plage, *Positif*, Sept. 1991, p59-63. - Michel Ciment, Hubert Niogret: Plus près de la vie que des conventions du cinéma – Entretien avec Joel et Ethan Coen, *Positif*, Sept. 1996, p12-17. - Jean-Pierre Coursodon: Un Chapeau poussé par le vent, *Positif*, Feb. 1991, p36-38. - Jean-Pierre Coursodon: Entretien avec Joel et Ethan Coen, *Positif*, May 1994, p20-23. - C. Gans: Interview de Joel et Ethan Coen, *Avant-Scène du Cinéma*, Nov. 1991, p1-5. - Bill Krohn: Entretien avec Joel & Ethan Coen et Barry Sonnenfeld, *Cahiers du Cinéma*, March 1991, p40-43. - Hélène Merrick: Les frères amis, *Revue du Cinéma*, Sept. 1991, p62-63. (on BARTON FINK). - Nicolas Saada, Thierry Jousse: Entretien avec Ethan et Joel Coen, *Cahiers du Cinéma*, Oct. 1991, p34ff. **(ger:)** Michel Bodmer: Gut und Böse an und für sich sind nicht interessant – Gespräch mit Joel und Ethan Coen, *Filmbulletin*, 5/1996, p37-40. (on FARGO). - Brigitte Desalm: Die Unzertrennlichen, *Steadycam*, No. 20 (1991), p57 (the Coens on BARTON FINK and their collaboration). - Heike-Melba Fendel: Die Herausforderung suchen, *epd Film*, July 1994, p20-23 (on THE HUDSUCKER PROXY). - Roland Huschke: Mama Coens verschrobene Jungs, *tip*, 4/1991, p38-40 (on MILLER'S CROSSING). - Peter Krobath: Die Details stimmen, auch wenn sie seltsam wirken, *Zoom*, Nov. 1996, p27-28 (on FARGO). - Marcus Rothe: Tödliches Geschäft, *Die Woche*, 15.11.96 (on FARGO).

II. On individual films

CRIMEWAVE

Reviews:

(eng:) Vincent Canby, *New York Times*, 6.6.86, pC5. - cart. (= Todd McCarthy), *Variety*, 22.5.85. - David Edelstein, *The Village Voice*, 10.6.86, p56. - Steve Jenkins, *Monthly Film Bulletin*, April 1986, p105-106. - M. McDonagh, *Film Journal* (USA), Sept. 1986, p47. - N. Norman, *Photoplay, Movies & Video*, April 1986, p23. - Tim Pulleine, *Films and Filming*, April 1986, p34. (fr:) Iannis Katsahnias, *Cahiers du Cinéma*, Feb. 1986, p58. - G. Lebouc, *Grand Angle*, May 1986, p27-28. - J.L. Manceau, *Cinéma* (Paris), 15.1.86, p4. - Jacques Valot, *Revue du Cinéma*, annual review 1986, p79. - Jacques Valot, *Revue du Cinéma*, Jan. 1986, p42. (ger:) A.B, *Berliner Morgenpost*, 14.4.85 (brief review). - Katta, *BZ*, 13.4.85 (brief review). - Jochen Metzner, *Tagesspiegel*, 11.4.85 (brief review). - RAI, *Filmfaust*, 45/1985 (brief review). - Claudius Seidl, *Süddeutsche Zeitung*, 18.4.85.

BLOOD SIMPLE

Screenplays:

Joel Coen, Ethan Coen: BLOOD SIMPLE and RAISING ARIZONA, London, Faber & Faber, 1996.

Reviews:

(eng:) R. Bishop, *Cinema Papers*, July 1985, p68. - P. Brenner, *Film Journal* (USA), Feb. 1985, p10-11. - James Cameron-Wilson, *Film Review*, Sept. 1996, p. - *Cinema Papers*, July 1985, p68 (brief review). - M. D'Menzie, *Metro*, Nov. 1985, p37-38. - *Film* (England), Oct. 1985, p12ff. - K. Geist, *Films in Review*, May 1985, p304-305. - Steve Jenkins, *Monthly Film Bulletin*, Jan. 1985, p17. - Pauline Kael, *New Yorker*, 25.2.85, p78-83. - K. Kreps, *Boxoffice*, May 1985, p59-60. - K. Quinn, *Cinema Papers*, Aug. 1992, p89. - Janet Maslin, *New York Times*, 12.10.84, p10. - Janet Maslin, *New York Times*, 18.1.85, p4. - P. Matassa, *Film Directions*, May/June 1986, p7. - M. Musto, *Saturday Review* USA, March/April 1985, p75ff. - Ian Nathan, *Empire*, Aug. 1996, p34. - N. Norman, *Photoplay, Movies & Video*, April 1985, p29. - D. Royle, *Films and Filming*, Jan. 1985, p34. - D. Shipman, *Contemporary Review*, June 1986, p325-328. - M.B. Silverman, *Variety*, 23.5.84, p, 22. - John Simon, *National Review*, 22.3.85, p55-56. (fr:) Y. Alion, *Revue du Cinéma*, Sept. 1992, p51 (brief review). - Thomas Bourguignon, *Positif*, May 1994, p24-26. - S. Braunschweig, *Cahiers du Cinéma*, July/Aug. 1985, p61-62. - *Cahiers du Cinéma*, July/Aug. 1985, p61-62 (brief review). - J. Chevallier, *Revue du Cinéma*, annual review 1986, p107. - A. Garel, *Revue du Cinéma*, July/Aug. 1985, p52-53 (brief review). - Colette Godard, *Le Monde*, 6.7.85. - R. Martineau, *Séquences*, July 1985, p32-33. - Y. Tobin, *Positif*, Sept. 1985, p75. - V. Vatrican, *Cahiers du Cinéma*, annual

review 1993, p30. (ger:) Frank Arnold, *Zitty*, 20/1985. - Ulrich von Berg, *Steadycam*, No. 7 (1986). - Cinema, 10/1985. - droste (= Wiglaf Droste), *die tageszeitung* (*taz*), 3.10.85. - Wiglaf Droste, *Volksblatt Berlin*, 4.10.85. - Norbert Grob, *Filmbulletin*, 6/1985, p31-32. - Günther Maschuff, *Wahrheit*, 7.10.85 (brief review). - pem, *Berliner Morgenpost*, 10.10.85 (brief review). - Carla Rhode, *Tagesspiegel*, 4.10.85. - Dirk Schäfer, *die tageszeitung* (*taz*), 7.2.89. - Claudius Seidl, *Süddeutsche Zeitung*, 26./27.10.85. - stuk, *Hannoversche Allgemeine*, 30.9.85. - ufs, *Der Bund*, 14.11.85. - U.K, *Basler Zeitung*, 23.11.85. - Kraft Wetzel, *Vorwärts*, 12.10.85. - Uwe Wittstock, *Frankfurter Allgemeine*, 14.1.86. - Renée Zucker, *die tageszeitung* (*taz*), 7.10.85.

Other sources:

(eng:) David Ansen: The Coens – partners in crime, *Newsweek*, 21.1.85, p74-75. - J. Coleman: Rules of the game, *New Statesman & Society*, 1.2.85, p33. - Richard Corliss: Same old song, *Time*, 28.1.85, p90. - David Denby: Where the coyotes howl, *New York Magazine*, 21.1.85, p51-53. - D. Elley: A NIGHTMARE ON ELM STREET PART 3: DREAM WARRIORS; BLOOD SIMPLE/RAISING ARIZONA, *Films and Filming*, Dec. 1987, p43 (about the soundtrack). - H.M. Gedult: Reflections on my first century, *Humanist*, July/Aug. 1985, p43-44. - S. Harvey: The 22nd New York Film Festival, *Film Comment*, Nov./Dec. 1984, p65-68. - H. Hinson: Bloodlines, *Film Comment*, March/April 1985, p14-19 (article and interview with the Coens and Barry Sonnenfeld). - J. Hoberman: The Glitz, the drab, and the baffling, *The Village Voice*, 22.1.85, p53. - Stanley Kauffmann: Starting with murder, *New Republic*, 25.2.85, p24-25. - J. Klemesrud: The brothers Coen bow with BLOOD SIMPLE, *New York Times*, 20.1.85, p17. - R.D. Larson: RAISING ARIZONA/BLOOD SIMPLE, *Cinema Score: The Film Music Journal*, Summer 1987, p149. - T. O'Brian: Private Spies, *Commonweal*, 5.4.85, p212-213. - R. Barton Palmer: BLOOD SIMPLE – Defining the commercial/independent text, *Persistence of Vision*, Summer 1988, p3-19 (detailed analysis). - Barry Sonnenfeld: Shadows and shivers for BLOOD SIMPLE, *American Cinema-tographer*, July 1985, p70-72, 74 (production report). - W. Weinstein: Coen Brothers outdo Hollywood with independent BLOOD SIMPLE, *Film Journal* (USA), March 1985, p8ff.

RAISING ARIZONA

Screenplays:

Joel Coen, Ethan Coen: BLOOD SIMPLE and RAISING ARIZONA, London, Faber & Faber, 1996.

Reviews:

(eng:) David Ansen, *Newsweek*, 16.5.87, p73. - Tony Ayres, *Cinema Papers*, Sept. 1987, p41-43. - John Barth, *Film

Comment, April 1987. - Vincent Canby, *New York Times*, 11.3.87, p24. - M. Clinch, *Photoplay, Movies & Video*, July 1987, p14. - Richard Corliss, *Time*, 23.3.87, p86. - David Denby, *New York Magazine*, 16.3.87, p60-61. - David Edelstein, *The Village Voice*, 17.3.87, p54. - J. Gardner, *New Leader*, 6.4.87, p22-23. - J. Greenberg, *Variety*, 4.3.87, p18. - K.R. Hey, *USA Today*, July 1987, p43. - A. Hunter, *Films and Filming*, July 1987, p38. - Steve Jenkins, *Monthly Film Bulletin*, July 1987, p214-215. - Pauline Kael, *New Yorker*, 20.4.87, p80-83. - *Listener*, 2.7.87, p37 (brief review). - J.H. Mahan, *Christian Century*, 1.6.87, p598. - M. Meisel, *Film Journal*, April 1987, p23-24. - Tom Milne, *Sight & Sound*, 3/1987, p218-219. - John Simon, *National Review*, 8.5.87, p52-54. - J. Summers, *Boxoffice*, May 1987, p44, 58. **(fr:)** *Cahiers du Cinéma*, June 1987, p14-16 (brief review). - A. Carbonnier, *Cinéma* (Paris), 22.5./2.6.87, p8. - A. Caron, *Séquences*, Aug. 1987, p83-84. - *Cine Revue*, 14.5.87, p22-25. - Jean A. Gili, *Positif*, July/Aug. 1987, p60. - Bill Krohn, *Cahiers du Cinéma*, May 1987. - J. Lhassa, *Grand Angle*, June 1987, p7-8. - Stella Molitor, *Première* (Paris), May 1987, p. - Jacques Valot, *Revue du Cinéma*, annual review 1987, p. **(ger:)** A.K. (= Andreas Kilb), *Die Zeit*, 5.6.87. - Michael Althen, *Süddeutsche Zeitung*, 2.6.87. - dlw, *Neue Zürcher Zeitung*, 24.6.87. - Otto Heuer, *Rheinische Post*, 5.6.87. - I.P, *BZ*, 13.6.87. - Olaf Krämer, *tip*, 12/1987. - Alexander Luckow, *Die Welt*, 11.6.87. - maho (= Manfred Hobsch), *Zitty*, 12/1987. - Arnd Schirmer, *Spiegel*, 1.6.87. - Daland Segler, *Frankfurter Rundschau*, 2.6.87. - ska (= Ruprecht Skasa-Weiß), *Stuttgarter Zeitung*, 3.6.87. - C.E. Voester, *epd Film*, July 1987, p35.

Other sources:
(eng:) J. Barth: Praising Arizona, *Film Comment*, March/April 1987, p18-20, 22-24 (production report). - M. Clinch: Invasion of the baby snatchers, *Photoplay, Movies & Video*, Aug. 1987, p 40-43. - David Edelstein: Invasion of the baby snatchers, *American Film*, April 1987, p26-30, 56 (article and interview). - D. Elley: A NIGHTMARE ON ELM STREET PART 3: DREAM WARRIORS; BLOOD SIMPLE/RAISING ARIZONA, *Films and Filming*, Dec. 1987, p43 (about the soundtrack). - R. Hill: Small things considered: RAISING ARIZONA and Of Mice and Men, *Post Script*, Summer 1989, p18-27 (on the relationship between RAISING ARIZONA and Steinbeck's novel). - Stanley Kauffmann: Japery, jeopardy, Japan, *New Republic*, 13.4.87, p24-26. - R.D. Larson: RAISING ARIZONA/BLOOD SIMPLE, *Cinema Score: The Film Music Journal*, Summer 1987, p149. - T. O'Brien: Young and tender – ARIZONA and FACING SOUTHEAST, *Commonweal*, 24.41987, p242-244. - J. Summers: From bloodshed to babies – the Coens go for laughs, *Boxoffice*, March 1987, p20ff. **(fr:)** Raphael Bassan: Les comiques actuels sont-ils des monstres? *Revue du Cinéma*, Oct. 1987, p12-13 (on RAISING ARIZONA and PEE-WEE'S BIG ADVENTURE).

- Michel Ciment, Hubert Niogret: Entretien avec Joel et Ethan Coen, *Positif*, July/Aug. 1987, p61-65 (interview). - Bill Krohn: Les indépendants et leurs sujets, *Cahiers du Cinéma*, May 1987, p70-73 (on SOMEONE TO LOVE, HEAVEN, RADIO DAYS and RAISING ARIZONA).

MILLER'S CROSSING
Screenplays:
Joel Coen, Ethan Coen: BARTON FINK and MILLER'S CROSSING, London, Faber & Faber, 1992.

Reviews:
(eng:) R. Alleva, *Commonweal*, 7.12.90, p720-722. - Vincent Canby, *New York Times*, 21.9.90, pC1-2. - Richard Corliss, *Time*, 24.9.90, p83-84. - A. Daws, *Variety*, 3.9.90, p75. - David Denby, *New York Magazine*, 8.10.90, p59-60. - Roger Ebert, *Chicago Sun-Times*, 5.10.90. - L. van Gelder, *New York Times*, 10.2.89, pC12. - G. Giddins, *The Village Voice*, 25.9.90, p60-61. - Richard T. Jameson, *Film Comment*, Sept./Oct. 1990, p32-33. - Steve Jenkins, *Monthly Film Bulletin*, Feb. 1991, p49-51. - Stanley Kauffmann, *New Republic*, 29.10.90, p26-27. - E. Kelleher, *Film Journal* (USA), Sept. 1990, p13. - p Klawans, *Nation*, 5.11.90, p537-540. - R. McKim, *Cineaste*, 2/1991, p45-47. - Tim Pulleine, *Sight & Sound*, Winter 1990/91, p64-65. - Robert Seidenberg, *American Film*, March 1990, p60-62. - John Simon, *National Review*, 3.12.90, p54-56. - M. Sragow, *Esquire*, Oct. 1990, p82-83. - Peter Travers, *Rolling Stone*, 4.10.90, p50. - C. Walters, *Movieline*, June 1991, p66. - J.M. Welsh, *Films in Review*, Jan./Feb. 1991, p46-47. **(fr:)** Jean-Jacques Bernard, *Première* (Paris), March 1991, p16. - S. Brisset, *Cinéma* (Paris), Feb. 1991, p37. - A. Caron, *Séquences*, Jan. 1991, p119. - Danièle Heymann, *Le Monde*, 28.2.91. - Iannis Katsahnias, *Cahiers du Cinéma*, March 1991, p36-38. - G. Marsolais, *24 Images*, Jan./Feb. 1991, p79-80. - A. Rakovsky, *Revue du Cinéma*, annual review 1991, p73. - Michel Rebichon, *Studio*, Feb. 1991, p10. - Philippe Ross, *Revue du Cinéma*, Feb. 1991, p23. **(ger:)** Frank Arnold, *Zitty*, 4/1991. - Lars-Olav Beier, *tip*, 4/1991, p41. - Jürgen Bretschneider, *Film und Fernsehen*, Feb. 1991, p50. - chp (= Christiane Peitz), *die tageszeitung (taz)*, 14.2.91. - Brigitte Desalm, *Kölner Stadt-Anzeiger*, 16.2.91. - Brigitte Desalm, *Steadycam*, No. 18 (1991). - Jan Dreier, *Prinz*, 2/1991. - Bodo Fründt, *Süddeutsche Zeitung*, 18.2.91. - Sabine Horst, *Frankfurter Rundschau*, 14.2.91. - Otto Heuer, *Rheinische Post*, 1.3.91. - Hellmuth Karasek, *Spiegel*, 7/1991. - Andreas Kilb, *Die Zeit*, 15.2.91. - köp, *Neue Zürcher Zeitung*, 14.2.91. - Bernd Lubowski, *Berliner Morgenpost*, 14.2.91. - Verena Lueken, *Frankfurter Allgemeine*, 15.2.91. - Christian Marquart, *Stuttgarter Zeitung*, 14.2.91. - Frank Schnelle, *epd Film*, Feb. 1991, p31-32. - Josef Schnelle, *film-dienst*, 3/1991, p 20-21. - Anke Sterneborg, *Tagesspiegel*, 14.2.91. - Reinhard Tschapke, *Die Welt*, 13.2.91.

Other sources:

(eng:) Geoff Andrew: On MILLER'S CROSSING, *Time Out*, 13.2.92, p30. - David Ansen: A Hollywood crime wave, *Newsweek*, 17.9.90 (on STATE OF GRACE, GOODFELLAS and MILLER'S CROSSING). - K.M. Chanko: Ben Barenholtz, *Films in Review*, Aug./Sept. 1990, p416-417 (producer Ben Barenholtz on his work with the Coens on MILLER'S CROSSING). - P. Cliff: Movie Trax, *Film Monthly*, Feb. 1990, p30 (soundtrack review). - H. Dudar: Gabriel Byrne, bound for MILLER'S CROSSING, *New York Times*, 16.9.90, p-20. - J. Flaus: MILLER'S CROSSING – A Film neither structured nor constrained by fashion, *Filmnews*, 3/1991, p8-9. - J. Gerard: Studio's tactics on a film, *New York Times*, 10.9.90, p9. - Marlaine Glicksman: Getting down to the bone, *Film Comment*, Sept./Oct. 1990, p34-45 (interview with John Turturro). - E. Kelleher: Circle Films, Fox Team for MILLER'S CROSSING, *Film Journal*, Sept. 1990, p5-6. - p Levy: Shot by shot, *Premiere* (USA), March 1990, p64ff. - C. Maude: Byrne free, *Time Out*, 30.1.91, p16-17 (interview with Gabriel Byrne). - B. Norman, *Radio Times*, 7.5.94, p44 (about Gabriel Byrne, particularly his work in MILLER'S CROSSING). - G. Smith: John Turturro finks twice, *Interview*, Sept. 1990, p44 (interview). - G.M. Tucker: MILLER'S CROSSING, *Soundtrack!*, March 1991, p18 (soundtrack review). **(fr:)** Thomas Bourguignon: Fugues grotesques: SAILOR & LULA et MILLER'S CROSSING, *Positif*, Feb. 1991, p30-35. - Jean-Pierre Coursodon: Un Chapeau poussé par le vent, *Positif*, Feb. 1991, p36-38 (interview). - Bill Krohn: Entretien avec Joel & Ethan Coen et Barry Sonnenfeld, *Cahiers du Cinéma*, March 1991, p40-43. - F. van Renterghem: Un cadavre sous le chapeau, *Grand Angle*, March 1991, p15-16. - Jean-Philippe Stefani: Au commencement était le verbe... et le verbe s'est fait chair, *Positif*, Feb. 1996, p92-95 (about the dialogue in MILLER'S CROSSING, RESERVOIR DOGS and THE USUAL SUSPECTS). - M. Sineux: Une ésthetique de l'égarement, *Positif*, Feb. 1991, p24-26. - Charles Tesson: L'aventure intérieure, *Cahiers du Cinéma*, Dec. 1992, p56-61 (a genre analysis of MILLER'S CROSSING and UNFORGIVEN). - Laurent Vachaud: Joel et Ethan à la croisée des chemins, *Positif*, Feb. 1991, p27-29. **(ger:)** Roland Huschke: Mama Coens verschrobene Jungs, *tip*, 4/1991, p38-40 (interview).

BARTON FINK
Screenplays:

Joel Coen, Ethan Coen: BARTON FINK and MILLER'S CROSSING, London, Faber & Faber, 1992. - BARTON FINK – découpage plan à plan et dialogues in extenso, *Avant-Scène du Cinéma*, Nov. 1991, p6-92 (French translation).

Reviews:

(eng:) R. Alleva, *Commonweal*, 27.9.91, p550-551. - David Ansen, *Newsweek*, 26.8.91, p57. - Anne Billson, *New Statesman & Society*, 14.2.92, p36. - Vincent Canby, *New York Times*, 21.8.91, pC11. - David Denby, *New York Magazine*, 26.8.91, p128-129. - S. Dickerson, *Modern Review*, Winter 1991/92, p12. - K. Ferguson, *Film Monthly*, Feb. 1992, p16-17. - R. Gibson, *Filmnews*, 1/1992, p11. - E. Grant, *Films in Review*, Nov./Dec. 1991, p406-407. - J. Hoberman, *The Village Voice*, 27.8.91, p70. - Richard T. Jameson, *Film Comment*, Sept./Oct. 1991, p26. - Steve Jenkins, *Sight & Sound*, Feb. 1992, p39-40. - Stanley Kauffmann, *New Republic*, 30.9.91, p26ff. - S. Klawans, *Nation*, 23.9.91, p350-352. - A. Martin, *Cinema Papers*, March/April 1992, p57-59. - Todd McCarthy, *Variety*, 27.5.91, p79. - A. Miller, *Premiere* (USA), Oct. 1991, p108. - M. Moss, *Boxoffice*, Aug. 1991, p101, 113. - Terrence Rafferty, *New Yorker*, 9.9.91, p76-78. - Richard Schickel, J.C. Simpson, *Time*, 26.8.91. - Peter Travers, *Rolling Stone*, 22.8.91, p71ff. - W. Weinstein, *Film Journal* (USA), Aug. 1991, p **(fr:)** *Avant-Scène du Cinéma*, Nov. 1991, p93-94 (extracts from reviews). - S. Brisset, *Cinéma* (Paris), June 1991, p10. - Jean-Paul Chaillet, *Première* (Paris), Oct. 1991, p20. - M. Girard, *Séquences*, Nov. 1991, p66-67. - Danièle Heymann, *Le Monde*, 27.9.91. - Thierry Jousse, *Cahiers du Cinéma*, Oct. 1991, p30-33. - G. Marsolais, *24 Images*, Autumn 1991, p20-21. - Martine Moriconi, *Studio*, Oct. 1991, p15. - F. van Renterghem, *Grand Angle*, Sept./Oct. 1991, p11-12. - Philippe Ross, *Revue du Cinéma*, July/Aug. 1991, p23. - Philippe Ross, *Revue du Cinéma*, Sept. 1991, p64-65. - *Séquences*, Sept. 1991, p32. - C. Viviani, *Positif*, July/Aug. 1991, p77-78. - Jacques Zimmer, *Revue du Cinéma*, annual review 1991, p21. **(ger:)** che, *Neue Zürcher Zeitung*, 26.9.91. - Brigitte Desalm, *Kölner Stadt-Anzeiger*, 12.10.91. - Angie Dullinger, *AZ*, 10.10.91. - Fritz Göttler, *Süddeutsche Zeitung*, 10.10.91. - Otto Heuer, *Rheinische Post*, 18.10.91. - Andreas Kilb, *Die Zeit*, 11.10.91. - Peter Körte, *epd Film*, Oct. 1991, p31. - Pierre Lachat, *Filmbulletin*, 4/1991, p39-40. - Verena Lueken, *Frankfurter Allgemeine*, 11.10.91. - Hans Messias, *film-dienst*, 20/1991, p20-21. - Hans-Joachim Neumann, *Zitty*, 21/1991. - Rainer Nolden, *Die Welt*, 11.10.91. - Angelika Ohland, *Deutsches Allgemeines Sonntagsblatt*, 11.10.91. - Milan Pavlovic, *Steadycam*, No. 22 (1992). - Erwin Schaar, *medien + erziehung*, 5/1991, p283-286. - Helmut Schmitz, *Frankfurter Rundschau*, 10.10.91. - Anke Sterneborg, *Tagesspiegel*, 10.10.91. - Christoph Terhechte, *tip*, 21/1991.

Other sources:

(eng:) P. Adamek: The Coen Bros. and BARTON FINK, *Filmnews*, 1/1992, p11. - Geoff Andrew: Too weird for words, *Time Out*, 5.2.92, p18-21 (interview). - Manohla Dargis: Double vision, *The Village Voice*, 13.8.91, p55-56 (profile). - Manohla Dargis: Is this the end? *The Village Voice*, 2.6.92, p70-71. - C. Eller: Fox handling BARTON

FINK with TLC, *Variety*, 17.6.91, p10. - C. Fleming: Platforming brings Fox pix up to speed, *Variety*, 23.9.91, p3 ff. - R. Grenier: Hollywood's holy grail, *Commentary*, Nov. 1991, p50-53. - Janet Maslin: Hollywood screenwriter's syndrome, *New York Times*, 25.8.91, p16. - John Powers: Finking it, *Sight & Sound*, Sept. 1991, p4 (commentary on the style and success of BARTON FINK). - William Preston Robertson: What's the goopus? *American Film*, Aug. 1991, p28-33, 46 (production report). - J. Shulevitz: Sounds like..., *New York Times*, 18.8.91, p14 (on the sound effects). - L.M. Thompson: Giving birth to the artist within – Barton Fink's nod to Stephen Dedalus, *Spectator*, 2/1992, p52-57. - J.M. Wall: The unexplained world of BARTON FINK, *Christian Century*, 2.10.91, p868-869. **(fr:)** Antoine de Baecque: Meurtre à l'Hôtel Earle, *Cahiers du Cinéma*, Oct. 1991, p36-37. - Thomas Bourguignon: L'illusioniste et le visionnaire, *Positif*, Sept. 1991, p55-56. - Michel Ciment, Hubert Niogret: Un rocher sur la plage, *Positif*, Sept. 1991, p59-63 (interview). - A. Di Guardo: Le Pearl Harbour du cinéma Hollywoodien, *Rectangle*, Winter 1991/92, p36-37. - R. La Rochelle: Le vaisseau fantôme, *24 Images*, Spring 1992, p22-23. - Marie-José Lavie: BARTON FINK et William Faulkner, *Positif*, Sept. 1991, p64-66. - Donald Lyons: Lubricating the muse, *Film Comment*, Jan./Feb. 1992, p14-16 (on BARTON FINK, KAFKA and THE NAKED LUNCH). - A. Masson: Le cauchemar du scénariste, *Positif*, Sept. 1991, p57-58. - Hélène Merrick: Les frères amis, *Revue du Cinéma*, Sept. 1991, p62-63 (interview). - Nicolas Saada: Barton Fink – John Turturro, *Cahiers du Cinéma*, June 1991, p29-31 (interview with Turturro, particularly about BARTON FINK). - Nicolas Saada, Thierry Jousse: Entretien avec Ethan et Joel Coen, *Cahiers du Cinéma*, Oct. 1991, p34ff. **(ger:)** Brigitte Desalm: Die Unzertrennlichen, *Steadycam*, No. 20 (1991), p57 (interview). - Georg Seeßlen: Strangeness oder: Das Leben kommt aus Büchern, *Freitag*, 25.10.91 (on BARTON FINK and PROSPERO'S BOOKS). - Karl Sierek: Das letzte Bild, *Meteor*, No. 1 (1995), p 89-94 (analysis of their most recent work).

THE HUDSUCKER PROXY
Screenplays:
Joel Coen, Ethan Coen, Sam Raimi: THE HUDSUCKER PROXY, London, Faber & Faber, 1994.

Reviews:
(eng:) R. Alleva, *Commonweal*, 20.5.94, p22-21. - Geoff Andrew, *Time Out*, 31.8.94, p59. - David Ansen, *Newsweek*, 14.3.94, p72. - R.K. Bosley, *Cineaste*, 4/1994, p64 (brief review). - G. Brown, *The Village Voice*, 22.3.94, p48-49. - J. Conomos, *Cinema Papers*, Aug. 1994, p68-70. - R. Green, *Boxoffice*, April 1994, p149, 157. - S. Klawns, *Nation*, 21.3.94, p390-392. - K. Lally, *Film Journal* (USA), April 1994, p30. - Todd McCarthy, *Variety*, 31.1./6.2.94,

p65-66. - Kim Newman, *Sight & Sound*, Sept. 1994, p 39-40. - D. Persons, *Cinefantastique*, 4/1994, p60. - John Powers, *New York Magazine*, 14.3.94, p74-75. - Richard Schickel, *Time*, 14.3.94, p103. - Peter Travers, *Rolling Stone*, 24.3.94, p105. - S. Warrick, *Modern Review*, Aug./Sept. 1994, p16-17. **(fr:)** Raphael Bassan, *Le Mensuel du Cinéma*, May 1994, p26-27. - Thomas Bourguignon, *Positif*, May 1994, p15-16. - *Cinéma* (Paris), 16.5.94, p1 (brief review). - Jean-Pierre Coursodon, *Positif*, May 1994, p17-19. - M. Delisle, *Séquences*, May/June 1994, p40. - D. Delval, J. Noel, *Grand Angle*, May 1994, p17-18. - D. Dumas, *Avant-Scène du Cinéma*, July 1994, p63. - M. Jean, *24 Images*, Spring 1994, p 54-55. - Jean-Yves Katelau, *Première* (Paris), June 1994, p69. - B. Nave, *Jeune Cinéma*, Summer 1994, p40-41. - Juliette Michand, *Studio*, Cannes special 1994, p12. - Vincent Remy, *Télérama*, 18.5.94, p22. - Michel Ribichon, *Studio*, June 1994, p34. - Nicolas Saada, *Cahiers du Cinéma*, May 1994, p94-95. **(ger:)** Michael Althen, *Die Zeit*, 10.6.94. - Carl Andersen, *Neues Deutschland*, 9.6.94. - Lisa Baum, *Zoom*, May 1994, p36. - *Berliner Morgenpost*, 9.6.94. - Heiko R. Blum, *Rheinische Post*, 11.6.94. - Eberhard von Elterlein, *Die Welt*, 9.6.94. - Franz Everschor, *film-dienst*, 11/1994, p31. - Gunter Göckenjan, *Berliner Zeitung*, 21.6.94. - Volker Gunske, *tip*, 12/1994. - Pia Horlacher, *Neue Zürcher Zeitung*, 2.6.94. - Sabine Horst, *epd Film*, June 1994, p40. - Roland Huschke, *Cinema* (Germany), 26.5.94. - Rupert Koppold, *Stuttgarter Zeitung*, 9.6.94. - Daniel Kothenschulte, *Kölner Stadt-Anzeiger*, 11.6.94. - Heike Kühn, *Die Woche*, 9.6.94. - Verena Lueken, *Frankfurter Allgemeine*, 9.6.94. - mn (= Mariam Niroumand), *die tageszeitung* (taz), 9.6.94. - Hans-Joachim Neumann, *Zitty*, 12/1994. - H.G. Pflaum, *Süddeutsche Zeitung*, 9.6.94. - Carla Rhode, *Tagesspiegel*, 12.6.94. - Josef Schnelle, *Frankfurter Rundschau*, 10.6.94.

Other sources:
(eng:) K. Bruke, D.E. Williams: THE HUDSUCKER PROXY, *Film Threat*, Aug. 1994, p60-61 (review and profile). - Brooke Comer: Byzantine business plot begets THE HUDSUCKER PROXY, *American Cinematographer*, April 1994, p36-42 (interview with Roger Deakins). - C. Eller: Coens – Silver uniting for HUDSUCKER, *Variety*, 1.6.92, p17. - John Harkness: The sphinx without a riddle, *Sight & Sound*, Aug. 1994, p6-9 (feature on the work of the Coens on THE HUDSUCKER PROXY). - A. McGregor, C. Carroll: Guys and dollars, *Time Out*, 17.8.94, p26-28 (production report and article). - W.C. Odien: The rise and fall of Norville Barnes, *Cinefex*, June 1994, p66-81 (about the visual effects). - William Preston Robertson: The Coen Brothers made easy, *Playboy* (USA), April 1994, p112ff. - M.J. Schiff: THE HUDSUCKER PROXY, *Film Score Monthly: The Film Music Journal*, April 1994, p14 (soundtrack review). **(fr:)** Raphael Bassan, Jacqueline Nacache:

Le grand saut, *Mensuel du Cinéma*, May 1994, p26-29 (review and article on Hollywood's self-referentiality in THE HUDSUCKER PROXY). - Jean-Pierre Coursodon: Entretien avec Joel et Ethan Coen, *Positif*, May 1994, p20-23. **(ger:)** Rudolf Benda (Ed.): THE HUDSUCKER PROXY, *Projekt Filmprogramm* 67. - Heike-Melba Fendel: Die Herausforderung suchen, *epd Film*, July 1994, p20-23 (interview).

FARGO

Screenplays:

Joel Coen, Ethan Coen: FARGO, London, Faber & Faber, 1996. *Avant-Scène du Cinéma*, Nov. 1996, p1-102 (screenplay in English and French, including extracts from reviews).

Reviews:

(eng:) Marianne Gray, *Film Review*, June 1996, p26. - Leonard Klady, *Variety*, 12.2.96, p78. - Todd McCarthy, *Premiere* (USA), March 1996, p22-24. - Devin McKinney, *Film Quarterly*, Autumn 1996, p31-34. - Ian Nathan, *Empire*, June 1996, p28. - Kim Newman, *Sight & Sound*, June 1996, p40-41. **(fr:)** *Avant-Scène du Cinéma*, July 1996, p82 (brief review). - Marco Blois, *24 Images*, Summer 1996, p46-47. - Jean-Pierre Coursodon, *Positif*, May 1996, p12-15. - Alain Dubeau, *Séquences*, May/June 1996, p45-46. - Christophe D'Yvoite, *Studio*, Sept. 1996, p10. - Bill Krohn, *Cahiers du Cinéma*, May 1996, p32-35. - Eric Liboit, *Première* (Paris), Sept. 1996, p21. **(ger:)** Andreas Becker, *die tageszeitung* (taz), 14.11.96. - Brigitte Desalm, *Kölner Stadt-Anzeiger*, 16.11.96. - Robert Fischer, *epd Film*, July 1996, p6 (brief review). - Gunter Göckenjan, *Berliner Zeitung*, 14.11.96. - Gernot Gricksch, *Cinema* (Germany), Nov. 1996. - Sabine Horst, *Frankfurter Rundschau*, 14.11.96. - Urs Jenny, *Spiegel*, 46/1996. - Michael Lang, *Zoom*, Nov. 1996, p26-27. - Pierre Lachat, *Filmbulletin*, 5/1996, p36-37. - Reinhard Lüke, *film-dienst*, 23/1996. - Ernst O. Mühl, *Neues Deutschland*, 14.11.96. - *Neue Zürcher Zeitung*, 15.11.96. - Hans Schifferle, *Süddeutsche Zeitung*, 14.11.96. - Jan Schulz-Ojala, *Tagesspiegel*, 13.11.96. - Christoph Schneider, *Basler Zeitung*, 16.11.96. - Hans-Dieter Seidel, *Frankfurter Allgemeine*, 14.11.96. - tkl, *Stuttgarter Zeitung*, 14.11.96.

Other sources:

(eng:) Geoff Andrew: Pros and Cons, *Time Out*, 15.5.96, p24-26 (interview). - Lizzie Francke: Hell freezes over, *Sight & Sound*, May 1996, p24-27 (interview). - Christopher Probst: Cold-blooded scheming, *American Cinematographer*, March 1996, p28-30, 32, 34 (interview with Roger Deakins). **(fr:)** Emmanuel Burdeau, Nicolas Saada: Les forces de L'ordre, *Cahiers du Cinéma*, Sept. 1996, p40-47, 49 (review and interview). - Franck Garbarz: Petits drames de la solitude - FARGO dans l'œuvre des frères Coen, *Positif*, Sept. 1996, p9-11. **(ger:)** Rudolf Benda (Ed.): FARGO, *Projekt Filmprogramm* 93. - Michel Bodmer: Gut und Böse an und für sich sind nicht interessant - Gespräch mit Joel und Ethan Coen, *Filmbulletin*, 5/1996, p37-40. - Peter Krobath: Die Details stimmen, auch wenn sie seltsam wirken, *Zoom*, Nov. 1996, p27-28 (interview). - Marcus Rothe: Tödliches Geschäft, *Die Woche*, 15.11.96 (interview). - Frank Schnelle: Tänze am Rande des Nichts - Über das Kino der Brüder Joel und Ethan Coen und ihren neuen Film FARGO, *epd Film*, Nov. 1996, p 21-26.

Filmography and Bibliography: Tillmann Allmer

Also available from Titan Books:

Dark City — The Lost World of Film Noir
The Alfred Hitchcock Story
Vertigo — The Making of a Hitchcock Classic
Millennium Movies — End of the World Cinema
Immoral Tales — Sex and Horror Cinema in Europe 1956-1984
Mondo Macabro — Weird and Wonderful Cinema Around the World
Images in the Dark — An Encyclopedia of Gay and Lesbian Film
and Video
The Bare Facts Video Guide

287

Le grand saut, *Mensuel du Cinéma*, May 1994, p26-29 (review and article on Hollywood's self-referentiality in THE HUDSUCKER PROXY). - Jean-Pierre Coursodon: Entretien avec Joel et Ethan Coen, *Positif*, May 1994, p20-23. **(ger:)** Rudolf Benda (Ed.): THE HUDSUCKER PROXY, *Projekt Filmprogramm 67*. - Heike-Melba Fendel: Die Herausforderung suchen, *epd Film*, July 1994, p20-23 (interview).

FARGO
Screenplays:
Joel Coen, Ethan Coen: FARGO, London, Faber & Faber, 1996. *Avant-Scène du Cinéma*, Nov. 1996, p1-102 (screenplay in English and French, including extracts from reviews).

Reviews:
(eng:) Marianne Gray, *Film Review*, June 1996, p26. - Leonard Klady, *Variety*, 12.2.96, p78. - Todd McCarthy, *Premiere* (USA), March 1996, p22-24. - Devin McKinney, *Film Quarterly*, Autumn 1996, p31-34. - Ian Nathan, *Empire*, June 1996, p28. - Kim Newman, *Sight & Sound*, June 1996, p40-41. **(fr:)** *Avant-Scène du Cinéma*, July 1996, p82 (brief review). - Marco Blois, *24 Images*, Summer 1996, p46-47. - Jean-Pierre Coursodon, *Positif*, May 1996, p12-15. - Alain Dubeau, *Séquences*, May/June 1996, p45-46. - Christophe D'Yvoite, *Studio*, Sept. 1996, p10. - Bill Krohn, *Cahiers du Cinéma*, May 1996, p32-35. - Eric Liboit, *Première* (Paris), Sept. 1996, p21. **(ger:)** Andreas Becker, *die tageszeitung (taz)*, 14.11.96. - Brigitte Desalm, *Kölner Stadt-Anzeiger*, 16.11.96. - Robert Fischer, *epd Film*, July 1996, p6 (brief review). - Gunter Göckenjan, *Berliner Zeitung*, 14.11.96. - Gernot Gricksch, *Cinema* (Germany), Nov. 1996. - Sabine Horst, *Frankfurter Rundschau*, 14.11.96. - Urs Jenny, *Spiegel*, 46/1996. - Michael Lang, *Zoom*, Nov. 1996, p26-27. - Pierre Lachat, *Filmbulletin*, 5/1996, p36-37. - Reinhard Lüke, *film-dienst*, 23/1996. - Ernst O. Mühl, *Neues Deutschland*, 14.11.96. - Neue Zürcher Zeitung, 15.11.96. - Hans Schifferle, *Süddeutsche Zeitung*, 14.11.96. - Jan Schulz-Ojala, *Tagesspiegel*, 13.11.96. - Christoph Schneider, *Basler Zeitung*, 16.11.96. - Hans-Dieter Seidel, *Frankfurter Allgemeine*, 14.11.96. - tkl, *Stuttgarter Zeitung*, 14.11.96.

Other sources:
(eng:) Geoff Andrew: Pros and Cons, *Time Out*, 15.5.96, p24-26 (interview). - Lizzie Francke: Hell freezes over, *Sight & Sound*, May 1996, p24-27 (interview). - Christopher Probst: Cold-blooded scheming, *American Cinematographer*, March 1996, p28-30, 32, 34 (interview with Roger Deakins). **(fr:)** Emmanuel Burdeau, Nicolas Saada: Les forces de L'ordre, *Cahiers du Cinéma*, Sept. 1996, p40-47, 49 (review and interview). - Franck Garbarz: Petits drames de la solitude – FARGO dans l'œuvre des frères Coen, *Positif*, Sept. 1996, p9-11. **(ger:)** Rudolf Benda (Ed.): FARGO, *Projekt Filmprogramm 93*. - Michel Bodmer: Gut und Böse an und für sich sind nicht interessant – Gespräch mit Joel und Ethan Coen, *Filmbulletin*, 5/1996, p37-40. - Peter Krobath: Die Details stimmen, auch wenn sie seltsam wirken, *Zoom*, Nov. 1996, p27-28 (interview). - Marcus Rothe: Tödliches Geschäft, *Die Woche*, 15.11.96 (interview). - Frank Schnelle: Tänze am Rande des Nichts – Über das Kino der Brüder Joel und Ethan Coen und ihren neuen Film FARGO, *epd Film*, Nov. 1996, p 21-26.

Filmography and Bibliography: Tillmann Allmer

Also available from Titan Books:

Dark City — The Lost World of Film Noir
The Alfred Hitchcock Story
Vertigo — The Making of a Hitchcock Classic
Millennium Movies — End of the World Cinema
Immoral Tales — Sex and Horror Cinema in Europe 1956-1984
Mondo Macabro — Weird and Wonderful Cinema Around the World
Images in the Dark — An Encyclopedia of Gay and Lesbian Film
and Video
The Bare Facts Video Guide

All Titan Books are available through most good bookshops or direct
from our mail order service. For a free catalogue or to order telephone
01858 433169 with your credit card details, e-mail
asmltd@btinternet.com or contact Titan Books Mail Order, Bowden
House, 36 Northampton Road, Market Harborough, Leics, LE16 9HE. Please
quote reference JEC/MO.